A Commentary on
THE MINOR PROPHETS

A Commentary on

THE MINOR PROPHETS

David Pawson

Anchor Recordings

Copyright © 2019 David Pawson

The right of David Pawson to be identified as author of this Work has been asserted by him in accordance with the Copyright, Designs and Patents Act 1988.

First published in Great Britain in 2019 by
Anchor Recordings Ltd
Synegis House, 21 Crockhamwell Road,
Woodley, Reading RG5 3LE

No part of this publication may be reproduced or transmitted in any form or by any means, electronic or mechanical, including photocopy, recording or any information storage and retrieval system, without prior permission in writing from the publisher.

For more of David Pawson's teaching,
including DVDs and CDs, go to
www.davidpawson.com

FOR FREE DOWNLOADS
www.davidpawson.org

For further information, email
info@davidpawsonministry.org

ISBN 978-1-911173-94-6

Illustrations of the Prophets by Eugene Spiro 1874-1972.

Printed by Ingram Spark

Contents

Hosea	9
Joel	23
Amos	49
Obadiah	115
Jonah	129
Micah	183
Nahum	263
Habakkuk	275
Zephaniah	337
Haggai	353
Malachi	377
Epilogue	399

This book is based on a series of talks. Originating as it does from the spoken word, its style will be found by many readers to be somewhat different from my usual written style. It is hoped that this will not detract from the substance of the biblical teaching found here.

As always, I ask the reader to compare everything I say or write with what is written in the Bible and, if at any point a conflict is found, always to rely upon the clear teaching of scripture.

David Pawson

HOSEA

HOSEA

Read Hosea

Ten years after Amos preached in Bethel, another prophet came who was to be God's last prophet to the northern ten tribes of Israel – God's last word, his last warning, and it is a real contrast to Amos's prophecy. It is affectionate rather than accusing, wooing rather than warning, tender rather than tough, mercy rather than justice, and this is God's final appeal before the ten tribes disappear. So we pay careful attention to it and there is a key word which unlocks the whole prophecy in Hebrew: chesed (qheseth); you pronounce the *ch* as the Scots pronounce "loch" and this word has no exact English equivalent. You see we don't have the Bible, we have a *translation* of the Bible and that has certain limits and there are never quite the exact word equivalents to this word *chesed* in the Old Testament or *agape* in the New Testament – there is not really an English word that communicates these unusual but very beautiful words. Let me try and fill it full of meaning.

It is essentially a covenant word. It is not something you have for everybody, it is something you have for those with whom you have a covenant relationship. The most common covenant relationship we have is marriage, so there is a commitment in this word. It does mean love but it has an awful lot of the word loyalty in it and true love is not true love unless it is loyal. The other synonyms that are used in the Old Testament for it are lovingkindness or faithfulness even – "faithfulness" is used sixty times for this word in our English Bible; "kindness" is used nine or ten times. It means unswerving love, undying devotion; it means one is so committed to someone you go on loving them whatever happens.

There is an old English word that used to be used – "troth". The only surviving example of that word is "betrothed"; there is a commitment in it; there is a loyalty in it, and it may be very significant that that word has died because that kind of loyalty has died and love is something without loyalty, something you can enjoy for a bit with someone and then drop. That is not *chesed*, not covenant love. The opposite of this word is unfaithfulness so in a church marriage service there are usually words like "keep thee only unto her" or "only unto him" – "as long as you both shall live". That is *chesed* – for better, for worse, for richer, for poorer – does not matter, that is irrelevant to the commitment.

Now the whole relationship between God and Israel is a covenant love and therefore, a *chesed* – stay with it. There was a man in the north of England whose wife shortly after they married left him and lived a pretty sinful life, picked up disease and the friend of this husband said to him, "Why don't you divorce her, she doesn't care that much for you, it'll never work out", and he said, "Never speak to me like that about my wife; I love her and I will love her as long as there is breath in her body." And when she lay dying of the disease she had picked up from her sinful life, his hands were held over her in prayer and he nursed her. That is *chesed*. That is God's love; that is what Hosea had to communicate to these people who didn't care about God's love at all. So on Israel's side the covenant meant loyalty to his commands; obedience was their part of the covenant. His part was to look after them, to protect them and provide for them, but their part was to obey him. But what he was looking for was glad, eager obedience that wanted to live the way that he wanted her to live, but that is what he did not get.

There is a group of Jews today who find delight in God's law. They are the happiest group of Jews I know and it is very interesting what they are called. They are called the Hasidim and that is made up of *hesed*, those who delight in God's law; those who are happy to obey it, not to do it grudgingly as a duty, but who see it as a delight. The longest psalm in the Bible, Psalm 119, is all about someone who delights in God's law – says it is great to have this. Well that is quite an attitude, isn't it? The burden of Hosea's messages are very simple. The Lord is saying: what has happened to our marriage? There was still *hesed* on his side, but none on their side now. What went wrong? It is a simple message and it is torn out of the pain of unrequited love. It is perhaps the most painful experience in the world to love someone and not to have that love returned; to want to love them and help them and they won't have it. Maybe you have known that pain of unreturned love.

How could Hosea understand God's feelings so well? The answer is that God taught him in the school of experience whose colours are black and blue. God often prepared a prophet through his marriage and gave him a personal experience of the feelings of God. For example, Jeremiah. God told Jeremiah: you must not marry; you must remain a bachelor because you have to tell Israel that God is now a bachelor – he does not have a wife any more. So Jeremiah had to learn, from the loneliness of not having a wife, how God was feeling without Israel, and that became his message. Hosea had the most extraordinary instruction in God through an experience of marriage. It is all in chapters 1–3 which are autobiographical and various expositions of Hosea have been given interesting titles, I have got two books on my shelf one is called *The Prophet and the Prostitute* and the other is called *Love to the Loveless*, which is a little phrase out of a hymn, but both of those sum up perfectly what happened to this man.

Again scholars argue as to whether it is fact or fiction; whether the order of events is right; whether chapter 3 did not come before chapter 1; whether Hosea knew what was happening beforehand or only realised afterwards what was happening. All these things are matters of discussion, and frankly you can get really bogged down in what I think is speculation. Let us take it in its plainest, simplest meaning. He married a prostitute. They had three children, at least one of whom was not his and was somebody else's. She went back on to the streets. He had to go and find her. He brought her home, put her through a period of discipline when he did not know her as a wife; and then courted her and started all over again and loved her. Those are the facts. The names of the children are very interesting. There were three. The first was called Jezrael or Yezrael which means "God sows it", and the biggest problem he had with that child was discipline – a very rebellious, unruly child who had to be disciplined. The second child was a girl called "Loruhama", which means not pitied, and she was a deprived child. She did not have love from the mother. The third child was called "Loami", which means "not my people". This was the child that Hosea didn't father. She already had another man, and this child was disowned. Those three adjectives I have given you (disciplined, deprived, disowned) all summarise how God was dealing with his people in Israel, and the names of the children were so important. I have not met any Christian parents who used any of those three names for their children, and when we get to Isaiah, *Maher Shalal Hash Baz* – I have never known a Christian to call them these names. We love Bible names for our children, but not these names!

That is all in chapter 1 about the three children. Chapter two is about the wife. It is very interesting that there are three things about her, but she was reproached by her own children for what she was doing. Her own children said: you shouldn't be doing that, mummy. So even the children could see what was going wrong, and she was punished. But she was restored later. There are the three "r"s for her – reproached, requited, restored. Chapter three is all about the husband, Hosea, and there are three things told us about him in there: first, that even when she was faithless to him he was faithful to her; he went looking for her after she left him with the children. Secondly, he was firm with her, and for a period he did not treat her as his wife; he brought her home but did not share the bed with her for a period. That was representative of the period of discipline in the exile that God was going to put the Jews through, before he restored her; Thirdly, he was feared. There was a healthy fear in his wife afterwards so she trembled, she feared him – and that was not a phobia, not a terror but it was a healthy fear that she had which would bring respect and loyalty back into her life.

Those chapters 1–3 tell the story. From then on, chapters 4–end are into the message that grew out of that, because God had given Hosea the message and now he was ready to go and tell Israel that was how he felt about her. So we can summarise the message of Hosea: it is made up of different sermons he preached, different prophecies he gave, all jumbled together so it is not easy to analyse. Nevertheless, we can put it together under various headings which give us the bones of it, as it were, and enable us to read it with understanding. Everything he says centres around these two headings: *human unfaithfulness* and *divine faithfulness*. It is the contrast between *chesed* and the very opposite in the people that forms the theme of his whole prophecy. God's controversy with Israel is this, and his compassion for them comes out in this. Those are the two words that Hosea uses: God has a *controversy* with Israel but he has *compassion* for them. This is God's problem: what do you do with a people that you love yet who are unfaithful to you? It is a real problem.

So we have a mixture of divine justice and divine mercy. First of all, Hosea does concentrate on seven sins of which they are really guilty. We can call them the seven deadly sins of Israel and show God's detailed knowledge of what is going on. The first is infidelity. They have become unfaithful in their marriages as well as unfaithful to God. It invariably follows; they are guilty of harlotry – they are going after other gods, like Hosea's wife after other men. Secondly, they are guilty of independence. God's chosen government was in Jerusalem but they had created their own royal line; they had set up their own independent kingdom – which is the essence of sin: we will not have you to rule over us, we will have our own kingdom; and they were in rebellion against God's chosen king in the south. So independence was a major sin. There was intrigue – there were lies and deceit, and people were making treaties outside the people of God, getting unequally yoked with unbelievers.

There was a whole lot of conspiracy – people talking behind each other's backs; people going behind each other and making secret agreements.

Fourthly, idolatry. The golden calf of Samaria figures large in Hosea's prophecy. The bull was a symbol of fertility, and it still is.

Next: ignorance. When they should have known about God, they did not; they could not be bothered to read their Bible; they did not want to know about God.

I feel that is happening in our country. You know, we have had Christianity here for nearly 2,000 years and people do not want to know. As soon as a religious programme comes on television, thousands of sets switch off. It is very reminiscent of all this: the idolatry, ignorance, immorality;

drunkenness, promiscuity, and violence. Those were things that Hosea picked out which was making it less and less safe for people to walk the streets at night in Israel.

Finally, above all: ingratitude. God redeemed them and they were so ungrateful; there was no thankfulness in them. In a series of pictures which would really stick in their minds, Hosea says: you are like mixed dough. That is when you mix flour with olive oil just before cooking it, but if you leave it and you do not cook it, it goes rancid and is horrible. He said that is what you are like: your passion is like a heated oven. He says you are like an unturned cake that is getting all burnt on one side and it is uncooked on the other – because they used to cook the cakes on top of an iron sheet on the fire like a griddle. He said: you are like a fluttering dove trapped in a net. That is vivid picture language.

But then he accuses the four groups of people responsible for this condition. He says the priests are the first ones responsible. They should know God, and they don't. They should be telling the people about God, and they don't. There were plenty of prophets in the northern part of Israel, but they were all false prophets telling people not to worry, that God would not do these dreadful things. That is what the people wanted to hear, and a false prophet always says "peace, peace" when there is no peace. False prophets say "Don't worry, it may never happen." That is a false prophecy. There were plenty of prophets saying "Thus says the Lord" but just telling the people what the people wanted to hear. I had to battle with this. You have got to be on your guard all the time. It is so easy for preachers to tell people what they want to hear; to want people to say 'What a nice sermon, thank you so much." But God needs men who will tell the people what they do not want to hear, and it is costly to do that.

The princes of this royal line they had set up also were

responsible. The other group that he singles out for particular condemnation are the profiteers who are making money out of real estate, and who were making money at the loss of other people who were poorer. That is happening today. I think it is very doubtful if a Christian can be in money exchange, shifting millions around with the terms of the market. It is the poor who lose out every time. When we gain money there should be a fair exchange of goods or services in value, so that both gain, but in fact there is an awful lot of gain going on that is purely at others' losses, and they do not get anything in return. That was what was happening, and Hosea singles them out as the corrupters of society.

Now Hosea says: suffering is coming to you. He says three particular sorts will come. First of all: barrenness. There would be miscarriages. Women would not even conceive or they would lose their babies. That is pretty tough – but God can do that. Then he said: bloodshed will come, loss of life, attacks; but ultimately (the same as Amos): banishment from your land.

That is the severer side of Hosea's prophecy, but it is not his main thrust, which is that God is still faithful. There is a statement in the New Testament about our relationship to Jesus. It is Timothy 2:12, and it says if we deny him he will deny us, but if we are faithless to him then he remains faithful. That might have been lifted straight out of Hosea.

Here is the good news: his compassion for them. This is the real heart of Hosea's word, and it is when I read chapters 11–14 that I am deeply moved by God's faithfulness.

God will punish them. You see, God cannot stand their professions of repentance. He sent his prophets to warn them of their doom. He did not want their sacrifices, he wanted their love; he did not want their offerings; he wanted them to know him.

Can you feel God's heart in that? That is the love that

cannot let them off; he has to punish them. But consider this, from chapter 11: When Israel was a child I loved him as a son and brought him up out of Egypt, but the more I called to him the more he rebelled, sacrificing to Baal and burning incense to idols. I trained him from infancy; I taught him how to walk. I held him in my arms but he doesn't know or even care that it was I who raised him up ... O how can I give you up, my Ephraim? How can I let you go?

You can't read this without emotion, and here is his final appeal in chapter 14: O Israel, return to the Lord your God for you have been crushed by your sins. Bring your petition, come to the Lord and say: Lord take away our sins.... That is the kind of prayer he wanted, not the prayer "Oh, he'll get us out of trouble".

Plenty of people cry to God when they are in trouble, but they don't ask him to take away the cause of the trouble. The book finishes: Whoever is wise, let him understand these things, and whoever is intelligent, let him listen; for the paths of the Lord are true and right and the upright walk along them, but transgressors stumble in them. That is one of the strongest appeals in the whole of the Bible to people who do not want to know about God's love.

Let us look finally at the application of this. How do we apply Hosea today? There is one huge difference between our situation and that to which Hosea (like Amos) spoke and prophesied, and we need to think this through very carefully. In Israel the religion and the state were one and the same thing. It was a theocracy. To be born into the state was to be born into the religion, and vice versa. That does not apply in the New Testament. In the New Testament, church and state are separated, and that may be summed up by Jesus' words "Render to Caesar the things that are Caesar's and to God the things that are God's", and so in a sense we now live in two kingdoms. I am a citizen of the United Kingdom according to my passport; I am also a citizen of the Kingdom of God. They are not one and the same thing, therefore we have to be rather careful applying prophecies of the Old Testament to a secular state today. Now we suffer from the complication of the fact that, since the Emperor Constantine, Europe has tried to combine church and state; tried to create Christendom, in which the Kingdom of God and the kingdoms of man are one and the same thing. So that to be born into England is to be born into the church and we have centuries of an established Christianity behind us. Actually, that may well cease in the future. The longest word in the English language is back on the agenda (disestablishmentarianism) and we may well see the separation of church and state. It could easily happen and then we would be back in a more New Testament position.

When, therefore, we see these prophecies which Hosea applied to both religion and state together, we cannot just take that and throw it at our government. That is rather important. The pattern, I believe, is this: what God said through the prophets to the non-people of God can be used as a prophecy to the government. The inhumanity, the riding roughshod over human rights, the legislation that makes the rich richer and the poor poorer. There are a whole lot of things in there that we can apply validly, but we must not expect the government to try to make people Christian by law. God has higher standards for his people than he has for others and it is a delicate line.

We have a shortage of Christian leaders and we should not expect them to establish Christian standards, but there are moral standards which are known to the conscience of humanity that we can expect and can agitate for. So I am just declaring this: these prophecies ought primarily to be applied to the church, and that is where our prime prophetic message should be. I fear that it is much easier for Christians to point out to the world and say: what wicked people you all are. It is very easy to do that. But in fact I believe that the prophetic word is more needed inside the church than outside right now, and that if the church were what it ought to be, that would begin to clean the nation up. But I am afraid we are getting known as a church that is all muddled up inside and trying to put everybody outside right. When we read prophecies we do see an amazing reflection of our society out there, but judgment begins at the house of God and we have to put these things right inside before we start trying to tell the world.

JOEL

JOEL

Read Joel 1:1-2:17
We do not know who Joel was, apart from the fact that he was the son of Pethuel – that is all it tells me. The fact that both the father's name and the son's have the two letters "el" in it tells me that they were a godly family, because in Hebrew the word "el" means "God". If you call your son with a name that has God in it you must have some real faith in God. I do not know when he lived, and the scholars have wasted a lot of ink trying to find out, and all of them say: we don't know who he was, when he lived, but we do know why he wrote this book – why he preached.

It was as the result of a terrible catastrophe in nature, which was causing widespread famine, and in vivid poetry we have a description of one of the most dreadful scourges of the Middle East: a plague of locusts. We do not get any of the horror of the word "locust" in the UK. If you lived in the Middle East and I said "locusts are coming" you would leave the building immediately and run for home. You would tremble; you would shake. Why is it that we don't have this horror here? For one thing it doesn't happen to us very often. The last time England had a plague of locusts was in 1869. Then the green leaves and blades of grass disappeared and the bark of the trees was eaten.

The other reason we are not scared of them is because we only see them as individuals in their solitary state. You might occasionally see one on its own in England. You certainly can see them in captivity. Just one is a harmless little thing, only about two and a half inches long. That is what this book is all about. It doesn't carry any disease. It doesn't attack humans. It doesn't bite. Why then should people be frightened of it? The little insect that flies around passes through about five different stages, changing colour at each stage from the hopper to the full swarming locust. That's it. Here is a description of it, which I got from the Arabs: the nature of ten larger animals is to be found in the locust – the face of a horse, the eye of an elephant, the neck of a bull, the horns of a deer, the chest of a lion, the belly of a scorpion, the wings of an eagle, the thighs of a camel, the feet of an ostrich, and the tail of a serpent. That shows you how seriously the Arabs take a locust swarm – how much they have thought about it.

Why should this be such a frightening thing? Why should people cringe in terror when they hear that the locusts are coming? The answer is in one fact only: the numbers that are coming. One or two locusts by themselves you would swat with a fly swatter but now I am going to give you some numbers which are so great that I think you will find it difficult to imagine. When they lay their eggs in the sand, they lay five thousand eggs to the square foot. An egg bed will cover many acres and every egg will hatch – that is the first fact. They then come out as hoppers, which cannot fly. They are tiny hoppers and you can get ten thousand hoppers to the square yard. The area covered by hoppers may be up to fifteen miles across. I hope you are trying to imagine this. A man in a Land Rover in Ethiopia drove fifteen miles over hoppers at ten thousand to the square yard.

The next thing is that when they change they are able to multiply their numbers one hundred times in one generation. With a kind of frantic orgy of copulation they produce millions, and you can have anything up to ten thousand million in one swarm. They then set off and they will travel two thousand miles before they die. Every day they will eat eighty thousand tons of vegetation – the weight of a cruise liner.

  Imagine a swarm like that descending on your county, and they are going to eat up eighty thousand tons of greenery every twenty-four hours. Now you know why it is frightening. I have only once been in a locust swarm. It was in Carnot, Nigeria. At midday the sun went out and I thought it was an eclipse, but it wasn't, it was the beginning of a locust swarm. Though they were flying at ten miles an hour, that swarm (which was small) blotted out the sun for three-quarters of an hour and they were just little insects. That is what happened here. It was such a severe attack that Joel said: "You aged men, did you ever know anything like this? Did your fathers ever have such a bad one? You children, remember this; tell it to your children and to your grandchildren. There has never been a plague like this."

  In Carnot I saw the poor Africans trying to beat the locusts off their little vegetable plots – the little bit of food they had grown for the next twelve months. In one day a million people can lose their food for a year to a plague of locusts. In a country where there are no supermarkets and just your vegetable patch, that is disaster. I am not trying to alarm you or to get you worked up, but you will never understand the prophet Joel unless you get the feel of the horror of this plague of locusts. Joel's description of the locust is an eyewitness account – he must have seen it.

  He describes the stages: the cutting, the swarming, the hopping, and the destroying. He describes their appearance like lions and horses, rather like the Arab description. He describes their number as an army, a nation, a host, a horde. He describes the sound of them like rumbling chariots and crackling fire. I can testify that that is exactly what it sounds like. He says, "Before them the earth quakes and the heavens shake." Now of course they don't physically, but when you are surrounded by millions of moving things there is nothing stable. You feel the earth and the sky. It is all just on the move because you cannot see anything that is still. It is a bit like being in an earthquake. The sun and the moon are darkened, yes; I have seen that. He is writing of what he saw. He describes their movements: they march in line; they do not jostle one another; each keeps to its path. Twenty million locusts can do that. It is an army marching up the walls climbing into houses. They just come on like a mighty army. You can beat and beat and beat, but it is hopeless and helpless even though you try.

This attack, he says, did four things. First of all, the plants were all eaten up. Even the bark of the trees was gone and the trees were white skeletons in a desert. I have seen that happen and I can testify to the accuracy of the description. He is not exaggerating. You cannot exaggerate with a locust swarm. He says: before them it is like the Garden of Eden; after them like a desolate wilderness. Not only did it affect the plants, it affected the animals. Now they have no pasture; they have nothing to eat and, beyond that, when the vegetation goes, as we know this affects the climate because the carbon dioxide cannot enter, the atmosphere is reduced, the rain stops, the moisture does not come and the water brooks dry up. That is why Israel has planted so many trees, millions of them – to get more rain, to change the climate and get shade, where the water can be conserved and kept in the soil. But when the vegetation goes, there is no water.

Both domestic and wild animals were crying for water and food. It is pathetic when you see a herd of cows crying for these things. The human beings are affected; the food and drink have been cut off before their eyes. The tiller of the soil sees the wheat and the barley gone and his granary empty. The dresser sees the pomegranate and the apple and the palm tree, the date palm and the vine all gone. They do not have enough to eat and drink. But now Joel says there is something else that is gone wrong. The offerings are no longer being brought to the house of the Lord. The cereal offering, the drink offering and the meat offering do not come. The priests are not being supported. The ministers of the Lord are not getting enough to keep going because there are no offerings. He tells them to weep like an old lady who remembers her fiancé who was killed just before the wedding in her youth, and who still mourns: to weep because God is not getting any offerings; the house of the Lord receives nothing.

That is the picture of the locust plague destroying. Now we come to the second thing that Joel wants to say. This plague is a *miracle*. It is not a natural event alone; it has been caused by God. It is a direct intervention of God in nature. I hasten to underline that he is not saying that every plague of locusts is an act of God. I know insurance companies call any natural disaster an act of God (and that you cannot claim on insurance for an act of God), but some disasters are acts of God and Joel has come to see that God sent those locusts. God can control a little insect like that. God made it, God can tell it what to do, as God controlled the whale in the book of Jonah in the story and life of Jonah – as he controlled the worm in the same life, he controls the locusts. God can tell that insect where to go. Men can't. We can only fly after the locust with a plane with a poison spray to try to stop them from going further, but God can tell the locusts where to go.

Now why should God send a plague of locusts? Before I answer that, let me point out that this miracle was not a blessing. Now that may sound a bit of an understatement but I mean to say this: this miracle was a curse. It was a direct intervention of God cursing his people. Why should he do such a thing? Some terrible wrong must have been done. Joel, looking at this plague, saw in it a foreshadowing and a foretaste of what he refers to as the Day of the Lord. What does he refer to? The Jews knew, and Christians know, that one day in the future distant history there is to be a day of reckoning and that God is to call people to account for their evil doing and is to deal with them. On that day Joel knew, as we know, the sun and the moon will be darkened. So when the locusts darkened it, he saw a foreshadowing, a foretaste and picture of the Day of the Lord that was coming. It is a warning: blow the trumpet in Zion. They didn't have air raid sirens in those days, they had trumpets, and when the trumpet was blown it was blown as a warning that locusts were coming or an army was coming.

Now Joel says, "Blow the trumpet in Zion", because God is coming. Tell the whole of the people of God. This is a godly punishment. God had done this once before. Do you remember in the days of Moses in the book of Exodus Moses went to Pharaoh and said, "God says let my people go," and Pharaoh said, "No I will not." Moses said, "If you do not, God will send a plague of locusts upon this land," and God did.

In Revelation 9 it tells us that at the end of the history of man when the trumpets are blown, when the fifth trumpet is blown, there came locusts on the earth. Locusts, those harmless little insects God can use for a day of reckoning.

Now what had they done? What terrible sin lay behind this? Was it idolatry? Joel may have lived in Elijah's day, and Elijah told the people of Israel, "Stop bowing down to Baal, to idols, to wrong, false gods." Was that what they were doing? There is not a word in the book of Joel about idolatry. Was it immorality that the later prophets like Amos spoke against – immorality in relation to business, in relation to sex, in relation to a number of other things? Was this what he was talking about? Was it immorality that caused God to send the locusts? There is not one word in this book about immorality. If it was not idolatry and not immorality, what was it? What possible reason could there be? It comes out in two phrases. First phrase: return to me—twice repeated, which means quite simply, the thing they had done wrong was to get away from God – that is all. Not into idolatry, not into immorality, they had just got away from God. They were God's people and God was no longer real to them and they drifted away from God. God's own people were no longer with God.

That is as serious if not more serious than idolatry or immorality. That is why today we who go to church and we who claim to be the people of God may falsely be complacent. An intelligent girl left a church that was active and prosperous, and seemed to do a lot of the things churches should be doing. When I asked why, her reply was very simple: "Because they left God out."

You can go to church, you can sing hymns, and you can have all the business of the church. You can be raising money. You can be running around doing your social service and you can leave God out. If we do then we deserve a locust plague too. We may not be guilty of idolatry. We don't set up idols and bow down before them. We may not be guilty of crude immorality, yet God says, "Return to me. You've got a long way away from me." Where is the blessedness I knew when first I saw the Lord? That is the question. Where is that so refreshing view of Jesus and his word?

That is the first phrase that gives me the clue. They had got away from God. The second phrase that gives me the clue is this: "Rend your hearts and not your garments," which means stop putting on an outward show of religion and get the inward reality. Now they went to church and they ripped their garments and they apparently were godly people, but deep down in their hearts they were not sorry at all for their sins. They recited the general confession and they ripped their clothes when everybody else did. Of course, that was the liturgy of the time. But the trouble was they had liturgy rather than life, the form of godliness but not the power of it, and it was all outside and God was sick of them rending their garments.

We don't rend our garments today. Garments don't matter but your heart does. What had gone wrong? They had got godless religion.

The best way to get away from God is to get "religion" – I mean religion in the sense of the outward respectability not the inward reality—that is a different thing.

An American lady came to a church in London and she was sitting there and she kept shouting "hallelujah" until finally the verger came and quietly said to her, "Do you mind not doing that here, it's disturbing?" But she said, "I've got religion." He said, "Well, you didn't get it here, madam."

I am not talking about that kind of religion. I am talking about the religion that is all put on; the outside, godless religion that doesn't meet God when it comes to worship. It meets plenty of people, and all the people that matter, but doesn't meet God. A church may be busy, engaged in so many activities that it doesn't have time just to sit and be still and "know that I am God". That is what Joel was getting at. That is what caused the locust plague.

There are three things wrong with godless religion. First, it is offensive to God. It is an insult to the Almighty to come to church and not meet God. Second, it is useless to other people; a godless religion can't help them and cannot change anybody's life. A man said to me, "If our lives as Christians do not provoke the right questions in other people, there must be something wrong with us," but godless religion doesn't provoke any questions. Thirdly, godless religion is dangerous to ourselves because we are deluded into thinking we are right with God when we are nowhere near him. Well now, this is Joel's charge: godless religion. Is the position hopeless? Is the situation beyond control?

No. They did not need to set up a commission and a locust control centre or work out how many priests they could now afford in the temple with the reduced offerings. What do you need to do? Well he gives them a specific programme of getting back to God. He doesn't leave it vague; he doesn't just say to return to God. He is saying: God tells you to do this, that, and the other.

What does he say? Here is the programme. The first thing is: you must come back to God, not just as individuals but together. If people of God have got away from God, the way to get back is for a group to get together and go back to God together. Call an assembly – not one of these happy assemblies where everybody starts with a funny joke, but a solemn assembly.

Proclaim a fast—one of the aspects of Christian piety most neglected today is the aspect of fasting. Some people even think it is only an Old Testament thing. It's not. You study the book of Acts in the light of fasting. You ask a missionary. Come and fast until we have got back to God – that is how a church gets back to God. In other words, even food is not as important as this. Drop your food, drop your meals, drop everything; call everybody, everyone needs to be involved. Call the elders; call the babies, even the nursing infants. Bring the bridegroom and the groom even though they re on their honeymoon. Get everybody together. This is absolute top priority. Call a solemn assembly come back to God together.

The second thing is the instruction for the ministers of the Lord: gird on sackcloth all night. Before the people come, let the ministers of the Lord get together and in the dark hours seek God. Then when the people have come, let the ministers weep between the altar and the vestibule, between the place where the people come in and the place where the offerings are given to the Lord. In their positions as ministers of the Lord let the ministers get together and weep between the vestibule and the altar and let them pray.

What kind of a prayer are they to pray? Even that is given to them by Joel. They are to pray for three things. First that the people of God may be spared in the mercy of God – there it is at 2:17, "Spare thy people, O Lord". The people of God need mercy when they have got away from God. It is the cry of a condemned man who knows he is guilty. The second thing they are to pray for is that those who have laughed and jeered and mocked the people of God in their weakness may be silenced and confounded. They are to pray that the people of God may no longer be a reproach and a byword and a subject of scoffing. The third thing they are to pray is that God may be vindicated and that they are to pray that nobody may be able to say again, "Where is their God?" In the twentieth century we lived to see a theology grow up called the "God is Dead" movement. That could never have grown up if the people of God were what they ought to have been. Where is their God? People are saying "God is dead." Why are they saying that? It is not because God is dead but because his people are. The outsider can't see God. He hasn't the faith to see God. He can only look at the people of God and see what is happening to them. What does he look at and see? In this nation he sees at least forty years which the locusts have eaten.

What I said in the 1970s applies to the church of Jesus Christ right through this land. For forty years the locusts had been nibbling away and the people of God had not got food. Said a man in a prosperous church: "I have not needed my Bible in church for nine years." The locusts have been eating the food and the people have only just been surviving.

I believe that God is saying to the church in this land:

"Return to me even now while the nation is still running away; even now return to me, come fasting." I would love to see the day when church leaders call us to a solemn assembly and spend the night before weeping; in that day fasting, and call us to seek the Lord. I must be honest and say, "Am I prepared to do it?" That was the calling of Joel.

Do you know what God's response was? God said: It will come to pass in the last days that I will pour out my Spirit on all flesh, your sons and your daughters shall prophesy and your young men will see visions; your old men will dream dreams. This is the need of our day – not for more organisation, not for more committees, not for more reports, but for the power of the Holy Spirit. Then the harvest would come again. What was the harvest that had failed in Britain? It was the harvest of people, the harvest of winning souls for Christ. That harvest cannot be reaped without the Holy Spirit.

Read Joel 2:18-3:21
Now supposing I were able to tell you everything that's going to happen to you during the next twelve months, would you want to know? Just supposing we could know all the future just for the next year, how would we feel about it? I think perhaps we would be torn between two desires. On the one hand we would want to know, on the other hand we would be afraid to know. It is strange, but in the times in which we live you discover that people have this same double attitude to the future. On the one hand you have people trying to find the future, on the other hand the mood of our day is a mood we call "existentialism", which means: forget the past, try to forget the future; live your existence in the present only and try to find meaning in the here and now. Try to get some kind of experience that will thrill you now. The Word of God could hardly be more different from this outlook. The

Word of God takes the line that unless you know the past and the future you will never be able to relate rightly to the present. You will not even understand the meaning of the here and now unless you know something about the there and then. This Bible is full of predictions about the future, many of which have already come true in detail, and some of which are yet to be.

The second half of the book of Joel is entirely concerned with prediction. It has become fashionable in our day to play down the predictions of the Bible, saying that prophecy is not "foretelling" but "forth telling." That is just talking nonsense. It is like talking about a square circle. The major part of the forth telling of the Word of God is foretelling what God is going to do; it is prediction. Prophecy is prediction, which is why in popular speech if someone says "I prophesy that..." he means: I will guess what is going to happen; I will tell you where this will lead.

Therefore Moses said that there is one test of a true prophet: whether what he predicts comes to pass. If it doesn't, he is a false prophet. A true prophet is one who predicts what does happen; a false prophet is one who predicts what doesn't happen. We are all familiar with false prophets. We have them knocking at our doors. They told us Christ was coming back again in 1914 and he didn't. They told us the end of the world was going to be in 1973 and it wasn't. You can soon tell a false prophet because they predict things that do not happen, and confuse and distort, but true prophets predict things that are bound to happen.

Of the three things which Joel predicts in the second half of his letter, two have already happened. So even the statistical chances are that a gambler could put a bet on the third happening. We are going to look at these predictions with the confidence that two-thirds of them have already been fulfilled. Now before we can go any further we have to read between the lines of the Bible. Sometimes that is necessary but we have got to be careful when we do it. There is something not written between 2:17 and 2:18. Joel had started by talking about a plague of those little locusts that came on Israel because they had got away from God – godless religion. They went through their religion without God. They still sang their psalms; they still went through all the routine, but God was not real. To show them that he was away from them, God was not only away from their worship, he withdrew from their daily life.

I thank God for his patience with this nation of ours. We have got away from God; as a nation we are much further away from God than we used to be. Yet God, in his mercy, has not yet withdrawn from us in our daily life, otherwise the supermarkets would be empty. Thank God for his mercy, and Joel told them that it was their godlessness that had caused it. Now v. 18 begins with a little word "Then", which implies just one simple thing between vv. 17 and 18. In v. 17 Joel told them what to do; in v. 18 God does something. What then has happened in between? I can come to only one conclusion—that the people of God did what they ought to do, otherwise God would not have responded; that the people of God, the priests of God, and the ministers of God got together and wept, they cried, and said: Lord we cannot go any further without you; Lord come back to us; we are coming back to you.

As I commented earlier, by the 1970s it could be said of Britain that the years had been eaten by the locusts for half a century. For the previous fifty years almost every denomination and almost every church had been reporting declining membership. The locusts had been attacking the people of God, and nibbling away at the things of God until we were only just hanging on. The nation's population was growing, and they needed God desperately more than they had ever needed him, and yet the Church, the people of God, languished and became the subject of jokes. Programmes on the television not only began to laugh at clergymen (and we deserved it for our pomposity), but they laughed at prayer. They made jokes about God and implied that God can do nothing. This is the world in which we live and the Church needs to turn back to God and say: "God spare your people that they may no longer be a taunt, a byword, a reproach among the nations."

In Joel 2:18, that word "Then..." implies that God heard something from his people. I mention this for a reason. The second half of Joel is packed with promises but we dare not claim a single one of them if we have not been through the first part of Joel. If we have never been brought low, if we have never come back to God and wept for our godlessness, then we dare not claim a single promise of God. "Then God was jealous for his people and had pity on them." Now when you turn to God and rend your heart and not your garments and are brokenhearted about the condition of his people, then God rends his heart. We now have a description of two deep emotions: jealousy and pity. Then God became jealous for his land and had pity on his people.

Some people think God is without feelings, but the Bible doesn't think so. God is a real person, that is why the Bible talks about the eyes of God, the ears of God, the nostrils of God, the mouth of God, the hands of God, the finger of God, the arm of God, the feet of God, the heart of God, the bowels of God, the kidneys of God. Not because we think God is a physical being but because we believe he is a real person and the functions of our body correspond to something utterly real in him. Where do we feel jealousy? Where do we feel pity? Here, the very words used are those for the kidneys and bowels of God. His jealousy and his pity – he feels deep down until it makes him feel ill almost—that is the picture.

I could never understand in the catechism that "God is a being without body parts or passion." I cannot understand the third part of that. The Bible presents me with a God who feels deeply, a God whose Spirit I can grieve, a God who can feel jealous. Now you notice that the response of God is not just his love. Some people speak vaguely of his love as if it is a sort of vague, overwhelming thing. Well, there is a love of God for the whole world, but there is a special love of God in the Bible for his people. It is called *chesed*, which means his married love, his covenant love. I hope I love other people besides my wife, but I have a special love for my wife, a *chesed* love, which means a love that has made certain promises which will not be broken.

God has a married love for his people. He has made promises to them. When you have a married love for someone then you are jealous and you say, "No one touches the one I love. No one laughs at the one I love. No one makes the one I love a taunt." If you really love someone with this kind of love you are jealous for them when anybody attacks them, when anybody ridicules them. God became jealous and as he looked at his people he took pity on them. That is what we need more than anything else today: the jealousy and the pity of God that spring from his married love for us; his jealousy for our reputation because his is bound up with it. If people taunt the people of God and say, "Where is their God?" it is God's name that suffers, and it is his reputation that is at stake.

So God in his jealousy and pity makes three predictions through Joel about the future. The first is a prediction of natural abundance for the people of Israel; that he will put right all that has gone wrong in the plague. Now in spite of the fact that locusts can do so much damage, two very simple things can undo the damage that locusts do. Number one, the wind. Number two: the rain. Why? Well first of all, even though their wings look quite big, you realise they are small in relation to the body, and the locust cannot really fly very strongly. It flies downwind; it can only go the way the wind goes.

In Israel the locusts came from the north and the locusts are called "the northerners" because they come down the north wind. When the wind is in the north the locust comes. When the wind is in the east in Israel the drought comes, a terribly dry wind from the Arabian Desert. When the wind is from the west the rain comes from the Mediterranean. When it is from the north the locust comes. God says: the first thing I will do, I will drive the northerner out of your land; I will drive him into the western sea, the Mediterranean; into the eastern sea the Dead Sea, and the stench of their rotting corpses will tell you it is over.

St. Jerome, in his commentary on the book Joel, describes such a locust plague, and says that, "For weeks afterwards they could smell the rotting bodies of millions of locusts on the shores of the Mediterranean and the Dead Sea." That happened in about the year 300 AD. So this has happened again and he describes vividly what God says he will do here.

The second thing that is needed is rain. In other words, God is saying he will send one wind to drive them away and then veer the wind around again and bring the rain from the west and it will pour down – the early rains in September that help to germinate the grain, the latter rains in April that swell the grain. You cannot have crops in Israel without the early and the latter rain. God says, "I will pour out my rain," and I know because of the records of the Old Testament that the locusts went and the rain came back, and God gave them plenty.

Look at some of the rich promises in this section; every one of them is a little gem. It is as rich in promises as a fruitcake in currants. Look at some of the negative ones. First of all: fear will go. "Fear not. Don't be afraid any more." Do you know that that phrase "Fear not" occurs 366 times in the Bible? As much to say: one for every day of the year and one for leap year if you are short."

Not only will fear go but shame and embarrassment will go. If the people of God are under the discipline of God then I am afraid they are afraid of the future. They are ashamed and there is a loss of morale. This is one of the things I notice as I travel the country speaking in churches: how many of the people of God have lost their morale and confidence. They are afraid of the future and they are ashamed of themselves. Fear will go and shame will go.

Now look at this lovely promise: I will restore to you the years which the locusts have eaten. That can happen on an individual level. I have known men and women who ruined their lives for ten or twenty years and yet when they came back to God, he gave them such power that in the next twenty years they did more than they could possibly have done in all those years. The years that the locust had eaten were restored.

In the 1970s I observed that for fifty years the church in this country had been through the years of the locusts, but I believe that he could restore the years that the locusts have eaten. We could see an influx into the church of Christ by the Holy Spirit of God that would more than make up for the tragic years we lost and the time that was wasted as we fiddled while Rome was burning. "I will restore the years and your people will be satisfied." It is tremendous when you meet satisfied people. Godliness with contentment is great gain.

We were striving and dissatisfied. We projected our dissatisfaction onto others, blaming them. Instead, God wants his people to be satisfied and have plenty. It is God's will that his people should never lack what they need. The normal condition of the people of God is not to be making deficit appeals but to be praising God for what he has given. That is the normal, and when God's people are right with God then the message is: "I will send you plenty." The promise of natural abundance would restore their confidence. "Then" he says, "You will know that I am the Lord, and other people will know it too." Prayer would turn into praise and they would rejoice and be glad.

That is the first promise. It was fulfilled for Israel and I believe that it is still God's will to fulfil this promise that our needs shall be met – more than met. We have a millionaire heavenly Father, with riches beyond comparison. The silver and the gold are his; the cattle on a thousand hills. How dare we think that he cannot supply what his people need together to do his will?

There is one very interesting omission in the second half of Joel. In the first half the plants suffer, the animals suffer, the human beings suffer and the priests suffer. In the second half the plants are restored by the rain, the beasts are restored by the food; the humans are restored by the grain, the wine, the oil, and the granaries that are full. But there is no word about the priests – not a single word about the ministers of the Lord. Why not? Because now, looking through his prophetic telescope, Joel can see something that God is going to do for all the people of God, not just the ministers. He can see a day when every person who belongs to the people of God will be a priest, and every person will be a minister.

Now, looking forward, comes this tremendous prediction of a baptism in the Holy Ghost, and it goes back to Joel 2:28ff. "It will come to pass in the last days," says God, "I will pour out my Spirit on all flesh" – not on the priests and the ministers but, regardless of age, sex, and class. "Your sons and your daughters will prophesy, your old men shall dream dreams, and your young men shall see visions. Even upon the menservants and maidservants in those days, I will pour out my Spirit." Some people are going to be surprised to find their own children prophesying and speaking the Word of God. I don't know which of these is the greater miracle. I think the one about the old men. After thinking of castles in the air in the early days (and maybe settling for a bungalow on the ground in their later years) to have an old man who has walked with the Lord for many years now being caught up in the Holy Spirit is wonderful.

"Even on your slaves, your menservants and your maidservants." In the early church there were many slaves who were members, and they were filled with the Holy Spirit – slaves who had no education, never mind theological education, preached the mighty works of God. Joel could see this too. Now why does this promise come here? It is not only God's will that his people should have enough material resources; it is also his will that they should have enough spiritual resources. It is not only his will that he should bless the people of God, it is his will that through them they should bless everybody else and that cannot be done with material resources alone.

Therefore Joel, looking into the future, sees that a day will come when the whole people of God, young and old, male and female, employer and employee, all of them, will have the capacity to preach God's Word, speaking forth the mighty works of God. They will know God's will and declare it. What is the gift of prophecy but to know the mind of God and to be able to speak it – to let your mouth be filled with his words? That is the gift. So what you see and hear from God you declare to others. Even if a church has all the material resources it needs, a fine building, all the money, all the stuff, it doesn't happen unless the Holy Spirit is there and so we are given this second great prophecy.

Again may I just give my own personal testimony? Let

me try and allay fears and to open your heart to everything that the Holy Spirit may have for you. There came a time in my own ministry when I discovered that my "trinity" was not the Trinity of the Bible. My "trinity" was Father, Son, and Holy Scripture. In other words, the question that came to me was this: how real was the Holy Spirit as a person? Not as a doctrine, not as something I learned in college, not as some "thing" I read about, but as someone I *know*.

You see, real Christian experience must be Trinitarian – not just to know God, but to know God in Jesus Christ and to know Jesus also; not just to know Jesus but to know the Holy Spirit, the other comforter whom Jesus sent to replace him in my heart.

Now I know that those three persons are so one and so close together that to meet one is almost to meet all three, but nevertheless, Christian experience can be lacking in this third dimension. Not that we are to talk about all three; they all want us to talk about Jesus and glorify him. But nevertheless, there comes a point where you realise that you do not know the third person as you ought, and I was driven to seek, to weep, and to ask until I knew him personally.

What I found then, what I discovered then of being filled with the Spirit I would covet for every single Christian. Now I know there is fanaticism; I know there is imbalance. I know that fellowships have been divided over this, and the devil must be laughing at it because if he cannot keep you out of an experience he will push you too far and too quickly into it and make you a fanatic. But neither reason is enough to justify our neglect of the third person of the Trinity. He brings power; he brings liberty.

A group of women after the Second World War in Germany came together. Many of them had suffered. They had lost loved ones, sons, and fathers. They came together in Germany in a place called Darmstadt, and there they sought the Lord. They asked the Lord if they could do something to sweeten and cleanse the continent of Europe after the wickedness of those war years. They lived together and they built a little community. They called themselves the "Sisters of Mary", not after Mary the Virgin but after Mary Magdalene, a sinner. Their influence has gone out through all the world. There they are on the Mount of Olives. I mention this because I once had the privilege of meeting their leader, Basilea Schlink. She was one of the most beautiful, loving, and quiet ladies I have ever met, and she was filled with the Holy Spirit of God. In that community, in that fellowship of Christians, the Holy Spirit is active, bringing his fruit and his gifts – for we are offered both in the scripture. It is not a case of either/or, we are offered both. Basilea published a beautiful, simple, scriptural little book, *Ruled by the Spirit*. You may feel at first when you read it that it is too simple. It is for the childlike, and the end of the book is a series of testimonies from those in that community who have discovered that the Holy Spirit is the most lovely person they have ever met because he is also the Spirit of Jesus. Read that book.

This is the fulfilment of the promise of Joel because the promise of Joel was not just fulfilled on one day. Some celebrate Pentecost Sunday as if we are celebrating something two thousand years ago that was dead and gone after that – just once and there it is. Then there are those who think the Holy Spirit comes along to us horizontally. Because we have some kind of continuity with the church of Pentecost, the Holy Spirit comes that way. He doesn't come horizontally he comes vertically to every generation. He is poured upon; he descends upon; he comes upon every new generation of Christians. "All those who seek, who hunger and thirst," said Jesus, "Those who go on asking, if you, being evil, know how to give good gifts to your children, how much more will your heavenly Father give Holy Spirit to those who go on asking him."

I don't want to see a fanatical fellowship that is unedifying and unloving, but I long to see more of the liberty, the power, the grace, the gifts, and the fruit of the Holy Spirit throughout the church. I say, "God, will you fulfil the promise of Joel in the church in Britain? Weld us together into a fellowship of love, power and a sound mind that is able to use and tap your supernatural resources." When God does this it is always a sign of the last days. For the pouring out of the Holy Spirit is the beginning of the end of the world. What happens when sons and daughters prophesy must continue and go on until the great and terrible Day of the Lord comes and the sun goes out and the moon turns to blood.

There is an urgency in all this. Since the day of Pentecost we are living in the last era of human history. The great and terrible day looms. What is our urgent task? It is here: that whoever calls on the name of the Lord shall be saved. That is our task. When people are filled with the Spirit I notice this, they no longer talk of any other name but Jesus. No one was ever saved by calling on the name of Baptists, Methodists, or Anglicans. No one was ever able to find power and life in those names. But those who say "Jesus" find power.

I would wish if I could make one change that I could abolish all man-made titles and labels, and just put the name of Jesus up and say, "This is a church of Jesus. We have come to you in the name of Jesus. We want you to know him and the power of his resurrection." Well that does happen automatically when people are filled with the Spirit. This is the name high over all, in hell or earth or sky; angels and men before it fall, and devils fear and fly; and whoever calls on that name will be saved.

The third chapter describes in local terms the final day of judgment by God. It describes it in terms that the people of Israel would understand. The Valley of Jehoshaphat is a valley full of cemeteries. There is a cemetery in the valley today. It is the Kidron Valley; the valley where invading armies camped before attacking Jerusalem.

In the most satirical passage in the Bible, God says: "Beat your ploughshares into swords. Come and attack me, you nations. You've attacked my people, well take me on. You have been taunting my people. You've made them a byword. You've scattered them. You've sold them for a prostitute. You've sold a little boy to have a good time; you've sold a little girl to get a bottle of wine. You've done this to my people. Are you trying to pay me back? Then fight me instead of them; come and fight me on the last day."

The vision here is of multitudes in the valley of decision. I used to think that meant in the valley where they must make their decision; it doesn't mean this. It is in the valley of God's decision. One day, whatever people think about God, whatever they say about God's people, he will decide what happens to them. In the Valley of Jehoshaphat, the place of judgment, it is God who will settle their destiny. In the light of that, how urgent it becomes for us to help people to call on the name of the Lord – that they may be delivered now before they face the valley of God's decision, that they may now make their decision to accept Christ as Saviour before he makes his decision to reject them.

You notice that the nations of the world are condemned for their inhumanity to their fellow men and for their antagonism to the people of God. You show what you think of God by what you say about his people. "Inasmuch as you did it not to the least of these my brethren you did it not to me." And over against the valley of decision, God's decision, is the mountain of delight, a picture of Jerusalem with milk and wine flowing, water gushing out from a fountain and filling that valley, the dry valley of Shittim below the city.

Through this we can see the city of God, the New Jerusalem, descending. It is a glimpse of the future, things yet to be. In the day when the Valley of Jehoshaphat is filled with the multitudes of the nations the city of God will be full of God's people, and strangers will no more walk through it, only his people.

Finally, we are told in this prophecy, that all the refuges of men (Egypt and Edom) will be desolate and a wilderness in that day, that all the cities people have built will be gone. I remember one day getting on the back of a horse and riding through a deep cleft in a ravine some three or four miles, in the Aruba, that dry valley where Lawrence of Arabia rode. We rode through this deep cleft, 150 feet deep, about 10 feet wide, which sometimes fills with water. We rode through and we came out in a hidden valley, the only entrance through this cleft. You could guard this whole city with two sentries.

We saw buildings carved out of the solid red sandstone cliffs. We saw the glory of a city that is now only inhabited by insects and jackals. It was the city of Petra, but in the Bible it is called "Edom", and God said, "Edom shall be a desolate wilderness." I sat on my horse and looked at the desolation. The grandest buildings I think I have ever seen – they must have been magnificent, but God says that all the things that people build and look to will become desolate because they are without him.

Here then is the final picture that Joel would have us take away. The ultimate outcome is that those nations, those people, those kingdoms of the world that have been against his kingdom will come to nothing. It is by the Spirit of God that we shall bring people into the city of God.

AMOS

AMOS

Read Amos 1–2

It has been said that Amos proclaimed a message so far ahead of his time that most of the human race, and a large part of Christendom, have not yet caught up with it. That is quite a statement. Why is it so relevant? We know the date when Amos preached this prophecy: around 750 BC. We know that because he dates it – two years before the earthquake, which was such a terrible one it was remembered 250 years later by the prophet Zachariah. But he also says it was in the days of King Uzziah and King Jeroboam. So we can pinpoint this prophecy in history. When you study the background of the social, political, moral and religious life of those days in that year, you discover that you are reading about modern Britain.

Let me give you a bit about it. There are two words that sum up the conditions behind this prophecy: peace and prosperity. Now in the Middle East there is nearly always war; it is the cockpit of the world because three continents meet there. But during this period they had not known a war for a whole generation. Young people had grown up who knew nothing of military threats, knew nothing of the hardships of war, and did not know what it was to be attacked. In our day, too, a generation has grown up that has not known either of the two world wars, and has not known firsthand what it is to live in other than a time of peace.

Not only was Israel free from external threat, from the big powers on their frontiers, in fact there was a bit of a stalemate between Egypt and Assyria. There was a peace between them. But not only that, they had known a pretty terrible civil war. Part of the nation of Israel had wanted home rule. They had got it, and there had been a civil war which divided Israel into two parts: ten tribes in the north which kept the name "Israel" and two tribes in the south which kept the name "Judah". These two brother nations had now come to terms and were living in what is called "peaceful coexistence".

So they were not fighting each other; there was no threat from outside, and no threat from inside. They had comparative peace and they had a false sense that there were no real problems; that they could go on muddling through. They also had a unique prosperity. They could now turn their attention from war machines, from conscription; they could now turn their attention to the import and export balance. They achieved a remarkably favourable balance of trade. They were on the routes of commerce. They bred a new class of merchants who really began to push up the import/export trade until the money began to flow in and they had affluence to a degree that the nation had never known before. The grandparents and great-grandparents, even under the days of King David, had not known such affluence as came now.

This started a drift of labour from the land to the city. Israel was in a state of urban development, with new housing estates springing up around Bethel, Samaria, and the other major cities. The farm labourers were leaving the fields and coming into the towns for higher wages in the trading and commerce that was going on. It was a consumer society, and the interests began to switch from necessities to luxury goods. Things began to be made in Israel that were not really needed. The status symbol had crept in and the status symbol of those days was a second house, what Amos calls "summer houses" – a cottage that you went to for your holidays.

The people getting the money had in many cases "risen from the ranks" as it were. There was now a new aristocracy, people who were at the top of the social ladder because they had money and for no other reason. Not the old aristocracy but the new one—the people with cash, the people who could buy things, the people who could panel their houses beautifully. This was the new aristocracy. Furthermore, the middle class was dying out and leaving two groups only: the "haves" and the "have-nots". The rich were getting richer and the poor were getting poorer, as inevitably happens in this kind of economic sphere.

The middle class was being squeezed out, and the middle class had been the backbone of Israel. This group was giving way to the wealthy aristocracy who had the money; and the working class hadn't got it. Those who were on salaries were increasing rapidly, and those who were on daily wages were going down and down because there was inflation and money did not keep up with its value. So those who were on fixed incomes were losing every day; those who were in business and commerce were going up and up, and developing all their wealth.

Now there were disturbing social developments from all this—the growing gap between these two groups, with fewer and fewer people in the middle to link them together in a healthy society. It was a world in which money began to talk too much and in which bribery and corruption became the order of the day, in which to do business you bribed someone. The bribery had crept from the business world even into the legal world so that if you went to court you simply paid the right man so much and your case went as you wanted it. The innocent were being sold for a pair of shoes. In other words, they could not even establish their innocence in the law courts.

Morally, the affluence had led to a permissive society. We are told among other things in Amos that alcoholism was now rife. People were drinking themselves silly in this affluent society. We are told that sexual laxity was rife and this comes up again and again in Amos. Morals in business and in every other way were rapidly degenerating. We are told incidentally even in business that the businessman could not even wait for the Sabbath to be over to get back to his business. The seven-day week was creeping in, and the business merchants of Israel were travelling seven days a week to get more business and didn't have one day a week for God now; they were too busy making money.

What was happening to religion? We are told that in religious realms all kinds of weird pagan ideas were getting mixed up. All kinds of wild interpretations of the faith were creeping in. I don't know if anybody then wrote a book claiming that orthodox religion was really the worship of the mushroom, but that is the kind of thing that Amos mentions: the kind of ludicrous, brazen, perversion of truth that introduced all kinds of strange activities. They were introducing erotic rites into the worship of God; they picked it up from Baal worship, that heathen fertility cult. They were bringing it right in to their orthodox worship of God and doing indescribable things in the temple in the name of God.

The priests and the prophets were also corrupt. Preaching was in decline. I remember seeing a large notice outside a church and I didn't know whether to laugh or cry at it. It said: "Special popular services – come and sing your favourite hymn", and then at the bottom in huge red letters: "No sermon." Now you could laugh at that but it is a symptom of the times. This is what was happening. They loved rites, they loved liturgy, they loved the temple, they came in big numbers, but they didn't like preaching, they didn't want to hear the Word of God and they told the prophets to shut up. The priests were corrupt because they were doing jolly well out of the affluence.

This was the situation and they remind me of the people

on the Titanic as it made its way across the Atlantic on its maiden voyage: drinking, dancing, having a good old time, quite unaware that within hours the ship would go down. This was the society here and there was nothing to disturb their complacency, their permissiveness and their affluence. People said to preachers, "Why are you so worried? Why do you think we're heading for disaster? We're not; we're getting on very well. We've never had it so good." That was how they talked and Amos says: "It was two years before the earthquake." Just two years they had before the earthquake to get right with God. God in his gracious mercy sent them a man to preach.

This is always his method. God has only one method of warning people of disaster to come: he sends a man to preach. It could be any man. It need not be an educated man. It could be a man from anywhere up the social ladder or down it, and indeed it was. Let us look now at the man that he sent: Amos. He sent this one man to this whole society to preach, to tell them that the way they were going was moral and religious disaster, and that if they went on this track as a nation they would be finished. I say in the name of God that if Britain goes on, on the track on which she is travelling today then as a nation we are finished and we may well live to see the end of what we have known.

Where did Amos come from? He came from the two tribes in the south and he was sent to Israel in the north. So he was a bit of a foreigner to them. He came not only from down south but down the social ladder. He was a man who was a farm labourer twenty miles south of Jerusalem in a little place called "Tekoa". Uneducated, without any social airs and graces, he was sent to this affluent set in the north to warn them about God.

Let me try to make it real. I want you to imagine that God got hold of a farm labourer from the Welsh mountains and sent him to stand outside a smart hotel in London, to shout: "Prepare to meet God." Incidentally, those words are a quotation from Amos so it is an apt illustration. Can you imagine what those people at the cocktail parties inside the hotel will think of this labourer shouting that? They won't listen. They will think he is a crank and will say, "Oh, it's another one of those." That was the task that God gave Amos. Take your hat off to Amos's courage that he went and did it. Two years before the earthquake, this little man went, and he preached a most devastating message.

How did he get that message? Was he a great thinker? Did he go to theological college? No, God told him what to say: "The words of Amos which he saw concerning Israel." It is almost as if God wrote them up on a blackboard and said: now this is what you must say; as if God wrote the message before his very eyes and vision. Probably that is what happened. Those familiar with the gift of prophecy will know that those who have exercised that gift have often said, "It was as if I just saw it written on the wall and I just had to read it off."

"The words of Amos which he saw concerning Israel in the days of Uzziah king of Judah and Jeroboam king of Israel." The other man in the Bible who reminds me of Amos is John the Baptist, that courageous, austere, isolated figure who preached with the same devastating warning about the coming judgment of God.

I am going to stay with that illustration of a Welsh farm labourer coming to the centre of London and preaching against the ills of our society. I will try to fit Amos into that picture to help you to feel that it is real. Now when he began to preach with brilliant understanding of his hearers, he did not begin by attacking them. Indeed, every parliamentary candidate could take a leaf out of his book as to how to approach a difficult subject. Like a boxer in the ring he went around the matter first. He boxed the compass and he spoke about all the nations round about, gradually spiralling in, coming nearer and nearer until a bang – he talked about Israel.

The first three nations he talked about were Damascus, Gaza, and Tyre – respectively in the northeast, the southwest, and the northwest. But if I am going to put it in the terms in which I have said, it is as if this Welsh farm labourer came to London and preached about France, Holland, and Belgium first, about their sins, and about what was wrong with them over on the other side of the channel, which could be quite popular talk to begin with.

He starts with Damascus, the capital of Syria. He says that Damascus is about to lose its place on God's earth; the Syrians have forfeited their right to live in God's sight. Why? Because they have been guilty of the most inhuman act of cruelty. To get more land they have expanded south into Gilead, they have captured the people, and then they did the horrible thing. They literally took a threshing sledge, which is a kind of heavy wooden platform made of cross beams fixed together, with iron spikes underneath, which is normally dragged over grain to separate the wheat from the chaff. They took these things, which they captured from the rich grain fields of Gilead, they took the people they had captured, tied them together, lay them down on the ground and dragged those over them until they were dead.

God said: you cannot live in my world and do things like that. Such inhumanity must be punished. I will not revoke the punishment. You are finished as a nation. The Syrians have completely vanished from the face of the earth. The Syrians we call Syrians today are not Syrians; they are Arabs living in the land that these people left, but they have gone. God told them, "You will go." Tiglath-Pileser was the man who took them away and who destroyed them.

The second nation is in the southwest: Gaza. God says through Amos: "Gaza, you will go," and the Gaza strip today is occupied by another people. These people have gone. These were the remnants of the Philistines, the last ones left that David had not defeated, and they were living in Gaza. There are no Philistines today. You can search the Middle East and you won't find a single Philistine. Why? What did they do? They took an entire people from their own land and they sold them into slavery to Edom. God hates slavery. He says: for that you forfeit your place in my world. Gaza goes.

The third one is Tyre. Now there is a city of Tyre today but it is not inhabited by the people of Tyre. Indeed you can see in Tyre today the ruins of their city. Thirty thousand of them were carried off into slavery. Why? Because they had carried off a people into slavery, a people with whom they had a pact, a treaty, and they broke their covenant word and they sent their friends off into slavery for hard cash. God says: you don't do that in my world and stay in my world. Tyre goes. Alexander the Great reduced Tyre to nothing and there wasn't a single soul left there.

Now before we go on I want you to notice two things. First, in every case this was not an isolated incident but a habitual outlook, "for three transgressions and for four". In other words: this is not just once you have done this, you have gone on doing it; it has become a habitual crime. The other thing I want you to notice is that in each case the judgment of God is described in one word: fire. A fire will come.

Now we move on: Amos moves closer in. He has been talking about three nations on the very fringe of their little world. Now he moves to three more nations who are in fact cousins — related to Israel. It is as if our Welsh farm labourer now begins to talk about southern Ireland, Northern Ireland, and Scotland. He is getting nearer. What does he say about these three? Edom – they are guilty; they have already been mentioned as slave traders twice, but they are guilty of a hatred and a ruthlessness that pursued their brother Israel without any pity and kept anger forever.

Now this may all seem a little remote but if anyone keeps anger and resentment against a relative forever then they are up against a judgment of God. That is a very common thing, but Edom kept up their hatred forever. You see, Edom came from Esau; Israel came from Jacob, and from then on they hated each other and they never let up on that hatred. Which is why, sadly, it is sometimes at a funeral that members of a family come together who have not spoken for years. They have kept it up all that time, and God hates that and Edom is to go.

Next Ammon — Ammon is guilty of something that is so indescribable that we can hardly bear to mention it, and it is that when they took over the land they took all the pregnant women and ripped them open to kill the foetus so that there should be no future generations of those people. That is a terrible act and God hates it and he says: Ammon, you go. There is a message coming out of all this: that the God of Israel is the God of the whole world, and God says to any nation that is guilty of such barbaric atrocities: you forfeit your right to stay in my world. If there is one thing written across the history of the human race it is that Amos was right, and that God does not suffer a regime guilty of this kind of thing to survive.

Finally Moab — they committed war on the dead, and not content with killing people they would then desecrate their corpses. That is an act of sacrilege in God's sight, even to any enemy.

Before we leave this first six nations let me underline a number of things. Number one, none of these are the people of God. Therefore, secondly, none of them knew the Ten Commandments. None of them knew God as he has revealed himself to Israel. But, thirdly, all are going to be judged by the God of Israel. Fourthly, he will not judge them by the Ten Commandments for they do not know them. He will judge them by the common laws of humanity. There is something built into human nature so that every person on earth knows what is human and what is inhuman.

Indeed, have you ever read Document A144? That is a marvellous document. It was produced by the United Nations Organization years ago and it is called the "Universal Declaration of Human Rights". It was not produced by Christians; it was produced by people from all nations, from all cultures, from all creeds. They were able to agree on what are the common laws of humanity and what are the rights of human beings. One of the statements in Document A144 is this: Every man has the right to be free and therefore slavery is wrong.

Now it is interesting that God has put within the human breast an understanding of humanity apart altogether from the Bible. It is by that instinct that God will judge the nations of the world. God is just and fair; he doesn't judge a person for what he does not know. If a man does not know the Bible God does not judge him by the Bible. If a man has never heard of Christ he is not judged because he has not heard of Christ, and Romans 1–2 makes that quite clear.

But men are judged by what they know of common humanity; of what they know instinctively in their nature is right and wrong, and everyone knows that. Therefore, they are judged. God's fire comes upon these nations not because they had rejected his revelation but because they had been inhuman. When I look out in this world, when I see the television pictures from so many places, I can see that God will judge all that by the common laws of humanity. We stand responsible to the God of Israel. Not one of the six nations I mentioned is left on the face of the earth. Any nation that is guilty of such inhumanity forfeits its right to live and will disappear from the scene of human history.

Now Amos moves closer still. It is as if our Welsh farmer now speaks about Wales, his own land, because now Amos speaks of Judah. This is getting rather close and rather hot. But at any rate they are still listening. They thoroughly approve of all these other nations disappearing and even perhaps Judah – that would solve a lot of problems. So they are still all ears. Amos is still preaching. Now what does he say about Judah? He says, "My nation, my own people, they are guilty before God not of inhumanity, they are judged by the revelation they have received. They are guilty of infidelity. They know the Ten Commandments; they know the statutes of God.

They know how God wants them to behave and they have done two things. They have rejected the laws of God. Why? Well I have no doubt that some people said they were impracticable, idealistic, old-fashioned, narrow-minded, out of date, that the Ten Commandments really belong to another era and that now we are grown up and responsible for self-discipline we could decide what was right and wrong. They rejected the laws of God and what did they put in their place? The lies of men.

They had developed a new theology and a new morality. They had men who were prepared to set aside the Word of God and give them their own traditions. So they were believing lies like this: you won't be punished if you break the Ten Commandments. These things are not really wrong; it is just that Moses said they were or thought they were. But now, in our day, we are enlightened. We are set free from the old taboos. We are free to do what we think is right. We no longer listen to the Word of God.... They preached this. They preached the new morality and different standards of behaviour, and even the people of God began to follow the new standards instead of the Ten Commandments.

So with utter impartiality and with strict justice, God says: "Judah you must go too, and even Jerusalem and her strongholds will fall," and they did. In the year 586 BC, Jerusalem was razed to the ground and the beautiful temple was gone. You see, God would not be fair if he let his own people off. He would not be a just God if he condemned other nations for sinning against the light they had and let off his own people when they sinned against the light he had given them. God is just and his own people Israel and the sufferings they have been through for all these centuries are a standing demonstration to one fact, which is written in the Bible again and again: God has no favourites. God is impartial; he is no respecter of persons.

Now this little farmer from Tekoa, standing in the city of Bethel, with all the people saying, "Hear, hear," and "Hallelujah" to all the downfall of their enemies says, "For three transgressions and for four of Israel I will not revoke the punishment." At last Amos has reached the crunch. He is almost moving in for the kill in his address. He has come right to the centre and he accuses Israel of insensitivity. They had become so hardened by affluence, so indifferent, that they no longer felt as they should towards people or towards God. They lived without feelings. Now let us see what he means by this.

I divide what he says in the rest of chapter 2 under three headings. They had become insensitive to God's present righteousness, to his past redemption, and to his future retribution. They no longer remembered these three things. Take the first: God is a righteous God. You cannot do wrong and get away with it with God. He is righteous, he is good, he is clean, he is pure, he is upright, and therefore he cannot stand anyone who is not.

Now what had they been doing? The first thing: they had

been exploiting the poor. So keen were they to get money and things that they had become callous towards people. It was not people who mattered any more, it was things: business, money, getting on, commerce, and trade. People? Well, they didn't matter. It was said of one businessman after he had died that he had climbed the business ladder by standing on the faces of those below him and licking the boots of those above him. What an epitaph! But that is what Amos is referring to.

Amos was saying: you have become indifferent to people. You are only concerned about your own income. So you sell the poor for a pair of shoes so that you can have something better to wear. You don't mind what happens to the person who made them. This is strong meat: things before people. They were not only insensitive to people, they were insensitive to God. He mentions horrible ritual orgies in the presence of God – people lying down beside the altar, having intercourse, and calling it religion. That is what he is talking about now. It is horrible.

He points out that they obviously haven't the first idea of what God is like to do such things. They come into the temple and get drunk. That happened, of course, once in the early church at Corinth, too. Lest we say, "Well that would never happen here," mark my words it is beginning to happen here and it is astonishing what this generation is beginning to do in the name of religion and even in the name of Christianity. So they neither saw the needs of men nor the nature of God. They were too busy getting things and living in a material world.

Not only were they insensitive to God's present righteousness, this was an act of utter ingratitude to his past redemption. God says, "Listen, I brought you out of Egypt. I gave you this land. I cleared the Amorites out for you." Incidentally, why did God clear the Amorites out? Because they too had become so inhuman and so degraded, and archaeologists have discovered this, that they didn't deserve to stay in Canaan. God said, "The Amorites lost this land; I gave it to you. If you're going to do what the Amorites did with it, out you go too." God is just and if he pushed the Amorites out because of their evil he must push the Israelites out for the same reason.

Not only did he destroy the Amorites, he raised the Nazirites. The Nazirites were a group of Jews who were total abstainers. God raised them up not because it was his will that everyone in the people of God should be a total abstainer but he raised up the Nazirites to be total abstainers to be a constant reminder to other people of the dangers of wine, of the fact that you did not need wine to live a full life, and of the consecration to God that is involved in self-denial. The Nazirites were among the people of God and God wanted them there. Though I do not believe that every Christian is under the law of God to be a total abstainer, I thank God for those who are voluntarily for the sake of their brother, and who do for the people of God what the Nazirites did.

Not only were the Nazirites raised up, but the prophets were raised up. So by the life of the Nazirites and the lips of the prophets they had constant reminders that God's standards were holy, and they didn't like it. Who does like people who prick your conscience? Who does like people whose lips and lives make you feel uncomfortable in what you do? So what did they do? "You made the Nazirites drink wine and you commanded the prophets, 'you shall not prophesy.'" They shut up the preachers and they made the total abstainers drink. That effectively took away their conscience and the conscience of the nation.

Not only that, God says, "But you're forgetting my future retribution. I will press on you like a cart full of sheaves crushes everything in its path. You will be oppressed by another nation. It doesn't matter how strong you are, how good a horse you have got, how fast you can run, you will not escape in that day." I've got to tell you now that what Amos said came true. Fifteen years after Amos gave them the warning, Tiglath-Pileser I came marching into Israel and he took many people away as slaves.

Still they did not come back to God, those who were left; and ten years later, in 724 BC, another Assyrian called Shalmaneser came, he wrecked Bethel, he wrecked Samaria, and all those towns vanished. In Samaria you can see the wrecked town that Amos predicted. It just went. God's people vanished from that country. The ten tribes of Israel became ten lost tribes and were taken away.

Now what has all this to say to us? Just this: if Damascus did not escape, if Gaza did not escape, if Tyre did not escape, if Ammon did not escape, if Moab did not escape, if Edom did not escape, if Judah did not escape, if Israel did not escape, what right have we to think that "Christian England" (so-called) will escape? We have no right at all. One of the things I see as I read my newspapers is that we are living under God's wrath in this nation. It is as plain as the Sunday newspaper headlines. Read them, and then read Romans 1. You are reading the same thing.

In an election I would rather elect a candidate, whoever he is and whatever party label he goes under, who fears God and who will seek in the political life of our country to do what is right by common humanity.

Amos talked about other countries, until he said: What about you? What about your nation? What about the things that are wrong in your country? What about the permissiveness that is the result of the affluence? That is what God is going to judge you for.

When people discuss politics, what a glorious opportunity that is to share with some of them what Amos says. "Without vision the people perish," and "righteousness exalts a nation," but "sin is a reproach to any people".

Read Amos 3–4

It is very interesting to see how public speakers fight to regain the attention of their hearers when their hearers are no longer listening. A speaker came to the men's club to give a talk entitled "The Art of Public Speaking", which I think is a bold thing to do anyway. When he reached his second point, which was "How to retain the interest of your audience" there was a loud snore from the second row, and the snores continued. Now chapter 3 in the book of Amos begins with the phrase "Hear this word" and chapter 4 begins "Hear this word", and chapter 5 begins "Hear this word." Now what does that tell me? It tells me that Amos was fighting every inch of the way to retain the attention of his audience. They had begun to drift away and it is very obvious why.

I tried to make this real and vivid by imagining a farm labourer leaving his sheep in the Welsh mountains and coming to London and standing outside a hotel and shouting, "Prepare to meet your God!" In those circumstances, a crowd might gather at first and then, when they heard more, they would drift away. But there were two reasons why Amos was losing his congregation and they were not captive in pews inside a church building and not really able to go out decently before the benediction. This was in the open air in Bethel. The first reason was, I think, his social background. Here was a peasant from the south challenging the sophisticated society men and women in the north. You can understand why they looked down their noses at this poor preacher—"Look at his clothes...." The second was that he was getting a little too near the bone. Having denounced all the other nations, and got their "Hallelujahs" and "Hear, hear"s, he now began to talk about their rotten society and they did not think it was rotten. He can see them beginning to drift away so he calls after them, "Listen! Listen to this word. It's a word from God. Hear this word," and he has to keep saying this: come back and listen. The word he is now going to say gets even more personal.

Verses 1–2 make a profound, yet disturbing statement that those whom God loves most in this life will be punished most in this life, and that is a most startling statement. It is a statement that is repeated right through the Bible, in the New Testament also: Hebrews 12, "Whom the Lord loves, he chasteneth" and, "If you are not chastened of the Lord, you are not a true son, but a bastard." Now that is New Testament as well as old. In other words, if you are God's people, you can expect more punishment from God in this life, not less. An unpalatable truth and I am not surprised he was losing his congregation.

But he begins this new word from God by saying, "You only, of all the nations of the earth, you are my special one; you are the one who is closest to me. You are the one nation that knows me as I know you and, therefore, I will punish you for all your iniquities." There is a sentimental notion around today that love and punishment are incompatible. May I say that far from being incompatible, you cannot have true love without chastisement. The moments when I knew how much my father loved me were the moments when he punished me, and if he had never punished me, I would now wonder whether he loved me. I would not have at the time; I didn't think it was love at the time. No chastening at the time is comfortable or pleasant. Whom the Lord loves, he chastises.

There is a further truth in this shattering statement and it is this: privilege brings responsibility, not permissiveness. If God gives privileges to Israel, that heightens the standard of behaviour he expects from them. They will be judged more strictly than other people because of the privileges of the knowledge of God and his Law that they have had. Very often people ask me, "What about those who have never heard?" They often imply, by the tone of their question, that God is unfair if he punishes them because they have not heard.

The answer is obvious: God will not punish them for what they have not heard. God is just and fair. We are not left in any doubt about that. But my trouble is that the people who ask this question are those who have heard, those who were brought up in Sunday school, those who do know enough of their Bible to know the truth, those who have been in church, and it is they who say this, trying to turn attention from themselves, who have heard, to those who haven't, as if this excuses them.

In Britain we have heard. We are a nation that has had privileges beyond many other nations. We have more translations of the Bible in English than any other language. We have more churches and chapels in this country in proportion to the population than almost any other country in the world. Christianity has been given to us from the earliest days. It first came with the Roman soldiers. This land has had the gospel for nearly two thousand years.

God was saying to Israel through Amos: you have had these privileges; therefore, I've got to deal with you. If your behaviour doesn't match your privileges, then I have got to deal with you because I cannot allow a so-called "godly country" to go on behaving like this. That was what was wrong with Israel, and that is what is wrong with Britain. I am not falling into the fantasies of British Israelite-ism and I am not saying we are God's chosen people, but I am saying that Britain has had more Christian privileges, I think, than any other nation or country in the whole world and what are we doing with it? "You only have I known," God says to Israel. Well he won't say that to Britain. He is known of us, but he would say to us: you have I given blessings and privileges that no other nation has enjoyed. This we have had.

Let us apply it personally. I find myself challenged thinking this way: when I think of the Christian upbringing I had, a home in which some of the greatest Christians in the world came to stay, and whom I was able to meet, a Bible that I knew since I was small, friends coming in and out of the family circle who were saints of God – what privileges. One asks, "What has one done even to begin to be worthy of such privilege?" Now there is the statement: Hear this word, you people of Israel, you only have I known. Think of your privileges; of all the people in the world, I have given you all this. Therefore, since your behaviour is so contradictory to your privileges, I must deal with you." It seems to me incredible that so called "Christian England," has now the world reputation of being the most swinging, sinning capital in the whole world.

Now we turn to vv. 3–15. There is an inevitable logic in the events that Amos now describes, so logical that he can appeal to the minds of his hearers and ask them rhetorical questions which, if they answer, they must answer in only one way. They are so clear. He is saying that the nation is moving towards doom inevitably; it is logical; you cannot stop it now. He asks these questions.

First of all, he says, "If you see two walking out together, do you think that is by accident?" There is a cause for every effect; there is a reason for every happening. Let me put this into simple language. If you have noticed one of our young men and one of our young ladies in the church walking together frequently, up and down the high street; you saw them in the north street, you saw them when you went down to the coast walking together, you saw them in the park, what do you say? You say, "There is an understanding; there is some reason for this," and the tongues start wagging. But you say, "There's a reason for that; they have made an appointment or they wouldn't be walking out together."

Amos says, "If you see two walking out together regularly" (and that is the verb – "Habitually walking together") "don't you jump to a conclusion and say, "There's a reason for this"? If you hear a lion roaring, you know there is a reason for that too. If you know anything about lions, you will know that a lion roars when it is sure of its prey or food. While it is stalking, it is silent, but when it is within reach of its food or prey, it roars and pounces to paralyse its prey. So Amos says, "If you hear a lion roaring, you know that it's pouncing"; it has sought its prey and found it.

Thirdly, "If you see a bird trapped in a snare, that has not happened unless there has been bait in the snare for the bird to get." A bird doesn't just fly into a trap; it goes for a reason. Fourthly, "If you hear the trumpet blow, doesn't your heart quake because you know the reason behind that?" Now the *shofar*, the Hebrew ram's horn trumpet, was the equivalent to the air raid siren in our society. Those of you who remember that wailing noise, do you remember when it started going up, wailing up; your heart missed a beat. Why? Because you knew there was a reason for that sound, and the reason? There were enemy planes crossing the coast from the channel and you knew it. You didn't see the reason, but you knew that lay behind the siren.

So now Amos says, "When disaster comes to a city or a nation, do you think God is not behind that? Can you not see that there is a reason for the disaster? Does disaster befall a city and God is not in it?" In other words, disaster should make us ask questions about God. When the nation gets in a mess, when we are in an economic crisis, should we not begin to ask what God is saying to us through this, instead of just trying to find some economic way out. Should we not ask what God thinks about our troubles at the moment?

Finally he says, "Do you think a chap like me, whose job

is looking after sheep, would travel all this way and get up in the middle of a town and preach like this if there wasn't a reason behind it? What do you think is behind my preaching? I will tell you. Just as certainly as if you see a young man and a young woman out walking together, you know there is an appointment behind it, so if you see a man like me getting up and preaching you know there is something behind it and it is this: the lion has roared, who will not fear? God has spoken; who can but preach? That is why.

Some people have had the impression that I am a preacher because I enjoy preaching, because I like the sound of my own voice or something like this, or because it is the cushiest job that was going for me. I have heard all kinds of things said to me like this, but I can honestly stand before you and say this: Why do I preach this stuff – is it because people like to hear it? No, I don't think they do, but because God has spoken. Who can but preach? If there is a word from the Lord in this world situation, you cannot keep your mouth shut about it. You have got to preach it. I was ordained to the ministry of the word, primarily; that was what the ordination was about, to preach this wherever and whenever there is an opportunity.

In vv. 9–11, Amos is telling us that God never does a thing without telling people first. Thank God he doesn't. By telling the prophets first, God reveals his justice, because the people will then know what the disaster means and he reveals his mercy by giving them warning. God never sends a disaster without warning people first through his servants. Otherwise, he would be an unjust God. Now he says an amazing thing. "Call the strongholds of... (actually it's Ashdod, which was the Philistines' centre) and to the strongholds in the land of Egypt. Assemble yourselves upon the mountains of Syria and look at what is happening among the people of God." In modern English, and putting it in reality today: send for people from other countries and let them come and look at the morals of London, Christian England. Amos is saying that the morals of this godly nation are lower than the atheist nations around.

In the Cold War period, one of the most challenging things that was said about Czechoslovakia was that the Czechoslovakian Christians were amazed that we in the West prayed for them. Why? Because they thought we had forgotten them? No. Because they said, "You are in a far worse state than we are and we have special prayer meetings for Christians in Britain and America."

Christians are stronger and holier in atheist countries than they are in the so-called "Christian West". Amos says, "Send the Philistines and the Egyptians to stand on the mountain and look at the riots going on in the cities of Samaria." One understands the challenge of Amos's words here; it is devastating.

Then he says, "They do not know how to do right." Ignorance is not innocence, because their ignorance is due to their own folly. They have so blunted their moral sense that they have become not immoral, but amoral. I hope you know the difference. There are three sorts of society: moral society, which does right; immoral society, which does wrong; amoral society, which doesn't know the difference. Amos is saying: you have not only become an immoral society, but have so blunted your conscience that you are amoral and people no longer know how to do right; they don't even know what right is. They have no conscience now about doing things that were once considered wrong even though they were done.

I would say this was the big difference between pre-war Britain and post-war. I am old enough to remember pre-war Britain, and then people who did wrong knew they were doing wrong. By and large, they knew they had transgressed or trespassed, climbed a fence into forbidden territory, territory that was forbidden by society as well as by God. We now live in a day in which the fences are down and in which you are not even conscious of trespassing when you are doing wrong. They do not know how to do right. The affluent society in Amos's day became the permissive and the amoral society, not knowing how to do right. God therefore says: they will be surrounded, invaded, taken. Within a generation they were.

Now Amos had been a herdsman, and a herdsman was under the law of Exodus 22. That law stated that a man was responsible for the flock to his employer and that if he lost a sheep he had to pay for it. There was one exception to this in the law. If a sheep was taken by a wild beast, the herdsman had to raise his rod and fight the wild beast off by hand and rescue a bit of the animal, and if he could produce a bit of the animal, he didn't have to make restitution because he was proving that he had tried to fight the wild beast off. Amos, remembering his days as a herdsman, could remember coming back with a leg or an ear of a lamb to prove that he had done what he could to stop the wild beast. In the same way, Amos is saying: Don't you realise that as a preacher I am seeking to prove that I have done what I could for this nation? Even if I have only an ear or a leg to show for it, even if I can only save just one or two people from this, it will prove that, as a herdsman, as a shepherd, as a pastor, I have done what I could. Indeed, that is every preacher's ambition that whether the world will listen and turn as a whole or not, if he can at least save something to prove that he did what he could, if there will be some people in heaven saved from the coming doom because he preached the word of God, then he has fulfilled his calling adequately as pastor.

So here is this pastor now; his shepherd's heart is coming out. He thinks that is all he will be able to rescue. As a shepherd has a leg or an ear of a lamb to prove that he did something to fight off what was coming, he believed he would have a little to show for his prophecy. But what would happen to the others?

First, their religious life would suffer. I don't know if you have seen a picture of a Hebrew altar. It was like a big, open box with a fire under a grate and the sacrifice was put on top. Then there were four literal horns at the four corners of the altar. These were places of refuge and you could hold a horn and nobody could touch you as long as you were holding the horn. In other words, your religion did give you security. In Durham Cathedral, there is a big ring knocker on the west door. At one time, if you hung on to that, you could not be touched legally. Religion has provided a refuge for people, a place of defence and safety. Amos is saying that when the land is invaded, the first thing they will do is break the horns off the altar so you have nothing to cling to in your religion.

The second thing he says is that their affluence will be hit badly. There were three sorts of luxury dwellings. When people had more than enough money for the house they lived in, what did they do? Some of them bought a second house so that they lived half of the year in the winter house, half in the summer house. Some of them said, "No, we'll stick to one house, but we'll decorate it lavishly," and they decorated it with ivory. Some of them said, "No, we'll not do that, we'll build a larger house", and they build a great house, far too big for themselves to live in. When you have more money than you need, you do one of those things with your house. You either get a second one, or you decorate the one you have too lavishly, or you extend it. Amos said, "The summer house will go, the ivory house will go, the great house will go." He could hardly be more direct and more practical; and the lamb will be swallowed. The tragedy is it all came true.

By this time the congregation is departing in great

numbers so Amos says again, "Hear this word. Come back. I've got more for you from God. Don't run away." Amos becomes even more practical. He gives them three reasons why God is saying all this. He goes into more detail. Now if you think preachers should speak in soft language and should be tactful and courteous, listen to him now speaking to the ladies of Bethel: "You cows".

Now that has become an insulting term of abuse today, but this is language of the prophets of God. If you think this is un-Christ-like language, let me remind you that Jesus said about Herod, "Go and tell that fox...." God calls a spade a spade, and God's language is most direct. The Authorized Version, in beautiful Elizabethan English, often shades this out and hides it, but the word of God came originally in the most blunt, direct language. Amos, watching the ladies in their evening dresses coming out of the large and great houses of Bethel and Gilgal, said, "You cows of Bashan." Now what is "Bashan"? It is an area in the Middle East that has the best grass, and when you wanted to fatten a calf or a cow for the slaughter, you sent them to Bashan and they got fatter and sleeker and then the knife came.

That is what he means. He looks at society and he is pointing out that they are just fattening themselves for a day of slaughter. He is very hard on the women. He makes out that they have descended to an animal level; that they are heartless and brainless and that all they are interested in is gratifying their desires and appetites. To do this, they have to push their husbands to get more and more money, to get on in business until they bring their husbands to a point where they oppress the needy and crush the poor to get enough money to satisfy their wives' insatiable appetite.

Is this unknown today? I talked to a lady who had just been converted a week before. I said, "What difference has it made to you that you've become a Christian?"

She replied, "I'll tell you what. I told my husband yesterday I didn't want that dishwasher after all. I only wanted it because they'd got one next door, not because I needed it. It's wonderful to be redeemed [that was her word] from the rat race."

Now this is practical and this is down to earth. "Hear, you cows of Bashan, you wives, pushing your husbands on to get more and more from this society. You will be taken away with fishhooks." I have seen in a museum a relief from an Assyrian monument which shows the ladies of Samaria being taken away with hooks in their lips and ropes pulling them. The Assyrians came and did precisely this. There they were; they were hooked on their own selfishness and they were taken away as if they were just animals. It all happened and it is there in stone for anyone to see.

Amos talks about the religion again. In the most biting irony and bitter satire, in perhaps the whole Bible, his message means: come and have a religious orgy; you love religion – pack the temple. Bring your offerings. Bring them every morning even though you only need to bring them once a week.

Why is Amos so sarcastic? For the simple reason that in an affluent society, religion flourishes. Religion does not go down in affluence; it tends to go up. Some of the best-attended churches in our land are precisely in this kind of situation. Why? Because people with means like religion, but it is a particular kind of religion. The kind of religion they love would be subscription lists with names. They like offerings with leaven. In other words, instead of asking what God would like, and bringing an offering of simple things, they must bring their own leavened food as an offering. But you notice there is one thing missing in vv. 4–5: no sin offering. That is the one thing that they don't want to bring.

If a preacher talks about sin and judgment, that is not

quite nice, so they don't bring a sin offering. They bring every other kind of offering in a patronising way. This is religion without tears, religion without repentance; this is respectable religion that is so nice, but is not real because it doesn't meet God – that is what is wrong with it. It is superficial religious affluence.

Why do people love religion? Well first of all, it is a good social occasion. You will meet everybody. Secondly, it stifles your conscience. The more freewill offerings you give with your name attached, then the more your conscience is stifled. You have done your bit; you support the church well. More than that, it feeds your pride and self-righteousness.

Thirdly, all the time they had been doing this in religion, God had been trying to break through to them. In their affluence, he had kept removing it, kept challenging it, and kept eroding it. Economically, everything seemed to be better than ever before, but again and again he sent an economic crisis to them. Again and again he sent a shortage to them. They didn't listen.

Now comes a series of five poignant, pleading, tragic, words from God. "I sent you clean teeth." In the Middle East in those days, they didn't use toothbrushes or toothpaste and a healthy sign was dirty teeth because you had food. If you met a man with clean teeth, it meant he had not eaten. I sent you a food shortage. You didn't think about me; you just went on. I sent drought and rain was patchy and three cities had to go to one for food. You didn't come back to me. I sent diseases on your crops. The ecology was upset. I am putting that in modern terms now.

The beginning of 4:10 refers to venereal disease: I sent an increase of that, but you didn't return to me. I put you to war and I slew your young men with a sword and you went through wars and you didn't return to me.

I recall that Winston Churchill's final volume of *The*

Second World War is subtitled, "How the Great Democracies Triumphed and Thus were Able to Resume the Follies that had so Nearly Cost Them Their Lives." Oh, we had packed the churches for days of prayer during the war, but when it was over and our young men were slain and buried in Europe, we did not return to the Lord.

God sent invasion, and they experienced something like Sodom and Gomorrah, a volcanic eruption – "And you were as a brand plucked from the burning." Yet they still did not return to him.

Now we are not saying that all natural disasters are from God. They are from God if he says they are. We are not saying either that no natural disasters are from God. But when disaster comes to a nation, the first question that nation ought to ask is: what is God saying to us through this? That did happen in the eighteenth century. There was an earthquake in Britain and the nation turned to God. The Reverend John Wesley preached one of his mightiest sermons I have ever read. It called the nation to think of God. Such disasters should have made them think of God, but it did not do so.

What was wrong with Israel, basically? They were prosperous and they had had peace. They had religion, but they never met God. Amos now finishes up: "Get ready to meet God." He has told them that the Assyrian is going to invade their land, but he doesn't say, "Get ready to meet the Assyrian." He didn't say, "Prepare to meet the enemy. Prepare to meet the Assyrian. Prepare to meet Tiglath-Pileser," the emperor who was going to come. He said, "Get ready to meet God." In other words, there is hope. If you will only get ready to meet God now, there is still hope that something can be done. If Britain today would only prepare to meet God instead of preparing to meet the next financial crisis, something could be done. This is the call of God and

I would to God it went out with ringing tones from every pulpit in the land and everywhere else. I would want to ask of every parliamentary candidate in a General Election: "What do you think of God?" It seems to me a more important question than any other we could ask.

How do you prepare to meet God? It depends entirely what sort of a God you are going to meet, doesn't it? (see v.12f.) Amos is saying that it is no use preparing to meet God with guns because this God creates the wind and made the mountains. It is no use preparing to meet God with excuses because he knows the thoughts and hearts of people so there is no point in preparing excuses and saying, "Well, Lord, it's happened because of this." It is no use preparing to meet God by trying to run away from him because he treads the tops of the mountains and you can't escape. Every man and woman must prepare to meet God some day. You cannot meet God with your money, your weapons, your social standing, your excuses – with anything. There is only one way to meet the God of hosts, the God of heavenly armies, earthly armies. It is the way of unconditional surrender. When you realise that God knows your thoughts inside out, when you realise that God can turn the morning into darkness and tread the heights of the mountains, and when you realise that the Lord of Hosts is his name, there is only one way to prepare. That is the way of coming and saying: "God, I absolutely surrender to you. I am yours to do with what you want. I give in. You have disciplined me. You have spoken to me. You have chastised me. Lord, I'm willing now to learn."

Read Amos 5–6
A sixteen-year old girl went out for a walk late one evening. She never came back and they found her body, stripped and assaulted, lying under the trees near her home. They presumed that she had gone out to meet one of her boyfriends

and there she was, a sixteen-year old girl starting off in life as an innocent little baby, growing up as a happy girl and now, they find her like that and there is nothing more can be done.

That is how Amos felt about the nation of Israel at this point. He is still having difficulty keeping his audience and I am not surprised because he has said some pretty horrible things to them. He has called the high society women "Cows of Bashan". He has accused the men of injustice, bribery and corruption. He has lifted the lid off this rotten society and he has laid it bare for everyone to see. Once again, he has to say "Hear this word; listen to me". But now a new note creeps into his preaching. It is the note of sorrow, the note of weeping. He says: "Hear this word, which I take up over you in lamentation."

The first lesson here is that we have no right to renounce evil unless we can also weep over it. We have no right to lift the lid off a rotten society unless we feel grieved that we have to do so. It is the prophet with tears in his eyes who can say the kind of thing that Amos has said. So now he says, "I look at this nation and I see it like a girl whose has been blasted, and who lies there, fallen and forsaken, and nobody can do anything about her."

Amos lived in the country. He was a shepherd. He must often have seen country girls leave the country and go to the large towns of Bethel and Gilgal. He must have heard how they went there to find real life and how, gradually, their purity and their personalities became corrupted and spoiled, until they were left looking years older than they actually were in some room by themselves with no one to help. He knew that this went on but he said it was happening to the whole nation. This nation is like a young girl lying there and it is too late to help. Fallen, to rise no more is the virgin of Israel. Forsaken, there is none to raise her up.

In other words, she neither has the help within herself or

the strength to lift herself up, nor is there anyone else who has the power to lift her up. She is bereft of internal strength and external aid alike. Now this is what made Amos weep and wail. This whole chapter is filled with tears and finishes with a prediction that one day, Amos, who is the only one crying, will be joined by an entire city and streets full of wailing.

I am reminded of that terrible moment when Jesus was the only one who cried. He rode into Jerusalem on an ass. Everybody was thrilled and happy. It was a holiday; it was a wonderful day. They were throwing palm branches around and throwing their garments down and shouting, "Hip, hip, hurray!" or "Hosanna", which was their equivalent. They were having a great time and out of that whole happy crowd, Jesus wept. He said, "If you had only known the day that God visited you. If you only recognised what was really happening, but there will come a day when you will all be weeping like me."

This is how God leads people to see society as it really is. Perhaps one of the greatest needs of our nation today is a group of men and women who will weep over the state of Britain while everybody else is having a great time. We need men like Amos who say: listen to the word of lamentation I raise over you; you are like a young girl whose life has been blasted to bits and she can neither help herself nor can anyone help her.

He then sees a series of visions – some about the future, some about the present. Recall that one of the features of his day was the drift from the country to the city. People were crowding into bigger and bigger urban areas: Bethel, Gilgal, Beersheba were all expanding rapidly. People were moving to the towns for three reasons. First, financial. There were better jobs, and better wages, and more money in the city. Secondly, they were moving in for military security and felt they would be safer in large towns where there were numbers who could defend themselves. Thirdly, because they had superstitious ideas about the religion of the cities, and felt they would be safe religiously if they were near the temples of Bethel and Gilgal.

Amos sees that, in fact, the city is the most insecure place to be for the future. I am old enough to remember the days when we set off, packed into trains, as children with little cardboard boxes hanging around our necks. In evacuation, children in the cities were being sent to Devon, the Lake District, to the country – anywhere to get them out of London. A number of you came to Guildford in those days to get out of London. The insecurity of the city was obvious in 1939 and 1940 and that was the place not to be when there was trouble.

Amos could see that although people were crowding into cities, those were going to be the most dangerous places. He says, "Don't go to Bethel, don't go to Gilgal, don't go to Beersheba – go to God. Seek God and live." He could see the cities decimated so that a city of a thousand will be a city of a hundred and a town of a hundred will be a village of ten. The warning is: don't run to the cities; run to God.

In America there is a deep valley in the hills with underground mansions. They have been dug out of the rock at tremendous cost and they are little palaces inside. People live in them and commute to work from them. They are digging down into these underground caves to live like animals in the rocks because they seek security. It is this kind of thing that Amos is addressing, and saying: seek God and live; stop running to human resources; seek God.

I tremble on Remembrance Day when I hear the people of Britain who never go to church singing "O God, Our Help in Ages Past". They come to these words: "Sufficient is thine arm alone and our defence is sure." It almost seems hypocrisy to sing that and then ignore that for the rest of the year and spend more on defence than on almost anything else. Now I am not saying we shouldn't spend money on defence; I am saying that the message for Britain today is this, "Seek God and live" or, "Stop singing such hypocritical songs every November 11th."

Why should we seek God? The answer is because the real enemy is God. The real enemy of every nation and empire is God. America may have its Arctic circle of radar early warning, but the real enemy is God. Radar doesn't tell you when God comes. Britain may have its defence system, but the real enemy of Britain is God. Nations rise and fall by his command, and empires come and go by his will. When God has written a nation off and when God decrees that an empire's days are numbered, there is no defence against that. Why not? Because God is the one who controls everything. Amos says God controls Pleiades and Orion. The stars are there because God put them there. He controls the day and the night. It is God who keeps the sea within its bounds and it is God who can bring a tidal wave and bring the sea over the land. It is God who keeps nature reliable and regular and because it is he who keeps it regular, he can also turn it round the other way and cause disaster to come.

We must remember that the God who saw that the sun rose this morning could have stopped it this morning. We must remember that the God who keeps the ocean within its limits can most easily set that ocean free. We are aware that if ice melted through a minor change in climate, the oceans could rise two hundred feet, which would obliterate perhaps two-thirds of the major cities of the world. Two hundred feet would cover most of London and it would cover almost all of Tokyo. That is the narrow limit in which we live in safety and we only live in safety because God keeps the oceans within their limit. It is God who controls the stars, the sea, and the wind. Therefore, to run to cities is a silly and useless thing to do once God has said through his prophets: "I am against you."

The second vision which he has concerns the breakdown of law and order, the breakdown of the judicial system of that permissive, affluent society of Israel. This is a situation that arises wherever people become selfish. Law and order begins to crack. What was happening in Israel? In those days they didn't have courtrooms or assemblies where the judges came. They sat in the city gate and if you go to an ancient city in the Middle East, there is the gateway, and either side are benches, and the judges sat in the gate. Amos says, "You pervert justice in the gate. You bribe the judges. The rich people get a better deal in the courts than the poorer people." I have lived in countries where someone with money can get the better defence and can bribe the witnesses – where a man of position can pervert justice. That comes, inevitably, in a society that is crumbling – justice goes.

Furthermore, there is a dislike of authority. In modern terms, a breakdown of relationships between public and police or, in this case, between the public and the judges. "They hate him who reproves in the gate and they abhor him who speaks the truth." There is a reluctance to be disciplined by authority. That is something we are beginning to see in the attitude to the police. I did not think I would live to see the day when the police would have to go out with face shields, shields on their arms, batons in their hands, and tear gas bombs. But we are seeing it. We need to pray for the police. They are suffering increasing difficulties in maintaining law and order and reproving the wrongdoer.

Amos says that God is a God of justice. Literally, reading the Hebrew as it stands, there were property owners extorting, so Amos says: you landlords, you have built houses of human stone, but God will see you don't live in them; you have planted lovely gardens and vineyards for yourself – you will never drink the wine from them because God is a God of justice and sooner or later we stand in his court.

The third vision he has in this chapter is of the total breakdown of society to the point where everybody is weeping and wailing in the streets, not knowing where to go, what to do, because society has collapsed and God has passed through the midst of the cities. It is a depressing picture. This whole chapter is a chapter of doom and yet, piercing the clouds like the sunlight shafts coming through a thundercloud, are three appeals through his tears: "Seek God and live." You notice it in vv. 4, 6 and 14. But in v. 14 it becomes: "Seek good and live." Now to seek God and to seek good are one and the same thing. You cannot seek God unless you are ready to seek good. "Seek first his kingdom and his righteousness."

In other words, it is sheer hypocrisy to seek God unless you are going to seek good at the same time. Someone who is unwilling to have his sins not only forgiven but removed, not willing to have his life straightened out when it is all wrong, is not a person who can seek God. God is good, and if I am going to seek him then I must seek good. He is a God of goodness, justice, and righteousness.

Otherwise, I would be tempted to seek God for the wrong reason. I would say, "God, I'm in trouble. I need you. Society is breaking up and this makes my life less comfortable. God, I'd like you to get Britain out of all her economic troubles." But unless we are at the same time prepared to say, "God, will you get Britain out of all her moral troubles", what right have we to ask him to save us economically? "Seek God and live; seek good and live." If we really mean business with God, we shall seek not only help in our troubles, but help in our sins as a nation. This is the message of Amos. You cannot find God unless you are ready to find good.

I remember trying to help a student, who said he had tried

to find God for some time and he had sought, and prayed, and gone to church and he couldn't get through to God at all. As we talked, the Holy Spirit began to show me what was the real barrier. I said to him, "Would you mind telling me about your personal relationships with people?" At first, he was almost offended that I wanted to pry into his private life, but I said, "I think if you're really going to get help, you'll need to share this with me." Then he did and he was in a relationship which God could never approve. No wonder he couldn't find God. He said, "I'm seeking God," but he was not seeking good. Therefore, because he wasn't seeking good, he couldn't find God. If you are really going to live, you seek God and good together. When he faced up to this and said, "Now God, you deal with this relationship," then he found God straightaway and he lived. That is the message of Amos: there is no shortcut to God past our sins. If we come to God, we must leave our sins behind.

Now we turn to the next section, and from wailing he turns to woe-ing and he takes on a sterner note. Now a "woe" is the opposite of a blessing; it is a curse. It is the opposite of a benediction; it is a malediction. Jesus himself often said "woe". He said, "Blessed are you, poor; woe to you, rich. Blessed are those who mourn; woe to those who laugh now. Blessed – woe; it is the other side of the coin.

Now Amos utters three woes, curses if you like, on the religious, political, and domestic life of the nation of Israel. Again, as I read these things, I found myself wondering how Amos knew about Britain – how he knew all this. Let us look first at the religious life. Outwardly their belief and behaviour were all right, but inwardly it was all wrong. They said and did the right things. They prayed that God would come; they prayed for the Day of the Lord. They said, "Lord, come – we want you." They gave offerings to God, burnt offerings and other offerings. God said: "I loathe it. I hate it."

Why? Well the first thing is they got the Day of the Lord wrong. They thought that if only God came, he would judge all the wicked people and they would be alright. How easy it is to do this. I recall again the national days of prayer during the war. I was quite young at the time. I remember being left with the impression that the Germans were the wicked people and the British were the good people and that we were praying for God to come and get rid of the baddies and leave us goodies alright.

I remember distinctly getting that impression from the prayers. I know now that there are sinners in Germany and sinners in Britain. I know now that there is nothing to choose between us as far as human nature is concerned. Whatever was happening then, in human nature there is nothing to choose. There is no such thing as the baddies and the goodies in this world. Yet we are always in our propaganda trying to say it is others who are bad. We are always trying to divide up and say, "Now God, come and deal with the baddies. Get rid of these wicked people." But when God comes, he deals with everybody fairly. If we are going to ask God to come and stop a war, we are asking God to deal with sin on our side as well as on the other side. In a vivid phrase Amos says: "It's as if a man is running away from a lion and meets a bear." It is almost a humorous situation, this. There he is, tearing across the jungle path, and a lion in the distance coming after him, and there is a bear standing in his path. He thought he was running to safety and he was running slap into something worse because, in fact, a bear is more dangerous to a man than a lion. It is as if a man was running away from a lion and managed to get into his house, and was puffing and panting, and leant with his hand against the wall and there was a snake in the crack in the stones that bit his hand and he died. Amos is saying: "You think that the day of the Lord will bring you out of trouble. It won't; it will bring you into worse. You think if God comes in answer to your prayer, he'll deal with all the wicked people around you. He won't; he'll deal with you. Therefore, your hypocrisy in praying that God will come is manifest. Now come to what you think is the delight of the Lord. You offer feasts, assemblies and offerings, and you play beautiful music. To God, your music is just a noise."

Singing praise to God may be beautiful musically, but to God it may be a noise. God does not judge our music by strict musical standards. He judges by other things. Therefore, what to us may be a sweet and a beautiful sound may be an utter noise to him. He may not delight in it. Our offerings of praise and thanksgiving may be beautifully worded and people may say, "What a beautiful service—how peaceful and worshipful." The real test of worship is: did God enjoy it? Did he delight in it? Did he love it?

What I get from all this is that there is a perilous danger of self-delusion in religion that you may think is beautiful and God may think is ugly; that you may think sounds good and God may say, "That's a noise"; that you may think, "God is thrilled with what we have done for him," and God says, "I hate it. I despise it; it's offensive and loathsome to me." Why? I will tell you in one sentence. Amos says, "Let justice roll down like streams. Let righteousness flow like a river." In other words, it is the life we live outside our worship that decides whether God enjoys our worship.

If I am a landlord extorting from the poor from Monday to Saturday, however beautiful my worship on Sunday, he hates it. If I am being unfair and unjust to people, if I am saying nasty things about them that are not true, if I am being a horrid person to live with at home during the week, God does not like my worship. It is self-delusion that he is enjoying it. Let justice and righteousness fill your life. Let standards of morality, let uprightness and integrity, honesty, and purity flow down like rivers through your life.

What he is saying is: let these things flow through your life into the society around, and then I enjoy your Sunday services; then I love your singing, and then I accept your offering. He reminds them that even in the days of the wilderness they brought offerings to God, but not for the forty years. They ran after other gods and they were unjust to each other and they broke the commandments during the week before the Sabbath came round. Only two out of two million survived the wilderness.

How can you worship a God of integrity on Sunday and be fiddling the accounts during the week? How can you worship God on Sunday and live a life of selfish indulgence from Monday to Saturday, only concerned with what I want? We can't do it.

That is the religious life. Now we turn to the political life and Amos says, "Woe to you, politicians – incompetents." First of all, there is their utter complacency in the light of social evil. One of the frustrations for us today is the complacency that is revealed in so much political life.

Amos's message is: you sit at ease; you feel secure – then look at the nations around and look what is happening to them. Look at Gath; look at these other places. Are you any different from them? Is your territory greater than theirs? Woe to those of you who live in your homes and indulge yourself.

In what way? First: a preoccupation with leisure: "You lie on ivory couches." Not only did they live for leisure rather than work, they lived for food. They were not even content that the lambs and calves should grow up and provide more meat. They wanted lamb and veal straightaway, before there was a chance for them to grow up.

Then: you just like music – idle songs – and you invent new kinds of music. We are so busy inventing electronic music and new kinds of sound just to amuse ourselves in our idleness. David invented instruments to praise God more richly; we invent idle songs, for ourselves.

Then he says: you like drinking too, and you drink wine by the bucketful; you are preoccupied with personal cosmetics and body toiletry. But you are not grieved over the ruin of Joseph.

Could you see anything more relevant than that – a society that is not grieved over a collapse of standards, over the breakup of family life, over the dishonesty that is so creeping through our society that every major firm and shop has a major problem with petty thieving and lifting things and taking them home? Amos says they will be the first to go.

What is behind all this? We come to the epilogue and God says, "What I really hate is your pride; I abhor the pride of Jacob." Then comes an awful picture of a city in which the plague has come and in which people are hiding their dead. They are scared stiff that God will punish them for hiding the corpses in their home. Here is a pathetic picture of a city hanging on to its dead because of the plague.

So finally Amos tells them they are silly, insane, so irrational, like a horse riding over rocks – an insane thing to do. You will never get far. It is like someone trying to plough the sea with oxen, an utterly foolish thing to do.

Amos then says, "You are so proud that you took a place called "Lo-debar". Here is a humorous and ironic comment. Lo-debar was a place in Transjordan which Jeroboam had taken. Do you know what the meaning of the word, Lo-debar is? It means "nothing". He is saying: you are so proud of having taken nothing. Your real political propaganda is all about nothing. It is an achievement that is no achievement. All your achievements are nothing and so God is coming to you and God is going to speak to you.

Amos has often been accused of being a prophet of doom.

He is, but he is also a prophet of hope. I sum up chapters 5–6 in two statements, which come to you as a message from God today: if you seek God now, you will find that he is gracious and you will live; but if you wait until God seeks you, you will find that he is just and you will die. That message goes through the whole Bible, from cover to cover. Amos only applied it in his day. I apply it in ours. I say to this nation: seek God now and you can live, for he is gracious; but if you wait until he seeks you out, you will die. I say it to every individual while there is still life and hope. Seek God now and live by seeking good as well, and living. But if you wait until God finds you, you will die. We plead with anyone who will listen.

Isn't it interesting that in one part of the Bible people are told that in a day when God seeks them, they will hide from him, and in another part of the Bible it says if you come to him now, you can hide in him?

Read Amos 7–8

Not only does God's truth come in words, but it came to Amos in pictures which he saw—visions. There are four visions, which now he shares with the people of Israel. The first is a vision of locusts, the second is of fire, the third is of a plumb line, and the fourth is a picture of a basket full of fruit. We are going to look at these pictures one by one and ask what God was saying in showing these pictures to the nation of Israel? Amos has already taken the lid off their corrupt society. He has shown how far it has gone from God in its religious life, its political life, its social life. Now he is looking even further, and in the visions, he is seeing where all this could lead to.

In the first vision, God shows him one possible punishment that he could use to deal with this corrupt nation and he shows him a plague of locusts. Now I don't need to say much more about that. We have thought about the damage they do but let me just remind you that a locust swarm can have twenty thousand million insects in it, which can travel two thousand miles, and every day they will eat between sixty and eighty thousand tons of greenery. That would absolutely ruin a nation in the position of Israel. There would be nothing left. Furthermore, the swarm would eat up the foliage before and after the nation, so that they would not be able to go to their neighbours for help. Furthermore, the vision that God shows Amos is of a plague of locusts coming between two crops. In Israel you can get two crops in the year, the early growth and the latter growth, but the early growth all had to go to the king as tax. That was the way they paid their dues in those days. The latter growth was what they had for themselves, after the king's levy. Here is a plague of locusts coming after the king's mowings and against the latter growth. Amos is so horrified he flings himself down on his knees and says, "Lord, please don't do this." He knows that Israel deserves it, so he pleads for mercy and says, "Forgive, I beseech you. Show mercy on this land. You will blot it out altogether if you do this. Jacob is too small to stand it; our reserves are too small.

A man who denounces his nation for sin must be one who can weep over that nation, pray for it, and beg for God's mercy on it. Applying that to our own nation, it is comparatively easy to say what is wrong with Britain. It is comparatively easy to see the immorality sweeping over us. It is not so easy to weep over our nation and beg for mercy. But someone who does has the right and the authority to criticise and to preach, because people will very quickly sense if someone does not pray for the people he denounces.

Now comes the amazing thing. God repents, and the word "repent" means changes his mind. God says, "This shall not be." Whenever you pray and say "Amen" that means "this shall be". Amos prayed and the response was God saying the opposite of "amen". Sometimes when we pray, we want God to say the opposite of "amen". We want him to say "this shall not be", and Amos is now telling Israel that he has saved them by prayer from a plague of locusts. I wonder if they believed him. I wonder if they said, "Thank you, Amos, for praying for us," or did they say, "Who's to know that the plague of locusts would have come anyway?" That would have been a typical reaction.

Amos went on to tell them of a second vision: fire. This was not a prairie fire, not a bush fire; the word means a volcanic eruption in which fire flows over the land; in which it devours the rocks underneath and then begins to devour the topsoil; the great deep and the land. So the land which has brought them food becomes just red-hot lava. Now this could happen in the Middle East – it is a volcanic area. Sodom and Gomorrah disappeared this way, under a volcanic eruption of fire. God let Amos know this is how he was thinking of dealing with this land: of sending lava over it and just obliterating it. Amos prays again and says, "O God, cease I beseech you. Jacob is too small! We can't stand that either; there will be nothing left." And for the second time God says that he will not do it. That volcanic eruption never came over the nation of Israel.

I want to point out the remarkable implications of these two visions and two prayers. The first implication is difficult enough; the second you will find almost impossible. Here is the first: prayer changes things. Now I find that a lot of even churchgoers believe that prayer changes people, but not that prayer changes things and that therefore there is no point in praying about things. To take a down-to-earth example, there is no point in praying about the weather, because prayer can't change the weather, because it can't change things; it can only work through people. But here we have prayer averting two natural disasters: stopping locusts and stopping a volcano. That is the first mazing truth that these two things tell us: that prayer can change physical things. Now it takes faith to believe that. Amos had that faith, and he believed that you could stop a locust plague through prayer and that you could stop a volcano erupting through prayer.

Here is the second, and I don't know what you are going to think of this: you can actually change God's mind through prayer. Now there are many who feel that prayer is simply to line yourself up with God's will; that prayer can't do anything about that will; that prayer is simply a way of surrendering to that will. This is the Muslim notion of prayer. "Islam" means to submit. "Muslim" means the surrendered one, and the Muslim attitude of prayer is this: their deity has made up his mind what he is going to do; there is nothing you can do about it. Therefore the height of prayer and piety is to submit to what God has already decided.

But if this is the word of God in Amos 7, prayer can actually change the mind of God. Why should this be? Because we can push God around where we want him? No, because God wants a fully personal relationship with us. This is the attitude of an earthly father to earthly children. There are certain things in which I want my children to come and talk a thing over with me and I may well change my mind. They may ask me to do a thing, and I may first say "no", but then if they change their attitude and come to me on a different tack, then it may well be that I will say, "Alright, now I will. I will change my mind and do this." Every parent has done that, because you want to lead your children; you want them to see things in a different way, and therefore, when they change, you are prepared to change. When they come to you with a different attitude, you are prepared to change your attitude. It is a real personal relationship. You still have full parental authority, but you don't impose it with an iron hand; you cooperate. Here I find the most amazing thing about the fatherhood of God: that someone can pray, and help God to change his mind, and that God will repent. That does not mean to be sorry for something wrong. To repent means quite simply to change one's mind. In fact, that's what it does mean in the Hebrew and in the Greek meaning of the word. It's made up of two words meaning "mind change". When it says "God repented" it means God changed his mind. Do you realise, therefore, that if God has made up his mind to judge Britain, that Christians getting on their knees and begging him to have mercy on this nation could change his mind concerning this nation? That is the reality of prayer. This is a conception of prayer which you will find only in the Bible.

God said, "I'm going to send locusts," and even though the nation deserved that, one man begging in prayer was enough to stop it! One man for a whole nation! I sometimes wonder if our nation is not in a far worse situation than it is, because some people are begging for the mercy of God for it and holding back the judgment of God. You can't hold it back forever; you can't hold it back altogether; but you can change his mind in the way it will come.

Which brings me to the next vision: God, in his infinite patience, says to Amos: "What do you see?" Amos says, "I see a plumb line." That is a piece of string with a bit of lead on the bottom. What is it for? It is not just to get a straight thing; it is to get an upright thing. For the plumb line of itself does nothing, it points to the centre of gravity. It lines up with something deep in the heart of the earth that is constant and fixed, and so the plumb line, pointing to that something, enables you to put up something that is upright. God is holding a plumb line against this nation. The plumb line is God's law. As one text in the Bible says: "It is by the straight edge of God's law that we see how crooked we are."

It is to test uprightness, because the plumb line of God's law points to the holiness of the heart of God. All of God's laws point to this holiness and are there to help us to build upright characters and an upright nation.

Have you noticed how the word "upright" is hardly used today? When did you last hear someone described as an upright person? Could it be that you hardly find many upright people today – that so many of us are crooked that we dare not use the word? The Bible is always using "upright" of an honest person of integrity. A plumb line was used after a building was built to see if it was going to fall down. You may have seen garden walls that were upright when they were built and gradually the foundations go and the wall begins to veer. The builder comes along, sets a plumb line on it and says, "That wall must be pulled down—it's dangerous. That wall's going to collapse any day," and down it has to come. God would say: I built this nation straight. I gave them my ten commandments. I built this nation upright. The foundations have gone and look at it Amos, look at the plumb line. It is veering over. This nation is going to collapse. Its days are numbered therefore I must pull it down before the danger comes.

Applying this to the nation of Israel, Amos then begins to describe the various parts of the wall that are beginning to fall. He says: your high places, your sanctuaries, and your royal family. What does he mean? He means the place of your leisure and social life, the place of your religious life, and the place of your government and political life; once again, the three things that have gone wrong. The high places were foul places. They were centres of black magic; they were centres of living for kicks; they were centres of sex.

The high places, if you read about them (and I am not going to elaborate – it is too horrible) were places that people went in their leisure to have a great time, and they had all kinds of perverted enjoyments there. The high places—on the top of mountains they did it, almost defying heaven to look at it. They were crooked and falling down. Their sanctuaries were crooked measured by the plumb line of God's law. In the house of Jeroboam the king and the government, the plumb line reveals that God must do something.

At this point, we have a little interlude. There is one man at this point who heckles, opposing Amos, and his name is Amaziah. He hated this farmer from the south. Why? Because Amos and Amaziah, confronting each other, are the prophet and the priest – the one concerned with reform and the one concerned with ritual; the amateur and the professional; the one who has a vested interest in his temple, and the one who is just a shepherd given the word of God. There is a real clash here between the vested interests of state religion and the preacher who has come with a pure word from the Lord.

Amaziah goes rushing off to the king and tells him there is a prophet who is conspiring against him politically. Do you remember that is what the Jews said to Pilate about Jesus – "He's stirring up trouble, he's starting a rebellion." This political charge is a typical way for the establishment to get rid of the preacher. It happens again and again, and so Amaziah, having told King Jeroboam about this, told Amos to get out of the country; that the king didn't want him; that the king had his own religion, thank you; and that there was no need for prophets to come here. I could almost say that Amos was the plumb line to Amaziah the priest. Amos's pure preaching showed up the corrupt religion, and Amaziah hated it.

Ever since, there has been a conflict between the word of God and established religion. I am not referring here to the Church of England but to religion that becomes established socially; religion that is accepted as simply part of the social set-up; religion that doesn't reform the society in which it is; religion that is just stuck on as a kind of respectability. Amos comes and clashes with that head-on, and Amaziah says: "Get out of here, Amos. We don't want to hear your preaching here." He almost could have said: we want comfort here; we don't like this kind of preaching – we don't want to hear about doom.

Amos replies with a simple, sincere, courteous testimony. Amos says: "I'm not a prophet because it's my career; I am no prophet. I'm not a prophet because of heredity; I am not the son of a prophet. I'm not a prophet because of my environment; I was a herdsman; a dresser of sycamore trees."

The contrast is with Amaziah, a priest. That was Amaziah's career – a priest because he was the son of a priest, brought up in the priesthood. Amos was not brought up that way; not there to earn bread but because God called him to be a prophet and commanded him to go and prophesy in Israel.

Every true preacher must be ready to say that. My father was a preacher and my grandfather was too, but that is not why I am a preacher. It was not my chosen career, and you cannot inherit preaching. Even though I was brought up in the environment, there was a time when I got right away from church and did not want to hear any preaching. I am not a preacher for that reason. A man only gets up to preach the word of God because God called him and commanded him to go somewhere and preach, and for no other reason. That is the only testimony a preacher can give, and if he is in it for a career or if he is in it because his father was in it or if he is in it because he was brought up in it, then he should not be in it. Amos makes it clear that in opposing his preaching Amaziah was opposing God who had called the prophet.

Amos then (in 7:16) challenges Amaziah: "Amaziah, you say, 'Don't preach against...'." Do you notice that little word "against"? I have had people come to me and say, "You know, you're all right when you're preaching *for* something, but I don't like you when you're preaching *against* something," as if it isn't the job of the preacher to preach against. In an age when we are all supposed to be tolerant of any and every religion, we are supposed to be saying nice things about each other, but there are times when we have got to say something against what is wrong. You must preach for and against if you are going to be a real preacher.

Amos speaks words against Amaziah (v. 17) and his family. Amaziah's wife would be reduced to becoming a prostitute on the streets to get a living. Amaziah's children would be slain by the sword. Amaziah would die in a land far away. Amaziah's property would be taken from him and be parcelled out to others. The nation he had served would go into exile. That is a terrible punishment. Why? Because it is a terrible crime. Why? Because Amaziah was supposed to be the representative of God in Israel, and there is no crime so serious as for the representative of God to tell God's representative to get out. The man who ought to have been leading people to God was telling God's messenger to take God's Word away. When that happens that is the most serious crime there can be, and that is why the punishment was so serious.

The fourth vision now comes, "Amos, what do you see?" Amos looked and he saw a basket full of fruit, but a particular kind of fruit – summer fruit. Summer fruit is the late harvest, and it doesn't keep. It goes ripe too quickly, and therefore you cannot store it. We have some fruits in this country very like this that you cannot store; you must eat them straightaway. Strawberries are like that – you just can't lay them by. In a week they would be rotten. There is a pun here, and I am afraid I cannot convey it to you, because the Hebrew word for summer fruit is spelled q-a-u-y-i-t-s, and the Hebrew word for end or climax; the end of things, is q-et-s. You pronounce them the same way. He says, "A basket of summer fruit, then the Lord said to me, 'The end has come upon my people Israel'." So the word for summer fruit and the word for end were derived from the same root word for the simple reason that summer fruit was near its end. It was ripe to the point of being rotten. God is communicating this to Amos: Look at this vision – I see this nation as a nation that is so ripe, it's going rotten. It is ripe for judgment; it's getting very near the end; it's getting near disintegration."

What did God see that caused him to say this? This time Amos does not pray and does not plead; he only has to agree with God; and vv. 4–6 carry an indictment of a society that is rotten because of its greed.

Amos draws attention to the exploitation of the needy. The have's and the have-not's were drawing away from each other. The poor cannot struggle against inflation and exploitation. This is Amos's word to those in Israel who were saying: "When will the new moon be over, that we may sell grain? And the Sabbath, that we may offer wheat for sale?" Furthermore, they were so anxious to make money they were prepared to be deceptive to do it. They made the ephah small and the shekel great, and dealt deceitfully, with false balances and weights. Amos is talking about cheating the customers, and his words are still relevant. When a nation leaves God out, it becomes obsessed with business, obsessed with gain, obsessed with greed, even to the point of deceitfulness in trade.

This shows us the kind of social conscience that we need to be developing, and so in 8:6 Amos challenges a monopoly. Some people wanted to control the poor; to be able to lend them money so that they were forever in their debt – wanting to be able to give them a pair of sandals on credit, so that there would be money coming in from them with interest. He is talking here about lending and credit sales. That is what was happening in their days, and people were forever in debt. When they had the monopoly they could sell the refuse of the wheat as well as the wheat itself, and they could sell anything. It is a picture of corrupt trade and business – people who cannot wait to make a bit more money.

So in vv. 7–14 God has "sworn by the pride of Jacob". People were proud of what they had done. They would boast of a sharp business deal; they would boast of how they did the other person down. God swears by the pride of Jacob that he will never forget anything they did. If they sold a thing for more than it was worth, he would not forget it. What is God going to do? He says, "I'm going to cause your land to rise and fall like the Nile" (8:8). When the rains fall on Ethiopia and come down the Blue and the White Nile, the Nile comes up, and then a few days later it goes down. God is saying that he is going to send an earthquake, and in that day the land will be dark; their feasts will be turned into mourning; and there will be mourning like for an only son. It will be a bitter, dark day in which you cannot see and which the land is rising and falling. He says it will be the worst famine they have had – a famine not of bread but of hearing the word of God.

I reiterate that I am not trying to apply everything in Amos to Britain. Some things don't apply but there is coming a famine to Britain of hearing the words of God, and when I say that, I don't mean that we're short of Bibles. We've got two dozen English Bible versions filling our shops. You can buy Bibles anywhere, but there is a famine of hearing the words of God because people cannot understand the Bible unless someone explains it to them. "How can I, unless someone describe and explain and teach me what it means?" said the Ethiopian eunuch to Philip.

There is a famine coming. Many Christian presses in this country have closed because they just cannot keep going – there is not enough market for Christian books. A large number of Christian magazines and periodicals have gone out of business. Why? Because there isn't a market, people do not want to read those. More than that, there is a shortage, a famine in Britain today, of preachers who will preach the word of God. Why is it that people will travel twenty or thirty miles to a church? The critics will say it is a personality cult, but they don't know what they are talking about. They never ask those people why they do it. Is it because they like one minister better than another? No, it is because there is a famine of hearing the Word of God, and people want to hear the truth. They must go a long way to hear someone who believes the Bible to be the truth, the whole truth and nothing but the truth.

The Bishop of Durham chaired an education commission, which has now this week produced its report entitled "The Fourth R." There will soon be a famine of hearing the word of God in our schools, because religious knowledge in ten years time will not be teaching the Bible—it will be teaching comparative religion and humanistic ethics. There is going to be a famine of hearing the word of God.

I passed through a large town where I saw one church that was a furniture warehouse, another that was now a supermarket, and another that was just boarded up. I thought: "When this city wants to hear the word of God, when they get to the point of wanting to know what God says about it, where are they going to go? The churches are closed, there'll be a famine of the word of God." God says here through Amos: "They shall wander from sea to sea, and from north to east". There will come a day when they want to hear Amos preach, and Amos won't be there. That is a worse famine than a famine of bread.

It would hit the young generation more than the old; the fair virgins and the young men who have gone after false religion will plead with their gods; they will plead with all their eastern mystics: tell us something. It is the young generation who do not even have the memories of the Bible; who don't even have memories of godliness; it is the young generation who'll be badly hit.

When I meet young people today, I find a generation that has grown up with no knowledge of Christian things; and who are going after this, that and the other, hoping to find satisfaction; trying meditation, mysticism, the lot. A university student asked me what I thought about mysticism. They were going to have yoga sessions at a festival in just a few days. The young people were searching to and fro, and there is a famine of the word of God.

We are not dealing with fiction but with fact. In the year 763 BC, two years after Amos said this, there came the most terrible earthquake to Israel, and it coincided with an eclipse of the sun at midday, 763 BC. The records are there, not only in the Bible but outside the Bible, and you can check up. In that year, the land rose and fell like the Nile, the sun went out at noon, and darkness came over a trembling land. If only they had listened; if only they had heard, because God is a God of mercy. He doesn't like doing these things to a nation. Why did he send Amos? The answer is: to plead with them to come back before it was too late.

No nation can afford to play about with God. You cannot defy God and get away with it. A nation that does not come up to God's plumb line will sooner or later fall. It is to this nation at this time that I say in the name of the God of Amos: "Seek God and live." Test yourselves by the plumb line, and confess that you are not upright and not straight. Come back and let the sunshine of his mercy break through once more.

Read Amos 9
The sins that Amos condemned in Israel are wrong anywhere, not just in that nation. This is terribly important: what Amos promises in the last chapter of his prophecy is not a promise that will follow a change of government, but it will follow a change of heart among the people. One of the things that any government has to face in England is the fact that they cannot do much, whatever they promise. As Studdert Kennedy used to say somewhat cynically, "A general election means one lot of sinners out and another lot in." In other words, what we need is help from God. We must not expect too much of a government of sinners in a sinful society until there is a change of heart among the people.

The people of Israel had a number of changes of government following Amos's prophecy and some of them were better than others. Now they did not have a democratically elected government; they had royal government; they were a kingdom, and they had a number of kings—some good, some bad, but what became patently obvious was that whether they had a good government or a bad government, the heart of the people did not change, and therefore the disaster came.

So I am not naively applying Amos 9 to our nation, indeed I must now say, that though there are remarkable parallels between Israel and Britain morally revealed in this prophecy, I now come to the point where these two diverge. Sin is a reproach to any people, but it is worse than ever in God's people, and Israel was a special nation; a nation called by God to live higher standards than anyone else, that people might know that God is a good and holy God. When sin enters that people, then it is a worse reproach than in any nation. The equivalent today is not sin in Britain, but sin in the church, for we are the people of God. Sin in any nation is a reproach, but this kind of attitude in God's people is worse than a reproach; it is bordering on blasphemy, because we bear the name of God.

In the final chapter, Amos has the last vision of all. It is a vision of destruction at first, and then it changes dramatically, like the sunshine coming out after the thunderstorm. It changes dramatically to a vision of a future that is prosperous, peaceful, and secure. We must ask at what point the change occurs, but first we must look at the first half of the chapter. It is not fair when you are reading the Bible to lick the jam out of the sandwich – to concentrate on the bits that are nice and comforting and exclude the bits that are not. You remember that Samson, at the end of his life, killed hundreds of Philistines because he put his great muscles around the two central pillars holding up the roof and he squeezed until the whole pagan house, in which he was, collapsed and killed everyone in it. Amos now sees God doing exactly the same thing. Now, of course, if you don't believe that God is this kind of God you will have difficulty with this and every other passage like it, but I believe that what the Bible tells us about God is true.

Amos says, "I saw the Lord standing beside the altar and saying, 'Smash the capitals that the thresholds may shake and this whole building may collapse on the people in it.'" He is talking of the pagan temple at Bethel where the people of Israel went to worship in their superstitious way. It is a terrible picture – of God reaching the end of his patience. They had gone too far, and he was ready to bring this down on their own heads. Their pagan religion was going to collapse, quite literally.

Now we don't need to take this as a kind of spiritual picture; this is a literal vision that he sees, and in the year 763 BC, it literally came true. The earthquake (that came two years after Amos said this) came on a day when there were thousands of people crowded into the large temple in

Bethel, and it collapsed on their heads. Some of them got out; the majority did not. So we are not talking about visions that are kinds of spiritual pictures, we are talking about fact and reality, except that Amos saw it two years before it happened.

Now in the next part of this chapter (to v. 10) we have three things said about God, which tell us something about the impossibility of escaping from him when you are on the wrong side. I have given them the theologian's labels. These are not words that you will find in the Bible, but they are useful ones that you may hear preachers use: God's *omnipresence*, *omnipotence* and *omniscience*. The word "omni" means "all". The word "omnipresence" means God is present in all places – he is everywhere. The word "omnipotence" – potency means power; omnipotence applied to God means he has the power to do anything. Omniscience: the *science* part of it means knowledge, it is where the word "science" comes from, and omniscience means to know all. God is everywhere in all places; he is able to do all things; he knows everything. Now if you have fallen foul of a God like that, how can you possibly escape? There is nowhere to run to; there is no power that you can have against him; there is no knowledge that he does not have about you.

It is this that Amos now bangs home with picture after picture. First of all: if you think you can run away from God, where do you think you can hide? You can hide from people. Sometimes if a child has done wrong they run away and hide in the bushes, or they run upstairs and hide under the bed.

Amos is saying: you people of Israel, you know you have done wrong. Where do you think you can hide from God? Even if you are not in the temple the day that it crashes, where do you think you can hide from God? He will find out where you are. You may dig into the world of the dead. That is what the word "Sheol" means. You may go and hide among the dead, and people think they can hide among the dead. This is why people commit suicide: they think it is a way out; that they can hide among the dead – but they can't. Though they dig down into Sheol and think they can hide among the dead, they won't.

You may go out into space, and the word for space in the Bible is the "heavens". You may get into a rocket and you may go straight out into space and keep on going. Do you think you can get away from God? No, you are just going into his presence, not running away. You may go and hide up in the mountains. Now this is what most people do in a time of crisis. They take to the hills, and the hill where people used to hide in Israel was Carmel – that twelve-mile long range of hills with caves and boulders. People hid there, and God would find them.

You might go and hide in the bottom of the sea. How could you do that? This was before the days of submarines, but God is saying in poetic language that you could get right down in the depths of the ocean (and that is deeper than the mountains, we now know) and you are no further from God; he can control the creatures of the sea who will come after you. Finally, you might even sell yourself into voluntary slavery so that you can be taken away into another land, and people may not be able to find you again, but God will. If he is omnipresent and you have done wrong, there is nowhere you can go to hide.

May I therefore straightaway add, lest someone be terrified by this thought, that if you have done wrong, the best place to hide is *in* God, not *from* God. Come and hide in God. You will never hide from God. You may hide your crimes from other people; you don't hide them from God. You may say, "Well, I'm going to emigrate to Australia or Canada", or, "I am going to get away and start again where nobody knows me," but you don't get away from God.

The second thing that Amos says is that it is not only inescapable, the judgment that is coming, because of God's omnipresence, it is irresistible because of his power. You cannot do a thing to stop God judging. Why not? Because God has a greater control of the world in which we live than we have, and he mentions three things against which man has still no control, even in our own times: volcanic eruption, earthquake and flood. God has powers at his control that we can do nothing about. Amos reminds us that the earth can melt. Suddenly the rock is red-hot and molten and there is nothing you can do about it. Suddenly the earth is quaking – rising and falling like the river Nile in Egypt. There is nothing you can do about it. Suddenly the sea floods in and inundates the land, and it only needs to rise two hundred feet to blot out most major cities in the world. Therefore if you think you can get away with wrongdoing with a God who is omnipotent, think again. His ways are irresistible.

Thirdly, not only is he sovereign – the LORD is his name – but God knows everything. It is what his eyes see that is the important thing. Now the people to whom Amos preached had made one terrible mistake. Because God had chosen them, they were special; they were different; God was going to treat them differently from any other nation, but when he looked down upon them he saw a sinful kingdom – not a kingdom living above everybody else, but a kingdom that was living below other people. Therefore he would treat them as he had treated the Ethiopians, the Philistines and the Syrians whom he had moved around on the map.

Now I can apply that to Britain. We have had privileges above other nations. We have got more translations of the Bible in English than any other nation or language in the world. We have churches and chapels by the thousand. We have many people preaching the gospel. Let us not think that because our Queen is crowned in a church, and because we claim to be a Christian country, that somehow that makes us special and that somehow disasters will not come to this land. Let me say what Amos says. If God sees a sinful kingdom, then God must treat that kingdom as every other kingdom. There is no special treatment for anyone, and indeed, even the people of God will come under God's condemnation.

Now at the end of this (v. 10) we are reminded that one characteristic of sinners is that they say: this will never happen to us. This disease is called "euphoria" and we are suffering terribly from it in this country. It is the disease that says, "It could never happen here; this would never happen to us." We are not in the earthquake zone. We are not in the trouble spots of the world. The things that are happening elsewhere could not happen here. Then suddenly we find they are. We find that rioting in the streets is happens in the UK.

Sinners say: "God will not visit our sins upon us. You can do wrong and get away with it. There is no day of judgment." But God says there is. God says, "I will shake the house of Israel with all the nations. I'll mix them all up and shake them all up together as you shake a sieve, but I will still not lose them because no pebble goes through a sieve" (v.9). When he shakes the Jews among the nations, he won't lose sight of them. His is not going to let Israel go altogether. "I will not utterly destroy the house of Jacob."

You tell me where the ancient Egyptians, Assyrians, Babylonians, Philistines and Edomites are today – I do not know. You tell me where Israel is today – I do know. God has shaken that little people among all the nations for two thousand years, but he did not drop them. He shook them as in a sieve, and other nations fell through and disappeared, but God's people stayed. One of the most exciting things to me is to live after 1948 and to see the name Israel on the atlas again. It is thrilling to see that God shook them as in a sieve, but they did not drop through. He shook them among all the nations so that they seemed to have been lost and all mixed up with the peoples, but there they are again.

Let me dwell on those three thoughts: God is everywhere, God can do anything, and God knows everything. That is either the most terrifying or the most comforting thought that you could have. If you are a sinner and on the wrong side of God, it is the most terrifying thought in the world – that God knows everything you do; and that you will never get away from him, even by dying, and that he has the power to punish. But when you get right with God and get forgiven, those very three thoughts become the most wonderful thoughts that you could have.

Read Psalm 139: "If I make my bed in Sheol, you are there. If I ascend into heaven, behold, you are there. If I take the wings of the morning and dwell in the uttermost parts of the sea, even there shall your right hand lead me." In other words: your omnipresence is the most wonderful thing of all. I can die, I can go out into space, I can migrate to Australia, and I am still with you.

Go further into Psalm 139: "You understand my thoughts afar off; even before a word is on my lips you know it altogether. You know when I get up; you know when I sit down; you know my down sitting and my uprising. You are acquainted with all my ways." That is a tremendous thought to the psalmist; he is thrilled – God's omniscience, omnipresence and omnipotence. "You knitted me together in my mother's womb. You decided how many birthdays I should have before there were any of them." The power of God: all these thoughts become to the believer the most precious, comforting and helpful thoughts you could have; to the unbeliever God's omnipresence, his omnipotence, and his omniscience are terrifying. This chapter is almost a travesty of Psalm 139. It is almost repeating the Psalm, but putting it on the unbeliever.

Now we turn to the future of Israel. It bursts out, and God makes tremendous promises. It has been said that the longest sentence in the English language is: "I will." It is a long sentence – lifelong. It is a promise – wonderful words that commit you permanently, deeply; words that you must fulfil. Now God says in 9:11–15, "I will raise up"; in v. 14, "I will restore"; in v. 15, "I will plant". The three promises concern three aspects of their life: their national life, their agricultural life and their territorial future.

Let us take them in order. First, God promises that some day in the future (he does not say what day; he says, "In that day" and leaves it there) he will restore two things. First, the royal family. God's will for Israel was that they be a kingdom, not a republic; but you cannot be a kingdom without a king. God says, "One day I will restore the booth of David...." That is, the royal family, the throne. He will build up the capital city, repair the walls and rebuild the ruins. They will have a royal family again, and it will be a king from the line of David. Now from the exile onwards, the people of Israel never had kings. They had a few in the days of the Maccabees, but they soon went and they were not of the line of David. People were asking, even in the day when Jesus went back to heaven, "When are you going to restore the kingship to Israel?" God promised that one day Israel would be a kingdom with a king again.

Secondly, not only would they have a king but they would have an emperor. Now a king is someone who reigns over his own nation; an emperor is someone who reigns over many nations. King David not only reigned over Israel, he reigned over Edom and a number of other nations that came within the empire. David was not only a king he was an emperor. Now I am afraid "imperialism" has become a dirty word today, and people think that it is a bad thing. It can be; it can be a very good thing. Now I am not going back and trying to praise the British Empire or saying that was God's will or anything like that. What I am saying is this: God's will for Israel is that she become an imperial power as well as a royal power. Neither of these has happened yet, but God has promised that "In that day" he will give them both. They will have a king and an emperor, and other nations will come under the throne of David.

The next thing is this: it is a picture of tremendous fertility, such fertility that in fact they are getting two or three crops a year and the reaper is coming along, and behind him the ploughman – just like that. I have seen that in only one country in the world – the ploughman following the reaper. It was in Israel, where already they are getting two and three crops a year. God says: "I will do this. The ploughman will overtake the reaper ... you will plant your gardens and enjoy the fruit."

"You will rebuild your cities and inhabit them ... You will make your gardens and plant your vineyards." If you want to see all that, go and visit Israel – it is very exciting! They are now doing exactly this. Notice that the increased fertility will not do away with work; they will have to work twice as hard. God will give them this, but they will plant, plough, reap and rebuild. I will do this; they shall do that. God never yet did things for us that excused us from work. He always gives us blessings that make us work the harder. I have noticed that when God blesses a church, you have to work twice as hard. You think that if revival comes, your problems will be over. Believe me, when revival hits England our problems will begin. The problems will be where to put the people, who will teach them, and how to spend the time counselling those who need counselling. When God blesses a church your work does not decrease. You will plant vineyards and you will enjoy the wine. You will make gardens and enjoy the fruit – but you will have to make the gardens; you will have to plant the vineyards.

The third thing he promises them is the most amazing. He will plant this people deep in the soil of their own land. The future of God's people Israel and their land are inextricably bound up together. That is why, even when the British government offered them a home in Kenya they said, "No. There is only one land where we can be ourselves." Then came the Balfour Declaration that gave them that land. Indeed, Israel and the land go together, which is why for two thousand years, when they greeted each other at the Passover, they said, "Next year in Jerusalem."

Then it became "Next year in the Old City." Now even that has changed, but this was what God promised, "I will plant them there." The earth is the Lord's and he gave the title deeds to his people, and it is that which overrides every other right to that little strip of land at the eastern end of the Mediterranean. God says: "I will plant them upon their land, and they shall never again be plucked up out of the land which I have given them."

To fix them in your mind, here are the three promises: that Israel would get a royal family that would also be an imperial family reigning over many nations; second, that their agriculture would be so fertile that two and three crops a year would be the normal thing; thirdly, that they would get their land back and would not be able to be plucked out of it again. Every word of that agricultural promise is fulfilled. They are back in the land. But will they be plucked out of it again? I can only say that I believe not, but that is an act of faith on my part. I have no proof of it, but I believe they will never again be uprooted from the Middle East.

The people of Israel are my brothers. They are going to be part of my future, and therefore we can see part of Amos's promises coming true physically in Israel and we can see part of them coming true spiritually.

Part of the promises you see on the map in Israel today. Part of the promises I can see in the church because we are not limited to one nationality, and we are God's imperial kingdom. The nations of the world are coming under his reign and under his throne, and when the kingdom is restored to Israel, the kingdom will be one kingdom of God, in which the throne of David is fulfilled through the son of David whom we know as Jesus Christ. God is fulfilling his promises in so many different ways, but all heading up together, until the day when the kingdoms of this world become the kingdom of our Lord and Saviour Jesus Christ. Then he delivers all up to the Father, and God shall be all in all. God is working his purpose out.

The book of Amos finishes exactly where most of the other prophets finish, and exactly where the greatest prophecy in the Bible, the book of Revelation finishes, indeed where the whole Bible finishes. The last chapter of Amos tells us that the human race is to be divided in two. Sinners who say, "Judgment will never come upon us; God will never touch us" will be set on one hand. Those who have remained faithful and believed God will be set on the other. Amos faces us in chapter nine with a clear division among the people of Israel. The book of Revelation finishes in the same way: earthquake, disaster, utter collapse of godless civilisation, a new heaven and a new earth, and a new city of God in which righteousness and peace will dwell forever. The future of the entire human race is reflected in the future of Israel in the days of Amos. There is to be a division, and it will be whether there has been a change of heart in people individually which will decide whether they experience retribution or restoration in that day of the Lord.

OBADIAH

OBADIAH

Read Obadiah

Obadiah was the first prophet whose message became a book in the Old Testament scriptures. The shortest book in the Old Testament, it is only one page – twenty-one verses. Maybe he only spoke once in his lifetime, yet his words have come down to us hundreds of years later. If you want a date for him, it is 845 BC and that opened a period of three hundred years during which prophet after prophet came and spoke and warned the people of God: don't go on like this. Joel, the second, was 835 BC, just ten years later. We know he was later because he quotes Obadiah and says that God has already said this to you. So we get them in the right order, and from other hints within the prophecies we know their dates. Joel used Obadiah's prophecy and built on it, and in particular picked up one phrase which Obadiah introduced, a totally new concept and the concept was: the Day of the Lord is coming. That concept, the Day of the Lord, goes right through all the major prophets and right through into the New Testament and it is a very important phrase which we shall have to look at in detail. It is the day when God comes to put wrongs right.

Now, the prophets had two messages: one for God's people of Israel, but they also had messages for the nations around Israel. They did not just speak from God to God's people, they spoke to other peoples, almost every one of them. In fact Obadiah didn't speak to Israel at all, but to one of Israel's neighbours called Edom, living south-east of the Dead Sea, and so his prophecy is entirely concerned with another nation, which is interesting. The first of these prophets didn't speak to Israel at all. We will have to ask why. Now we know very little about him. We know his name which means the worshipper of Yahweh, or the servant of Yahweh, but to worship is to serve and we still say we are holding a worship service on Sunday morning and so serving God and worshipping are the same thing in the Bible and he is called the servant or worshipper of Yahweh, *Obad jah*, but we call him Obadiah and that is all we know and most of his word is a prediction about the future. It came to him, he says, as a vision, so he was wide awake, but he saw this picture, he saw it happening and he describes what he saw very clearly, so it is a visual rather than a verbal message and he is one of the seers of Israel who could see things happening before they occurred.

Now this state of Edom was in what became called trans-Jordan, over the deep crack valley of the Jordan and the Arabah valley over on the other side. Under King David, Edom became a sort of satellite, and so David conquered Edom, it came within the empire, but the people of Edom still lived there and as soon as the empire of David began to shrink, as soon as things began to go wrong, Edom immediately sought its own freedom and rebelled against the kingdom of God, represented in the King of Israel. So that is where they lived, south east of the Dead Sea and they had two cities. One was called Bozrah, and the other was called Sela. We now know that as Petra, and I am sure you have heard of the amazing buildings there. It was right on one of the most important roads of the Middle East – the crossroads of the world, where the road from Africa to Asia crosses the road from Europe to Arabia, and the road down the far side of the Jordan valley was called The King's Highway. It was up that road that Moses had led the people of Israel, but the two cities of Bozrah and Sela were on that road, and Petra, as we call it now, is a most unusual place. I remember years ago going to visit it once. I left Amman and we actually drove down through the desert, down The King's Highway, alongside the railway that Lawrence of Arabia was always blowing up and we went right down past Bozrah and came to near the place, then we had to leave the car and get on some old mangy horses covered in dandruff. We climbed on these horses and went through a narrow crack in the mountain – you could touch both sides of it at points. It is called the Siq and we rode for miles through this crack. The rock was on either side of us; it is just a crack and very dangerous to go through when there is a flash flood after a rainstorm. We saw a car washed away through there and people had been drowned, so you have got to go when it is dry and then ahead you suddenly see a temple about the size of St Paul's Cathedral carved out of the rock – red sandstone. You then turn right and you come out into a large open circle where there are a thousand temples and they too are carved out of the rock, all round this huge empty circle in the middle of the mountains; and above them is one mountain, about maybe two thousand feet high, just towering with sheer cliffs, and this is Mount Seir, the old city of Sela where the people of Edom lived, and the prophecy of Obadiah is all about that one mountain.

The architecture is superb. We could climb up to the top of this peak and from there you could see the Dead Sea in one direction and the Red Sea in the other. It is incredible, and all around the circle are the carved temples. When you go inside they are as big inside as they are outside and there is nothing propping up the ceiling, and the walls are the most amazing shades of red, purple and green sandstone. It really is a fantastic place to visit and it is totally deserted, and then in the middle you see Mount Seir. It is impregnable and the Edomites lived there. You find altars of human sacrifice where they offered humans alive to their gods, and you can see all the houses carved out of the rock and other little temples. They were literally cave dwellers – but such caves. The temples you see there now do not come from the days of Edom. I have to add that they were built by the Nabateans centuries later, but I will come back to that. But the Edomites lived in the fortress right up on top, and of course it was impregnable and they were proud of this. No-one can bring us down, they said. Obadiah quotes that. Their pride – we are invincible. I am reminded of Captain Smith of the Titanic: "God himself couldn't sink her." What a dangerous thing to say! Edom said: God himself couldn't bring us down. Obadiah's message is: you are going to be brought down. O proud Mount Seir, you will be brought down.

That is the background to this amazing place. Now what is significant here is that the God of Israel is the God of other nations. That really was a radical thing to say in those days when every nation had its own god and they believed the God of Israel was just the God of Israel and other nations had nothing to do with him. But the God of Israel was the only God there is, and he will not only judge Israel he will judge every other nation too – that is the message, and the God of the Christians is the only God there is and he will judge people of every other religion too. Do you believe that? It is not easy to believe that in what is called a pluralist society, when everybody has their own god. But if there is only one God, and if the Creator of the universe is the God of Abraham, Isaac and Jacob, then the God of Israel is the God with whom every nation will have to deal and to whom every nation will have to give account. That is the revolutionary message of the prophets. They did not just speak to Israel, they spoke to everybody. Our God is going to judge you too – that is the radical message of Obadiah. Everything is under his control. And of course that is the message of the

New Testament too. When Paul spoke in Athens, on Mars Hill, he said God allots every nation its time and space. It is God who draws the map. It is God who brought the British Empire to an end. When I was a boy, the school atlas was red. You could travel right round the world and never leave British soil. It was the empire on which the sun never set. So what happened to this great empire? The answer is that we washed our hands of God's people Israel, and God said if you can't look after my people you can't look after anybody, and within five years the empire went. I believe that was one of the clearest examples of the hand of God. Because one of the other principles that comes out in these prophets is that God judges other nations by their attitude to his people – that that is the thing that is most important to him: how did you treat my people? In the Old Testament days this meant: how did you treat Israel? But in these days it also means: how did you treat the church? And God will judge the nations of the world for how they treated his people. That is written on history; it is written large, and the first nation to be so judged was this nation of Edom, for what they did to Israel.

Now this is a very interesting principle: what we do to God's people we do to God. Jesus picked up the same principle: "inasmuch as you have done it to the least of these my brethren, you did it to me". When he said "my brethren" he means Christians there; he is not talking about anybody – the word "brethren" is only used in Matthew's Gospel for Jesus' disciples, and Jesus said: touch my disciple, you touch me; laugh at them, you are mocking me.

Saul of Tarsus learned that the hard way on the road to Damascus. A voice said "Saul, Saul, why are you persecuting me?"

"Who are you Lord?"

"I am Jesus of Nazareth" – and Saul didn't say "but I am not persecuting you, I am persecuting the Christians" because he realised in a flash that what you do to Christians you are doing to Jesus of Nazareth.

Now that is a profound principle: what you do to God's people you are doing to God; they are the apple of his eye and that is the most sensitive part of God to touch as the iris of your eye is the most sensitive part of your body. It is a principle of judgment of all the nations. Now that God's people are in every nation of the world, every nation is having to decide their attitude to God's people. On the Day of Judgment, that will be a major factor.

In fact, at the very beginning when God called Abraham, he said: Abraham, whoever blesses you I will bless and whoever curses you I will curse. Now that principle comes out in prophet after prophet when they speak to other nations, and that is why most of their prophecies are to nations that had contact with Israel, that lived around Israel and that therefore had taken up an attitude towards Israel – an attitude that would cost them their future destiny.

We are beginning to realise there is an awful lot in Obadiah. Very simply it divides into two parts. The first part, (vv. 1–14) is that one nation is going to be judged, namely the nation of Edom. In the second part he sees all the nations being judged. It is an expanding vision.

First of all, one nation will be judged. "Edom", by the way, means red and of course the city is made up of red sandstone but that is not why it is called red. We will return to that. First recall that Mount Seir was that huge rock in the middle of what we now call Petra, which was easily defended. I remember going to Hitler's "eagle nest" in Berchtesgaden where he had built on the top of Berchtesgaden and the walls are four feet of granite. It is an impregnable place, and from there you can see as far as Munich, it is an amazing place and yet twenty years later he was committing suicide. It is astonishing how man likes to build high and get up there and say 'I am it'. Ever since Babel, man has tried to do this. There is a race on to build the tallest skyscraper in the world.

Obadiah says: the nations are going to destroy you. Unlike burglars they won't just take the things they are interested in, they are going to take everything from you and unlike grape pickers who always leave some things behind, there will be nothing left behind but you. You will be humbled; you will be brought down. You will lose your territory. You will lose your status because God hates pride in men. It is the one sin that really gets God – when man is proud, when he thinks he is everything, when he thinks he is invulnerable. It is almost inviting God to bring that person low.

Why? The answer is because Edom despised Israel. You see there are two sides to pride. One is that you have a very high view of yourself. But inevitably the other side is that you have a low view of everyone else. You cannot have a high view of yourself without a low view of others because you are just the same really, and if you put yourself up, you have to put others down, and in particular, Edom lifting itself up in pride on the top of Mount Seir, looked down – literally looked down on Israel; but they despised Israel, and this hatred went back a long way as most conflicts do. Conflict in Northern Ireland goes back three hundred years. The conflict in the Middle East between Arab and Jew goes back to Isaac and Ishmael. It seems as if the more closely people are related the more they can hate each other. If you have not been close you cannot really hate and that is why when a marriage breaks up there can be more hatred there, and more contempt, than if they had never known each other

It is because Edom is actually Esau – that is why Edom means red, because Esau had ginger hair and the Edomites were direct descendants from Esau. You will remember Jacob and Esau and if you read that saga then you understand the later pride and contempt in Edom – Esau's descendants.

So Esau's descendants had settled on the east side of the rift valley and Jacob's descendants settled on the west side, and they glared at each other, but it is interesting that God forbade Israel ever to have a wrong attitude to Edom. You will find in Deuteronomy that God says you must always treat the Edomites right because you must remember that Esau was Jacob's brother and God commanded brotherly love toward Edom on the part of Israel.

That is why Obadiah, in this prophecy against Edom, says you should not have treated your brother as you did, because what happened was this. As soon as the empire of David began to crumble, the Edomites rose up and anybody who attacked Jerusalem or Israel, anybody whether it was Philistines or Arabs, later the Babylonians, the Edomites did not just stand by, they joined in. And when the Babylonians came they had a horrid habit – they were a very barbaric people. They would take babies by the foot and smash their brains out on the rocks, and the Edomites joined in and egged them on: go on, do it to them, and all their hatred and jealousy and resentment of centuries came out. When the Philistines came against Jerusalem, the Edomites joined them. When the Arabs attacked Jerusalem, the Edomites joined them. When the Babylonians came the Edomites joined them. They took every opportunity. Of course they weren't strong enough themselves to do much, but when they saw somebody else, they were quickened to the fight and took the side of everybody but Israel, and they were brothers – Jacob and Esau – and God condemns them for their lack of brotherly love. You shouldn't have had that attitude towards your brother Israel, taking advantage of their weakness, taking advantage of their enemies' attacks; you should not have done it and God is going to judge you for it.

A question occurs: did they hear what Obadiah said? If they heard it, did they heed it? Well, the first part is all about Edom, but half way through Obadiah changes from the third person to the second, from talking about Edom as "him" to talking about Edom as "you", and it looks as if Obadiah had the courage to go to Petra to tell them to their face: you shouldn't have done this. If he did, no wonder the prophets were killed – and they were, one after the other, but he obviously went to Edom and he told them.

What happened to the Edomites after that? Their history is very complicated, but in the sixth century BC the Arabs attacked them and they had to flee; they left their city and moved over the rift valley into the Negev desert, and the Negev was renamed Edomia after the Edomites who had come, so they now left their cities. They were now living as Bedouin in the desert as it were; in the Negev they were Edomites but they built up their wealth there and then came a day when an Edomite from the Negev, a descendant of Esau, went to Rome and talked to Julius Caesar and said "Would you sell me the throne of Israel in Jerusalem?" The Romans sold him the throne and his name was Herod – Herod the Edomian, the Edomite – and now he was King over Israel. The Edomite Herod the Great, as King over Israel, said now: I am going to build greater buildings than the Nabateans are building in my old city Petra – because by now these great temples were being carved out of the rock – and so that is why he rebuilt the temple in Jerusalem. That is why he built his palaces everywhere. That is why he built the palace on Masada. The Edomite was now king of the Jews, and when the Wise Men came and asked where is he born, the King of the Jews, can you imagine why he was so angry? He was not having a Jew on this throne: Edom has conquered; I am Herod the Great. He killed every boy in Bethlehem, and his son was the Herod who killed John the Baptist. This Herod was the one to whom Jesus had nothing to say at his trial; his grandson was the Herod who was eaten by worms in the Book of Acts, and his great-grandson was a man called Agrippa who died in the year AD100 without children. The Edomites had disappeared. There isn't a single Edomite in the world today, and it all happened because Obadiah saw it happen and said it would happen. It is an amazing story, isn't it? How the Jacob and Esau thing nearly killed Jesus. Jesus himself stood on trial before an Edomite. It tells you this: God takes his time about judging people, because from Obadiah to their final disappearance is 910 years. God doesn't judge quickly, but he does judge.

A German poet picked this up in 1653, and here is Longfellow's English translation:

> The mills of God grind slowly
> But they grind exceeding small
> Though with patience he stands waiting
> With exactness grinds he all.

God takes his time, he is slow to anger, but when God says he will do it, he will do it – maybe a thousand years later, but he will do it. Where is Edom today? Gone. Where is Israel today? Back in her land. If you don't believe in the God of Israel I don't know how you explain this and so many other things.

From this judgment of Edom, Obadiah saw that one day all nations would be judged; that the God of Israel will hold every nation responsible, and especially for their attitude to his people, and then he adds a most amazing thing. One day, Israel will possess Edom – because that part is included specifically in the land that God promised to his people and one day they must have it, and Obadiah saw that. Now it is over two and a half thousand years later and it has not happened yet, but the promise included all that part of the fertile crescent between Gaza and the Euphrates and includes this part, and he saw it coming. He saw there would be no survivors from the house of Edom, but that their land would be possessed by its true owners, and in the last part, vv. 17–21, he sees Israel expanding to the north into Ephraim and Samaria, to the south into the Negev, to the east into the Edom hills, and as far as the Mediterranean coast in the west. He saw it and he describes it as if it has already happened because he saw it so clearly.

What has all this got to do with us? There is a Jacob and an Esau in every one of us, and if you read the Epistle to the Hebrews it says to Christians: don't be like Esau – sold his birthright for a pot of soup and he cried, his tears flowed afterwards. He was full of regret and full of remorse but he was never able to repent, and the New Testament says don't be an Esau, be a Jacob. Jacob wrestled with God until God lamed him, but he got the blessing and it is from Jacob that God's people Israel came; and the Edomite has disappeared from history. Esau lived for the present, for the immediate satisfaction of his physical desires, and he lost his future to that which is exactly the attitude of the Herod, son of Herod the Great. He was a man who was so sensual, so eager to satisfy his own lusts that he gave away half his kingdom to a dancing girl, or was ready to; and she said I don't want half your kingdom, I would like the head of John the Baptist, and he gave it to her. That is the Esau syndrome. The Esaus of this world live for this world only. They don't care about the future, they are only concerned about the satisfaction of their desires in the present. Well there is an Esau in every one of us, but don't let him out. Be a Jacob, the man who was broken by God, became a prince, and his name "Israel" is now on the map again after two thousand years. Remember that when God speaks he keeps his word; when he says he will do something he may not do it by next Tuesday, and that makes us impatient. Lord, when are you going to do it? You may have to wait a thousand years, but if God says he will do it, he will do it, and that is why we can trust his word. Little Obadiah – a minor prophet, but everything he said will come true.

JONAH

JONAH

Read Jonah 1:1–16
Next to the book of Genesis, the book of Jonah has been attacked more than any other book in the Old Testament. On the one hand, there are those who treat it as one huge joke and there are many such jokes. I have heard them all, but I am not going to repeat them. There are many people who have treated this book with ridicule, flippantly, and have thought anybody who still believes this must really be out of their minds. Indeed, a denominational newspaper berated me, a man of my intelligence, still believing that Jonah was true.

The other attack on this book is a serious one, not a flippant one. It is an attack made by many school teachers when studying this book with their children, and alas, many ministers. This serious attack is a claim that this book is not concerned with fact, but only fiction. It is seen as a parable, a tract, a story that somebody thought up. It is being taught in schools and even churches as an earthly story with a heavenly meaning.

So I want to begin these studies on Jonah by giving you four reasons which convince me that Jonah is historically true – that it actually happened. That does not mean I am the sort of credulous person who would believe anything. A Christian once said to a man who challenged him on the book of Jonah, that if the Bible said that Jonah swallowed the whale he would still believe it. That kind of attitude is simply making difficulties where there are none. The Bible doesn't say that, so fortunately you don't have to believe it.

The Bible does say that a great fish swallowed Jonah, and that is not only credible, it is important to accept for the message of the book.

Now here are my four reasons. First of all, when I read this book it is presented to me as history. It is presented to me in exactly the same form, speech and manner as every other book of history: the books of Kings; Chronicles. They describe real places, real people, real events; and in exactly the same tone of voice, and exactly the same manner, with exactly the same language. We are told here about real places. Joppa is real, Nineveh is real, Tarshish is real. We are told about real people. We are told about real events, and I am quite sure that anybody reading the book of Jonah as it stands would never have come to the conclusion it was fiction. It is presented to you as a slice of history.

Second reason: Jonah is mentioned elsewhere in the historical books of the Old Testament. He is mentioned in Kings. He has the same father there as he has here – Amittai. He is presented there as an ordinary person, and funnily enough, those who think this book is fiction accept Jonah in the other book. Why accept him in one place and not the other? This is just ridiculous.

A third reason is that the Jews always accepted Jonah as history. From the very beginning they believed they were reading about a real person.

But the fourth and final reason, which for me is absolutely crucial: the Lord Jesus himself believed and taught that Jonah was real. In fact, the Lord Jesus himself, Son of God, faultless in his humanity, said, "As he was in the belly of the whale three days and three nights" – historical event; "I will be in the belly of the earth three days and three nights" – another historical event. Furthermore, lest people say that our Lord Jesus was simply accepting the current view to accommodate himself to their ideas, let me point out that one of the things the Son of God once said was this: "Those who refuse Christ now will one day meet the men of Nineveh, who will point at them and say, 'we repented even before Jesus came. We repented over Jonah, why can't you repent over Jesus?'" So our Lord Jesus not only accepted the fact of Jonah as past history, he said the men whom Jonah converted will be there in the day of judgment, facing those who with far more evidence of the truth have still not accepted it. So for these reasons, we are dealing in the book of Jonah not with fiction, but with fact.

Why is it important to say all this at the beginning? Because the whole message of the book of Jonah changes if you treat it as fiction. If you treat it as fact, the main figure in the story is God. If you treat it as fiction, the main figure is Jonah. This is a book about God primarily; it is a book about what God does, and that is the main message. If God did not do this, then this book is not a reliable guide to God. The book was written not to tell us about Jonah, or about Nineveh, but to tell us about the kind of god God is, by telling you what he did.

There is only one reason I find why people refuse to accept this as truth. When you get behind all their arguments you find there is only one reason, namely that the book contains five miracles. If we are going to say that every book in the Bible that has miracles in it must be fiction, then the Gospels and Acts would be fiction, to say nothing of the Old Testament. You will find that those who start by saying Jonah is not true will finish up by saying some very much more serious things even about Jesus. The message is: God is the sort of God who did these five things in the experience of Jonah.

I divide the book up into three sections: the *great tempest*, the *great fish* and the *great city*. I am quoting from the book. It is a book of greats, and the first great is a great tempest. We first of all look at Jonah and God in the great tempest. Then we shall tackle that whole problem of the whale. I will give you some scientific information about that as well. Then we look at the greatest miracle of all: the great city that repented.

I am going to approach the first chapter from two angles: first of all through the experience of Jonah, and then through the experience of the sailors. Both times I am going to ask: What did they see of God in their experience? What did Jonah find out about God? What did the sailors find out about God?

Now let us take Jonah – the prodigal's progress; the runaway preacher; the man who would not do what God wanted him to do. There are four steps down for him, and they begin with the step of *disobedience*. All trouble of this kind begins with that single step of not doing something that God wants us to do. God has every right to tell Jonah where to go and what to say, for Jonah is a preacher, a man of God; Jonah is a man who has given his life into God's hands, and Jonah is a man whom God has called to preach to other people. God has every right to say: you must go there; whether you want to or not is beside the point; you must go there, and you must say this. As I have mentioned before, one of the subtle temptations every preacher has is never to preach against anything or anyone, only to preach for things and people. God said to Jonah, "Go and preach against..." and he had every right to tell him to do so. A preacher should not preach against unless God has told him to, but he had to go and preach against, whether it was popular or not. Jonah didn't go—he knew he ought to, but instead of going east to Nineveh, he went as far west as he could go. Do you know where Tarshish was? It is on the coast of Spain. It was as far away as he could get; and you notice that this was a deliberate planned act of disobedience. It says that he rose, he went, he found a ship, and he paid for the ticket. That man knew what he was doing. The journey from Jerusalem down to Joppa, the nearest seaport, gave him time to think, but every step he took hardened his resolve to get away from God. Quite deliberately, he turned his back on what God wanted him to do and set off in the opposite direction.

I wonder – did he honestly think that he could get away from God? He ought to have known better than that, but it says "to flee from the presence of the Lord". That phrase in the Old Testament usually refers to the temple, the place where God tabernacled among his people; the place where God lived; the place where God met his people, where worship was offered, where prophets went to pray. It was from that presence of the Lord that Jonah fled. If as a child of God a person is in a state of disobedience, the last place they want to be is among God's people where they worship. Invariably, a man at odds with God is at odds with God's people. Invariably, we don't want to go near church. We go in the opposite direction if we are in a state of disobedience. We don't even want to be anywhere near the place of worship, the place where God's people meet to pray and to praise. It is so typical, and so understandable that he fled.

You notice that there were plenty of sailors around to help him, and one of the things that life teaches us is this: when you have set yourself on a certain course, both circumstances and companions will combine to help you along that course. If you have said, "I'm going against God," you will find people who will help you to go against him. There will be those who will be glad to take your money and help you on your way. There will be circumstances that combine to help you to get away from God. Jonah found, as soon as he decided to go, that there was a ship just waiting, and sailors waiting with their palms out for his money. You find that the way of sin, once you've decided to go on it, is a way that has help from circumstances and companions to go along the road.

The other side of that coin is a wonderful one – that if you have decided to obey God and to go his way, circumstances and companions are now there to help you that way. Either way you go, you will find circumstances, help and companions are there to assist you. So Jonah got his one-way ticket. I am quite sure that when he went up to the ticket office at Joppa, he said, "Single please," but God had the return trip arranged as we will see.

Now we come to step number two – *distress*. Sooner or later, disobedience leads to distress. Peace goes; something happens that disturbs. God lets you go so far and no further. God is wonderfully patient with us, but he does not let us go all the way. Maybe Jonah thought he was having a wonderful trip. The sea of the Mediterranean was like a millpond; the sun shone; he decided to go below and have a nap, and he thought everything was over.

I think the key word in the book of Jonah is "but". You may have noticed the word "but" twice already: "But Jonah rose to flee"; "But God sent a tempest". You'll find it is full of buts. In a sense it is like a gigantic chess game. Every move that Jonah makes, God makes a move, gradually helping Jonah to see that God is the one who is going to win the game, and that Jonah, as a child of God, must accept God's lordship in his life. So God makes the first move, and miracle number one takes place: the miracle of sending the great wind and the tempest that beat on the ship.

I want you to notice that when that distress came, the first people to suffer it were the sailors. None of us lives to himself, and whether we are going the right way or the wrong way, the people around us are going to benefit or suffer accordingly. If we are going the way of God, then the people who meet us day by day, even the people sitting on the same bus are going to be helped. But if, on the other hand, we are going in a way of disobedience and going wrong, other people may suffer before we do.

I have lived long enough to see that happen again and again – that when a man is deliberately turning his back on God and going the wrong way, it is often others who have the first wave of distress, and this is what is happening here. The sailors get it. They would not have had that distress if Jonah had not been disobedient, and already his sin is beginning to spread out in an ugly circle of ripples affecting other people, and there is Jonah, sleeping down in the boat.

Now there are two sorts of sleep; there is the sleep that you can have in which you are absolutely right with God, in complete trust in him and have nothing to fear. That was the kind of sleep that Jesus had when he lay in the boat on Galilee; and there is the sleep of those who have thought that God is right out of their lives and a million miles away and they don't have to think about this. Both people can sleep peacefully: one because God is so real and near to them, and the other because God is so far away from them. It is the people who are in between who can't sleep, who know that God is real, but haven't got near enough to him to trust him. Those are the people who worry.

There are many sinners in the world who sleep very soundly indeed with not a worry in their minds. There are many people who spiritually are sound asleep, because God is so far away to them that they don't even consider that he is anywhere near. These are the two kinds of sleep: the sleep of death; the sleep of life; the sleep of sin and the sleep of faith, and here it is the sleep of sin. The difference is this: if we are asleep because we are trusting in God, he will let us sleep on; but if we are asleep because of disobedience, God will sooner or later wake us up.

The words that the sailors use to Jonah are exactly the words that Paul uses to sinners in the New Testament,

"Awake thou that sleepest". Wake up. Take notice of the condition you are in; take notice of the circumstances. God is wanting to say something to you; he wants to deal with you; wake up! Do you notice that Jonah woke up and he couldn't pray? Of course he couldn't – when you are on the run from God you can't pray, and those pagan sailors praying to their own idols and gods, whatever they thought existed, said to Jonah: you pray to your God as well; we're praying hard to all of ours. Jonah could not pray. The only person on board ship who couldn't pray was the man of God. It is a terrible picture that a man of God should so get away from God that when pagans challenge him to pray he can't, and he doesn't.

The third step down for this poor man was the step of *disgrace*, "Be sure your sins will find you out" – publicly as well. There will come a day when every sin committed comes home, and whatever excuses, however we try to wriggle out of it, we can't. The sailors began to ask why Jonah was not praying. Who was he? Where was he from? They instinctively felt that there was something wrong with this man, and so comes the point of disgrace.

The sailors knew only one way to find out what God thought: to cast lots. I don't know if they used dice. They had dice in those days. Here comes the third miracle now, because when they toss those dice up, God turned them. God controlled those lots. When they fell on the deck and they looked down, it was Jonah who was indicated by the lots. God had uncovered him before other people, and Jonah now confesses his sin. But it is a typical confession. It is vague; he doesn't admit a thing more that he can help, and in fact he manages to be so diplomatic that he passes the fear on to them, and gets them worried about themselves instead of him. He does not for one moment admit what it is that is causing the trouble. He simply tells them that he believes it is his God who sent the tempest.

As a Hebrew he believed in a God who was not just a little God of his nation. He believed in a God who made the heaven and the earth and the sea—everything. Then, Jonah, why did you try to run away from him if he is that big? Here is a case of a man who has got the right words in his mind, who can recite the right creed but doesn't live by it. If Jonah feared the God who made the sea, he would never have got on that boat. If Jonah was really true in saying "I fear the Lord" he would have gone to Nineveh. He is reciting a creed. He has all the right words, but is not living by them. It is a half confession, and half confessions are not enough. Only little by little does he bring out what has gone wrong.

Now comes *disaster* for Jonah. The sailors are human and humane. They struggled to get him out of it, but they said, "What shall we do?"

He said, "There's only one thing you can do and that's throw me in the sea."

Now at this point I want to ask: was Jonah right in saying this, or to put it another way, why did he ask to be thrown in the sea? You know the one thing that was needed, the one thing that God was waiting for, he never got. What is the one thing that Jonah could have said that would have put it all right? The thing that God wanted was Jonah to say, "I'll go to Nineveh, Lord."

We find a typical reaction of Jonah here. It is going to happen again in chapter four. Jonah is always the one to escape if he can; to get the easy way out. Jonah prefers death to going to Nineveh. Later he is going to say again, "Lord, let me die rather than see Nineveh." Jonah asks for death as a way out, and God takes Jonah at that. He deals with Jonah, but he doesn't let him find the way out through death. So they threw Jonah in the sea, and the storm ceased, and the great calm came – another miracle. Now the sailors are terrified of God. They had been frightened of the sea, now they are frightened of God.

I am going to look at this whole chapter from the sailors' angle. They were certainly not Jews; they were about their routine business, doing their business in great waters. Suddenly their whole lives have changed because of one passenger, and it is a dramatic moment. When they had set off on that voyage, they had no idea what was going to happen. Now there were six things about these men which are typical of most men on the earth. They represent the great mass of men who do not yet know God personally.

The first thing to be said about these sailors is this: they were *religious*. Most men are. I have only met in my lifetime about half a dozen genuine atheists. Most of them are a bit like the one who said, "I'm an atheist, thank God", and when you study it seriously, they are not really. These sailors each had their own god, and when they got in a real jam, they prayed. Most men do. You talk to anyone who was in the war, and you ask what happens when men are really up against it. They pray. Men may be religious deep down, but religion does not save. You notice that they prayed, but the prayer was not a prayer of faith, it was a prayer of fear. Most people pray when they are afraid, but that is not a prayer of faith. They all prayed to god, but not the real God, not a God who existed, a god of their imagination; a god of their own construction. Like the disciples in the storm, they were desperate.

I suppose this is why fishermen are superstitious. In the Shetland Islands where I began my ministry, the fishermen were very superstitious. They would not take a pig or a parson on board a boat when they left harbour, and you can draw your own conclusions from that. There was one village there where thirteen fishing boats set out one night and only one came back, and the village was populated by women in black. When you are really up against the mighty ocean especially in a storm, you are religious all right.

The second thing about these sailors which is so typical of men: they were *respectable*. What do I mean by that? I mean that each of them was quite sure it must be one of the others who had done something wrong. Is this not typical of unredeemed human nature? We are quite sure that somebody has been doing something wrong for the world to be in the state it is. Wonder who it is? Let's cast lots to find out. Now they were partly right – it was Jonah's fault – but you notice that not one of them examined his own heart. None of them began to say, "Well I've done some things that were wrong. I deserve this." No, they were good, respectable people who were quite sure there was evil in the ship, but not in them.

Thirdly, they were *reasoning* men. They were prepared to argue with the man of God, to discuss things with him, to find out what he believed. You notice that their conversation, their discussion, got deeper and deeper: question one, "Who are you?" – mere curiosity. Question two, concern, "What have you been doing?" Question three, conviction, "What must we do about it?" Now you see their discussion got deeper and deeper, and men are prepared to discuss, but now comes the key thought here: they are *resistant* men. When it comes to the part of telling them what they must do, they are determined to try to avoid doing it. I have spoken to so many men who are just like this. Religious, yes, when they have been in a jam they have prayed. Respectable – reluctant to admit that they might be responsible for any of the world's troubles. Reasoning– yes, ready for a discussion; a discussion that can go deeper and deeper, until the point is reached where you say, "Now this is what you must do about your need," and at that point they resist.

Do you notice what they try to do? The first thing they tried to do was throw the cargo overboard to lighten the ship. I am going to press that a bit far maybe allegorically, but

I can see a man saying, "Look I'll give you a subscription for the church. Will that do? I'll offload some of my money. Will that do?"

The next thing they tried was to row hard to get to land by their own efforts, and this is the instinctive thing that a man does when he is told there is only one way to get peace with God. He says: "I'm going to get there by my own efforts. I'm going to pull myself there. I'll manage to be good enough. I'll manage to do enough good deeds. I'll get there under my own steam. I am the captain of myself. I am the master of my fate." That's a typical male reaction, but Jonah was too heavy. All the cargo was not as heavy as Jonah in that boat.

Guilt is the heaviest thing a man can carry, and the way to get rid of guilt is not to try and get rid of your cargo and your possessions, and it is not to try to get there, however hard you try. There is one way, and that is God's way. God was trying to say to these men through Jonah that you don't get rid of guilt except through death. There is only one way and that is the sacrifice of death for sin. There came a point where these men became repentant men and said: "O God, you've chosen this way, then we will come your way," and they added a prayer of forgiveness, for their own forgiveness, and they threw Jonah into the water.

At that point, they became aware that God was utterly real. Up to that point, they had not been sure whether he really did exist, but they were going to try it to see. Now they were absolutely sure, and do you notice what we may now say about them? They are now *reformed* men. They are now men worshipping the true God. They are men who are making vows. What does that mean? It means that each sailor was on his knees saying, "God, when I get back to port, I'm going to worship you. God, when I get back to my family, I'm going to tell my family that you're the real God." They made vows—vows for the future, promises for the rest of their life. They had been face to face with God.

It is still the same way that we deal with guilt. In chapter 1, I see a picture of my little ship of life, tossed around in storms. Why? Because I am a disobedient child of God. The load I carry that is causing it all is my guilt. How can I ever get rid of that? How can I ever get that calm in the storm that I want, the peace that I long for? I can try giving my money and my time and my energy to God; jettisoning the cargo that I have wanted to keep to myself – that doesn't do it. I can try rowing hard; I can try struggling to be good, to be Christ-like. That does not get me any nearer the shore. God would say that I need a death to cover guilt. I don't have a Jonah though, to throw overboard. I cannot throw myself overboard. What can I do?

One greater than Jonah is here. Jesus has died and the calm that I can sail into is a calm that comes from knowing that Jesus was offered for my guilt, and that God sends the great calm of forgiveness as a result. I know I am reading a spiritual meaning into the story, but I think it is there. When they threw Jonah into the sea there was a great calm and they made vows and promised that they would belong to the true God evermore. It was not the end of Jonah. God had not finished with him.

Read Jonah 1:17-2:10

The little book of Jonah has been the test ground for some people's faith. People have said, "You don't still believe that?" Not only is the word of God about Jonah questioned, but God himself is at stake. For there are statements here about God. Are they true? Is God like this? Can God control the fish, as well as the weather, as well as the worm in the last chapter?

Now I begin at a very mundane level by asking two questions: could a whale or a great fish swallow a man;

secondly, has it ever happened within known history apart from the Bible?

Take first the question: could a whale swallow a man? We all know that whales are air-breathing mammals. They are almost unique among the creatures of the great deep. Dolphins and porpoises, I believe, share this honour. The arctic whale could not swallow a man. It lives on minute creatures in the sea, which it filters out from the water. Its throat just could not take a human body, but the arctic whale is never found in the Mediterranean. The whale found in the Mediterranean is the sperm whale or cachalot. This, in fact, has a much larger throat which is quite big enough to swallow. Furthermore, it swallows a lot of sea water and a lot of creatures in it through the large throat, then immediately something inside its throat sorts out the food from the water. The water is expelled and the food passes on to the stomach. But the entrance to the stomach is too small for a human body. Between the throat and the stomach is a large pouch called the laryngeal pouch. This is the main centre of breathing. Food passes straight through this pouch. If it is small enough it goes on into the stomach. If it is too large it sticks there. It is here that the air is taken in. It is perfectly feasible for a man to survive within that pouch for some time. He would of course be without food, but for some days he could certainly survive. So in theory at any rate it is possible, if for example this great fish were a sperm whale. It doesn't state that it was. There may be other creatures that could do this but we know of at least one that could.

The second question is: has it ever happened? Well there are two cases within recorded history of such a thing happening. The first was in 1758 and the details are not very well authenticated. It is there; there is an account. The full details are not given so we are not able to check up. But there is one from the year 1927, which is certainly attested by a

Mr Ambrose Wilson which you can look up if you wish. It happened off the Falkland Islands. A whale overturned a boat which had a number of sailors in it. They had been trying to harpoon it, and in fact the whale swallowed one of the sailors.

Three days later they opened up this whale, having caught it on the deck of the whaling ship, and to their utter astonishment found the man doubled up in this pouch and found to their even greater astonishment that he came around and that he did recover. His health was not in too good a state for the rest of his life and one remarkable thing was that his skin was bleached a dead white colour by the gastric juices to which his body had been exposed. It remained that way for the rest of his life. What does all this say? Simply that Jonah didn't have a monopoly of this bizarre experience, but it doesn't yet deal with the miracle. The real miracle is not whether this could or did happen. The real miracle is that God made it happen at just the right moment.

Jonah didn't have to swim around till 1927 in the hope that it would happen. The statistical odds against it happening at the right time in the right place are so immense that I think anybody will realise the real miracle is in the words, "And God prepared a great fish." This was not a chance accident as it was in both the other cases. It was a deliberate planned event. Having said all that I think we must be careful to let the Bible speak for itself and to see what it does say and what it does not say about this unusual event lest we create unnecessary difficulties for ourselves and say that things are in the Bible that are not.

I give you an illustration of this. For example there is a widespread idea that Eve gave Adam an apple. You will never find that anywhere in the Bible. There is a widespread idea that three kings came from the east to visit the baby Jesus at Bethlehem and you'll not find that anywhere in the Bible. There is this idea that Jonah was swallowed by a whale but in fact that is not in the Bible at all. A great fish – yes. It doesn't say what species it was and in fact we can't know what it was because nobody ever saw it except poor old Jonah from the inside and you don't get a very good idea of what species you have come across from that vantage point. Even more serious is this: it seems to me quite clear from the language in chapter 2, when studied carefully with an open mind, that at some point in this experience Jonah died and that the miracle we are studying is not a miracle of survival but a miracle of resurrection. When we look closely at the language involved, you will realise why I affirm that.

Now let us look at the Bible itself and ask what it says. Most of this part of the study is of an amazing prayer. Considering the circumstances in which it was offered to God it is a prayer that should command our close study and attention. Some scholars have told us that this prayer shows that the book of Jonah is the concoction of a committee because this prayer is made up of parts of eleven different Psalms: Psalm 18, Psalm 31, Psalm 42, Psalm 69, Psalm 142 are all quoted in the prayer. So some scholar got the bright idea of saying that somebody has concocted the whole story. He wanted to construct a prayer and so he pulled little texts from here and there, put them together, and here is Jonah's prayer. There is a much simpler explanation than that, and it is this. When you are really praying, when you are really in distress, when you're praying from the heart, you will discover that phrases and snatches of readings and hymns come naturally to your lips. If you have been a regular worshipper of God, if you have regularly joined in worship with God's people, prayed and praised as they have done, some of the hymns that you have sung will come back to you in moments of distress and you will sing them to yourself. This is a perfectly normal experience. The fact that you use other people's words in a prayer does not make it less of a prayer. It makes it more of a prayer because their experience and yours are being offered together. What they have said about life is true for you too. May I commend to you the practice of reading a Psalm every day for yourself? You will find again and again it expresses just what you want to say. Now Jonah was a man who loved to go to the temple. We know that from the prayer. He loved to go every Sabbath and worship God with his people and sing the hymns and sing the prayers. No wonder then when he is in this situation he finds himself recalling words from the services that he used to attend. But let us look at this prayer a little more carefully. Some of the tenses of the verb puzzle people. In this prayer he is talking about a deliverance that is already passed and yet he is still in the belly of the whale.

He has a real problem. He says, "I called to the Lord [past tense – not I am calling] and he answered me." He further says, later in the prayer: "Thou didst bring up my life...." He had been saved already, and here he is still in the whale. How do we explain this? Some people say it is because this was related later by Jonah; he is telling someone about it. He is saying later: this is what I prayed, and as always when you are telling about a vivid experience and reliving it as you tell it to someone else, the tenses of your verbs change. But I think there is a much more obvious explanation for it than that to be found within the prayer itself. When was Jonah delivered by God? When was he saved? The answer is not when he came out of the whale but when he went into it. When we grasp that, the prayer falls into place and everything he says in that prayer becomes meaningful.

Now I get that from the prayer itself and it is quite astonishing how many people have views on Jonah who have never studied the book properly and who have never really looked at this prayer and never studied its wording which is very important. Our usual conception of what really happened is probably based on our own imagination. Now I remember as a boy when I heard this story I saw a picture. There was the boat, here the sailors, and over he goes, and in mid-air is Jonah and popping out of the sea is a large sea creature with a big open mouth.

I am sure you have seen this kind of picture in your mind and drawn it, perhaps in Sunday school. But you know this is not what happened. We can tell from the prayer what did happen: Jonah was drowned before ever the fish appeared. The sailors never saw it. Before it did anything at all, a great deal happened. The language is vivid; it is the language of a drowning man who believes the end has come. They tell us that drowning men see their whole life in a flash. I don't think that could possibly be true. But, as Dr Johnson said, "It could have a wonderful power of concentrating a man's thoughts and certainly one or two key thoughts would come into his mind." True to life, it happens here.

Notice the language. He talks first of being cast into the deep and there he is floundering. He probably couldn't swim because the Jews hated the sea and very few of them could swim. He is conscious of being thrown into the deep, into the heart of the seas, and as he is thrown he says, "The flood is round about me." He is conscious only of water all around him. Then the waves and the billows pass over him but his head just keeps popping up. Then he says, "The waters closed in over me...." All this is happening so quickly, in a series of phrases. The waters closed in over me, the deep was round about me ... and as he sank through the waters his hair got caught up in some seaweed.

You notice the phrase "Weeds were wrapped about my head" and the word he uses is "seaweed" in the original language. The seaweed was around his head at the roots of the mountains. He was conscious of being among the rocks at the bottom of the sea. Now that was about his last thought as he sank down to the bottom of the seabed – and how deep or shallow it was I wouldn't know. It was fairly near land. Land was in sight because they rowed hard to reach it, but he sank down to the roots of the mountains where they go straight down into the Mediterranean Sea and there, caught in the seaweed, his last moment of consciousness comes.

Now in between this description of being thrown into the water, the waves crashing over him but managing to struggle up again, and then becoming weaker and sinking and going down in the sea, he describes the thoughts of his mind as he went. There are not many – there wouldn't be time, but there are one or two very important thoughts. One is, "I shall never see the temple again." For the first time it comes home to him that the temple is part of his past. He used to love to go there. He had been running away from it when the sailors took him to Tarsus. Now he knows that he will never again worship in that place and sing praises to God.

I suppose that when he ran away to Tarsus he had an idea that in a few years, after it had all blown over in heaven, he might come back and worship again and sneak into the back unnoticed. Now he realises he never will again. "I am cast out from thy presence, how shall I again look upon thy holy temple?" That was one thought as he went down. Another thought was that he was going to die. He wasn't just going down into the water. He was going down to the land whose bars close over you forever. He describes that place as Sheol, Hades, as the pit, the realm of the departed, those who have died. He knows perfectly well he is dying.

He prays from the realm of the dead. The first prayer offered on board the boat he wasn't praying. The sailors were praying like mad and they said, "Why don't you pray to your God?" He knows it was no use. Now in his drowning moments he is face to face with truth and the prayer for salvation comes from the world of the dead, "Out of the belly of Sheol I cried." He died and his spirit prayed to God. It is the only case in the Bible of a prayer from the dead being answered and it is the prayer from a servant of God. This prayer was offered before he entered the whale. It was in the distress of drowning and in the disembodied state of separation of spirit and body that that produced that from the belly of Sheol – from the dead, Jonah cried.

He knew from the Psalms that even if you go to Sheol you are not beneath or beyond the reach of God. "If I ascend into heaven," says Psalm 139, "Behold you are there. If I make my bed in Sheol, if I die and go down to the dead you're there too. You can reach me there. Wherever I go on earth..." There is only one place you can go where God can't reach you and that is hell. But hell is different from Sheol or Hades. God has the keys of death and Hades; so has Christ. So the prayer came first from "out of the belly of Sheol" (2:2).

Now at that point and only at that point and not before, with a dead body lying among the seaweed at the roots of the mountains, at that point God answers the prayer of a dead man and brings him back to life in a most unusual way – that great fish comes; let it be a sperm whale, we can't be dogmatic but it seems as if that was likely – and it picks him up. Now you may say that was a profoundly unnatural thing to do.

I knew a trainer for Marineland in California, training whales and porpoises to do tricks. He showed us a film of his pets there, and one of the sequences I found remarkable. A whale and a porpoise shared a huge tank. They did all their tricks for the spectators. Being mammals they are highly intelligent. One day the porpoise died and sank to the bottom of the tank. The whale was terribly upset. What happened next was filmed. The whale came swimming down to the bottom of the tank, picked up the porpoise in its mouth, swam back up to the top, and for three days tried to get it to breathe again by pushing it through the surface of the water. That is amazing. I could see old Jonah being pushed up again there, this deep instinct for air, for life. That is precisely what happened at this point only it didn't happen naturally or by instinct. It happened because God was in charge of the situation.

The whale took up Jonah, and it seems that at that point through a miracle of resurrection (not survival) God gave him his life back and brought body and spirit together, and as we have seen he would be able to survive those three days and three nights. Now he prays about something that has already happened, a deliverance he has already had. He now knows when he came to, realising that he was in some living creature, that something incredible had happened, that God had not accepted his resignation as a prophet, that God had not let him go, that God was still going to deal with him, that God had literally heard that dying prayer and indeed that dead prayer from the belly of Sheol, and spirit and body had come together. It is not the only resurrection in the Old Testament. There are two or three others. There are more in the New Testament when body and soul are brought together by God again. So here he is, alive. No wonder he speaks in the past tense. I cried, he says, out of the belly of Sheol. I was dead, drowned, and God reached down there and he answered me and here I am.

Jonah was thrown into the deep, the waves and the billows crashed over his head, the waters closed over him, and down he went into the seaweed and the roots of the mountains. You can see it all. He thought he would never see the temple again. In the whale he realises he will. Now there is a tremendous note of hope. "Thou didst bring up my life from the pit, O Lord my God." Now he realises he is going to get a chance to go back and pick up the threads and start all over again. He finishes the prayer with a tremendous shout of triumph, "Deliverance belongs to the Lord!" Now how could he shout that when he was still in the whale? The answer is precisely because he was. He had taken a single ticket to Tarsus and God had the return trip all arranged. Three days and three nights were needed to get back to Joppa. Now the most important thing about this prayer and the most significant from beginning to end of it is this: here is a man who turned to God in the worst extremity of his life. You notice that he accepts God's justice completely. He doesn't blame the sailors for throwing him in the water. He said "thou didst cast me into the deep". He doesn't blame the sea for drowning him. He said "thy waves and thy billows went over me." He acknowledges absolutely that he deserved to die, that it was just, but he cried to God for mercy. It is great when someone says: I deserve to die but I plead for life. I deserve your justice but I ask for mercy. I deserve the worst you can give to me but I ask for something of the best.

When someone prays like that, God answers. When someone recognises the justice and the mercy of God together, God listens and does something. So he prays to God. Most people pray to God when they are in a jam. Most drowning men do. Talk to sailors in the navy who have been near drowning and they will tell you they pray. Somebody said to me: "I have really prayed in my life twice." They told me of two very deep and dangerous experiences during the First and Second World Wars, when twice in their life they really prayed.

Now the difference between Jonah and that person would be that Jonah didn't just pray when he was in a jam. Here is a profound little word of advice that somebody once gave me: get your anchor down before the storm begins. The man who can pray most effectively in a crisis is the man who has prayed before. Jonah's prayer reveals that he has the right idea of God and he knows the right way to pray when he is in the crisis because he has been praying regularly in the temple. I want you to notice further that Jonah says, "When I am out of all this I will pray again. I will offer sacrifices of thanksgiving in that temple when I get back." He says this now, "What I have vowed I will pay." What is he referring to?

There was a day, years earlier, when Jonah as a young man was called of God to be a preacher. Jonah made a vow that day and said: God, I'll be a preacher; I'll go anywhere you want me to go; I'll speak to anybody you want me to speak to; here I am, I vow my life; I offer it to you." He has broken that vow by going to Tarsus. Now he says: God, I'll go back and I will pick up the threads of that vow and I will do what you have told me to now.

It would be wonderful if some crisis in your life brought you to the point where you said, "What I have vowed I will pay." So many of us said as young Christians: Lord, we want to do anything you want us to do; we'll go where you want us to go; we'll speak to whom you want us to speak. Now we may have settled for middle age Christianity when we don't do that.

Jonah now sees the point of going to Nineveh because in his prayer he says (v. 8): "I can now see that those who pay regard to vain idols forsake their true loyalty." In other words, I know now why you wanted me to be a missionary. I know why you wanted me to preach, because people who don't know the truth have forsaken their true loyalty to God. They worship vain idols and so it is all coming back. Here is a man being called again to the mission field.

I suppose the most wonderful thing about this story is this – that God is so patient with us that he will have us back again. God could have called any other prophet, any other man or woman on earth to go to Nineveh and preach in place of Jonah. God could have called another but he didn't.

He still wanted him. Jonah had let God down, betrayed him and run away from this, but God still wanted him. If you have been a Christian for many years, you have known the patience of God when he has called you back and said: "I still want you. I know you've let me down but I want you back again to go on doing this for me" – the marvellous grace of God.

We have gone through the prayer, and I must come now to the final verse. The Lord spoke to the fish and it vomited out Jonah upon the dry land. It came right inshore to do so. I am going to tell you a rather funny thing. The Children's Bible includes a delightful story of Jonah, and there is a picture of the whale just pushing off into the distance. Jonah is left standing on the shore. My younger daughter studied that for a long time and looked up to me in all seriousness and asked, "Where's the sick?" She was very anxious that someone had not been true to the details. I use that for this reason: her little mind as a child was saying there was something wrong with the picture; that it seemed not to be true to the Bible. She was not the only person to feel that way. I am trying to be utterly true to every detail of the story, and when you do it becomes a wonderful story. I do not know where this happened. Whales can certainly come inshore and they can certainly regurgitate. I don't know where it happened. I would guess not far from Joppa. God has his way of bringing you back to where you went wrong – to the place you lost your confidence, to regain it. You notice that Jonah's exit from the whale was once again commanded by God. You notice that God can speak to fish. God spoke to the fish and there was Jonah. I have no doubt that his flesh was bleached. I have no doubt that people asked him why it was. I have no doubt that he told everybody who would listen: Do you know what happened to me? I ran away from God, and do you know how he brought me back? I can imagine people saying to him, even in those days when they believed more than people today: do you expect us to believe that? Do you expect us to swallow such an incredible story?

It was Jesus Christ himself who was once approached by a group of people who said to him: give us some sign; give us something to see; give us some miracle that will prove to us you are the Son of God. Jesus said: As Jonah was three days and three nights out of sight, out of mind, entombed in the deep, I will be buried in the heart of the earth three days and three nights. I am expanding here, but I am sure Jesus meant that as Jonah came out of that whale with the marks of death upon him, so Jesus would come out of the tomb; and as the resurrection of Jonah was the sign to the city of Nineveh, the resurrection of Jesus would be the sign to the whole world. Jesus added elsewhere that even if someone rises from the dead people don't believe. I am afraid that is true.

Jesus called himself a greater than Jonah. Jonah rose up from the grave. He rose up from death. He rose up from that drowned corpse at the bottom of the Mediterranean and he rose up from that tomb of the belly of the whale. Jonah had been dead and buried, and Jonah rose up and a whole city believed that it was true and accepted his story. Jesus, the greater than Jonah, rose up from the tomb and there are people today who in the face of I think incontrovertible evidence deny that Jesus is alive today.

There is a parallel—both deaths were due to the justice of God. Both deaths were, in a sense, judicial murders; executions. In both cases God raised from the dead. In the one case the death was a man for his own sins; in the other case the Son of God for everybody else's. Both deaths and resurrections – of Jonah and Jesus – led to the good news of God's love and mercy being taken to the Gentiles.

Read Jonah 3

In this chapter there are three wonderful miracles, and they are all of the same kind. They are all miracles of repentance. I hope you don't feel flat when I say that. In fact, there are four miracles altogether. In fact, there are thousands of miracles in chapter 3. There is, first of all, Jonah's repentance – that is a miracle. There is, secondly, the repentance of the people of Nineveh, and there were two million of them. Thirdly, there was the repentance of an oriental king, and that is a miracle. Then the final miracle is the most amazing of all: God repented. We are going to go through these miracles of repentance one by one. But first, what is repentance? I find that so many people still have the idea that repentance is a change of attitude. Certainly the Greek word *metanoia* from which the word repentance comes means literally a change of mind. It is basically to think differently, to change your mind about God, about yourself, about life, about everything. It begins with a re-think: instead of seeing yourself as somebody pretty good you see yourself as somebody pretty bad. Instead of seeing God as someone you should have as little to do with as possible you see God as someone you should get to as quickly as you can. This is a change of attitude but if it stops there it is not full repentance. The change of attitude must lead to a change of action if it is to be full repentance. The Bible would put it like this: it must bring forth fruits worthy of repentance but in simple language: change of attitude must produce change of action.

When people came to John the Baptist and said they wanted to be baptized, he said: if you repent. He explained what this meant. If they had too many clothes, they should go and give some away to those who do not have enough clothes. Someone fiddling the accounts and cooking the books at work needed to go and put their finance straight. A bully should stop fighting. Now this is not just a change of attitudes, it is a change of action, and repentance covers both.

In every one of these four cases of repentance (Jonah, the Ninevites, the king and God) you find a change of attitude followed by a change of action. Take Jonah, we know that he changed his attitude right there inside the whale. In the belly of that whale he changed his mind. But I want you to notice one thing that he didn't decide to do. He did not say: now I can go back to Nineveh. He never mentioned it inside the whale, and like a lot of other people he had the wrong idea that forgiveness lets us off our responsibilities and it does nothing of the sort. It enables us to go back and fulfil them properly. Forgiveness is not an easy way out, it is the right way out.

So Jonah got back to his own land. He went to worship God and there he was – forgiven and back in the temple.

God said: "Jonah, back to Nineveh......" It was to be back to the job he had run away from. Forgiveness doesn't set us free from our responsibilities, it puts us in a position to fulfil them again and to do them properly. Jonah learned that forgiveness is as much concerned with your future as your past. It is as much concerned with the positive side of doing right now as the negative side of having the wrong forgotten. It is as much concerned with obedience as disobedience.

God just doesn't forgive us so that we can go right back into it and do it again. It is not like a man falling off a pier and you saved him from drowning by diving in and rescuing him, and he shook you by the hand and thanked you warmly and then turned around and again walked back in and shouted, "Save me!" – and then repeated that. Sooner or later you are going to say to that man: "I don't think you want saving." I think God has the right to say this to some of us sometimes. We say, "Lord forgive me for doing this," and as soon as we have got forgiveness we think we can go right back and do it again. That is not why he forgives us.

Jonah, back to Nineveh – not only back to God but back to the job that he told him to do. If this sounds a bit tough on Jonah it was wonderfully patient of God still to be prepared to use him. He could have sent someone else but he gives him another chance.

The mandate – that was to go to a large and evil city. We are told only two things about it here: it was a great city and it was a wicked city. We now know from archeology, digging around in the dust and ruins of Nineveh, just how big and how evil it was. Let us consider these two things. First of all its size; I wonder if you have studied the excavations that have been made since 1841. Guarding Nineveh there were fifteen hundred towers, each two hundred feet high. The wall was so wide that three chariots could be driven abreast along the top of it. These battlements took 1.4 million slaves eight years to build and many of them died in the process through overwork. We are told in chapter 4 that there were 120,000 children in the city who were not yet morally old enough to discern right from left and wrong from right, which indicates that there must have been, on a rough estimate, 2 million souls living inside those walls.

It was a great city and one man was sent to it to conduct a crusade. There were no posters. There was no vast arena. There was no gigantic organisation. There was no big finance. There was nothing but one little man with an unnaturally white face – Jonah; I am referring to what the whale would have done to him, not to his cowardice though I would think that added to it. But he went there and faced that city.

Not only was its size forbidding, its sin was even more awe-inspiring to one preacher. We now know from the archaeology that this was one of the most sinful cities there has ever been – affluent, luxurious, and decadent in its culture. For amusement they tortured people to death and there are bas reliefs sculptured on the ruins showing the ways in which they did this. It was a cruel city of violence where you did not dare to go out at night. It was a city of luxury and malice, murder and plunder. It had been built up by plundering others, and when you have built a city like that you must defend yourselves against those who will come and plunder you, hence the towers and the walls. Jonah was told: you go and preach to that city. I think perhaps I would have run away to Tarsus, but Jonah went. His mandate was to go to that most difficult place you could go and preach. I have the feeling that every Christian has a Nineveh in his life. It may be someone at the office; it may be a relative. It may be a "Nineveh", and you say: "God, I'll talk about you anywhere else but that's the one place I'm not going to go. That's too big for me, that's too bad for me." God sometimes says: go to the very place you would rather not be, and preach there.

God says, "Tell them what I tell you." Jonah was not to choose his text or sermon. He was not to have any say in the message but simply to tell them what God said. That is every preacher's job. I think in a preacher's life there comes a crisis, and I remember the time it came to me, when you have to decide: are you going to preach what God tells you or what the people want to hear? Are you going to shape your message according to the audience or are you just going to say, "Lord, whether anybody comes or nobody comes, what you tell me to say I'll say." It is a crisis in a preacher's life when he comes to this point because pressures of the "customer" can be brought very subtly to bear upon a preacher.

The churches, I suppose, are the one sort of place where the customer is not always right and where the man who is dealing in the things of God must say, "God, what do you want me to say tonight?"

Jonah's message had to be one of unrelieved doom and death and damnation for a city. That is not a popular message and people don't like it and they can easily get upset. God said, "Yet forty days, and Nineveh shall be overthrown!"

Can you imagine someone from far away marching into the centre of London and saying: "Six weeks and London will be annihilated by nuclear bombs." What would happen? They would say, "Hyde Park Corner is the place for you." If he went on doing it they might send for the police or a doctor. But Jonah, a little lone figure, came striding through the desert that day, came in at the gate beneath the vast towers and walked into the city a certain distance, and then stood in the street and he said: forty days God gives you and this whole city will have gone. Now it is marvellous that he arose and went. The message was one of doom and disaster, so much so that, because of his experiences both on the ship and in Nineveh, Jonah's name has become a nickname for gloomy people who bring disaster. "Oh, you're a real Jonah," they say and this man spoke of disaster.

But it is not unrelieved doom because there are just some little sparks of light in this message. The first is: why should God have told Nineveh this if there was no hope for them? There was no point in sending Jonah if there was no hope at all but the glorious thing is that the very terms of the message imply that there was a chance, otherwise why announce it? There would have been no point in announcing it – it just adds to their suffering if there is no possibility of avoiding it. Right through the scripture, forty is an interesting figure. It is almost invariably used for a period of testing. Forty years in the wilderness; forty days in the wilderness. It seems as if God sees this term "forty" as a fit period of testing, of probation.

So he says forty days, and then Nineveh would be gone. Why should God say that? Because God is holy and when a city gets as low as Nineveh had got, then literally, to use Bible language it stinks in God's nostrils and he must deal with such a blight on the face of his earth. Now comes, I think, the biggest miracle in the whole book. The people of Nineveh believed God. There has never been another case in history of such a thing occurring. It is unique. I have never known any such thing happen on the scale on which this happened before: that a man of God brought a city of two million people to its knees. I know we have been privileged to see so-called city-wide crusades, but let's face it, even when the biggest place in a city is jammed, it is only a tiny percentage of the people in that city.

There has never been a crusade to touch it. Jonah, a little foreigner coming in from some little state away in the west came and preached. The whole city came to its knees. I notice the statement says, "They believed God." It doesn't say, "They believed Jonah." That in itself is a remarkable statement. They didn't say, "Jonah what you say is true." They said, "This is God speaking to us." They believed that when God says a thing he means it. Somebody has asked me, "Wasn't there a lot of fear in their faith?" The answer is: yes – what is wrong with that?

People talk nowadays as if fear is a wrong thing. It can be a healthy thing. I wanted my children to be afraid of the traffic. I wanted them to be afraid of fire. I wanted them to be afraid of a lot of things. It is a healthy thing to be afraid. The fear of the Lord is the healthiest fear you will ever have. If you have never been afraid of God then I wonder if you have even begun to understand wisdom. The fear of the Lord is where it all begins. To be afraid of God is the point at which a man comes to himself and says, "I'm not as I ought to be." Well now, in this faith there is fear. No doubt about that. They are afraid of God. Now let me distinguish between a healthy and an unhealthy fear. A healthy fear is something that leads you to the right kind of action but an unhealthy fear is something that paralyses you.

Mary Slessor, the great missionary, as a girl was afraid of traffic. She was so afraid of it that she would not leave her house alone and she dared not cross the street. It became a phobia. It paralysed her and it became a neurotic fear that prevented her from doing anything. Do you know that Mary Slessor by the grace of God got into a canoe one day, went up a river in east Africa to face cannibals and almost certain death, and that was the girl who didn't dare to cross the street alone. Isn't that amazing? Why? Because she found a healthy fear – a fear of the Lord, which put her straight.

Now what's wrong with the Ninevites fearing the end of their city? – Nothing at all. It didn't paralyse them. They said, "What do we do about it?" Their faith coupled with a fear led to a fast. I am going to make a provocative statement now but I think possibly the reason why we don't fast as we should is because we don't fear the Lord as we should. Fasting has dropped almost right out of Christians' thinking and yet Jesus told us to do it as he told us to pray and to give. Why don't we fast more? I think because we don't fear the Lord enough, because we don't take him seriously enough, because we still want our Sunday joint after we have worshipped – and they fasted.

These were people who were living in the lap of luxury. They had great food. We know this from the records we have now found. They fasted and they took off their beautiful clothes. They pulled on sackcloth, realising that their clothes did not matter. They put the same thing on – in God's sight all were sinners – and they fasted. Think of a whole city doing that.

When you get to the Day of Judgment, you will meet people of Nineveh. They will accuse others of not believing because they have had far more opportunity than the

Ninevites to believe. All they had was one little foreigner coming to tell them their city was going to be destroyed, and they all believed. There are people who have heard of Jesus – never mind Jonah – and still they don't believe God, still they don't repent, still they don't turn back to him. "The men of Nineveh," said Jesus, "will rise up and judge Capernaum." Capernaum had Jesus himself but did not believe.

The next miracle we come to is the king. Jonah started at the bottom and worked up. Jonah could have said, "Well now, this is an important message God has given me. I had better make for the top, make for the key man who has influence over everyone else. It is amazing how we think like this. The world may think like that, but God doesn't.

When God sent his own Son into the world he didn't send him to a palace but to a stable. When Jonah went to Nineveh he didn't go to the palace he just went to the streets, to the ordinary people. God has a way of doing this. The early church began among the slaves, the dregs of society. It seems to me that it is God's method to start at the bottom and work up. Every worldly movement tries to go the other way, starting with the man at the top and he can influence everybody else. Jonah just started in the street with the nobodies and it worked all the way up until the king heard of it.

The king was used to giving absolute orders. This was no democracy or constitutional monarchy but a despotic dictatorship. The king would say "Come", and everybody would come running; and "Go" and they would all go running. This man heard about a little preacher in the streets, and he realised that before God he was responsible for leading this city, and that his leadership had been utterly corrupt. The king stepped off his throne. You can't stay sitting on your little throne when God steps into your life. The king took off his robes – you have no glory of your own when God becomes real – and he put on sackcloth and sat there. Then he called a national day of prayer.

I don't want to throw stones or to criticise but where is the national leader today who will call Britain to prayer and fasting? We need it more than ever. We needed it during the war. Where is the call for national days of prayer now, when we need to ask God to be delivered from selfishness and sloth. Where is the man at the top who will say, "Let us seek God? Our nation was great when we sought God as we should." This man did it, and Nineveh was a miracle of grace.

Now there was something good about this call to prayer, to cry mightily to God. It is always good when a leader of a nation acknowledges that there is somebody above him to whom he is responsible, and calls the nation to acknowledge that someone. But what was bad in his call was this: you cannot make people good by Act of Parliament. You can't decree penitence. No Prime Minister could get a law through Parliament that every British person must be penitent. Fortunately, he was too late – they already were penitent. There is something rather humorous, rather ironic, about this chap issuing this order. I can imagine somebody coming in saying: "It's all right, you don't need to, they are all in sackcloth." He was too late. God saw to that. The people were penitent not just because the king told them but because they really were.

Now what did this king believe to do such a thing? The answer is he believed that God is just and that God is angry with violence and wickedness, and that he must punish it until people perish. But he must have believed that God was merciful as well or he would have never said, "Who knows, he may change his mind." Now this is the picture of God, which is an accurate picture, that Jonah must have conveyed to those people under this pagan king (who was an astrologer who believed that your fate was fixed in the stars and who consulted his horoscope before he did anything). This man came to believe that there was a God who was just and merciful, who had every right to obliterate his city and yet to whom you could cry mightily. So the whole nation turned to prayer. He said, "Who knows...?" I would want to say to the king of Nineveh: "We know that it's worth crying to God mightily."

We know that God can forgive. How do we know? – Because we are living the right side of Jesus. He was still in the pagan darkness where it was worth trying, as many people in this country are today, who say, "Who knows, it might be worth trying church. It might be worth trying to read the Bible. It might be worth trying prayer." People come to God as a try and think it may be worth trying. Who knows, we might get something. But the person who knows Jesus will not say, "Who knows....?" He will say, "We know – it is worth going." And so he went.

We come to the most difficult miracle to believe in the chapter: God repented. He didn't repent when he saw how they felt. He didn't repent when he heard what they said. He repented when he *saw what they did*. I want you to notice that what God is looking for from us is not just a different feeling but different behaviour. He saw what they did, proof that they wanted to be free from their sin; they turned away from their luxurious living and they stopped their violence. They knew perfectly well that turning over a new leaf would not save them, but they did turn over a new leaf to show they wanted to be saved and that is what repentance means.

We have the most amazing thing: the unchangeable God changes his mind. I think most of us were brought up to believe that God never changes. From one point of view he doesn't. There is no shadow cast by turning with God. That is a reference in the Epistle of James to the fact that every other heavenly body moves and casts a moving shadow as it moves. But there is one in heaven who doesn't, and that is God. He doesn't change at all. God never changes in his love. God never changes in his justice. He never changes in his mercy. Thank God that he doesn't. I am a creature of moods but he does not change; he does not have moods.

It is the same God Abraham met, and Isaac and Jacob. He doesn't change but he does change his behaviour. His character never changes and therefore if the situation in which he finds himself changes he must change his behaviour as anyone of consistent character must. A God who is just and merciful must behave differently according to the situation of the people to whom he is related. If they are running away from him, he must be just. If they are running back to him, he must be merciful to be consistent, to be unchangeable.

So God, who said "I am what I am" is the God who repents. It is a personal, dynamic living relationship. God can change his attitude, and when he does he changes his action and the evil that he was going to do he does not do. There is hope. "Who knows," said the king, "He might change." We can say we know that he will change if you do. If you repent and cry to him for mercy you will find he changes. If you are not right with God then he must be a just God to you, a God of whom you will be afraid, a God before whom you will perish one day, a God who will punish you. But the moment you turn around and show God that you really mean it by your acts, that you want to live a good life, that you want to turn over a new leaf, that you want to be saved, you find immediately that he is waiting with open arms for you and you may think you have found a different God. You haven't. God has changed towards you because you have changed towards him. My Bible tells me that all the way through. What a wonderful thing to believe in an unchangeable God who changes. It is a paradox, but it is true and God repents.

He has no joy in the death of the wicked, and if a man will begin to meet him even halfway, (like the father in the parable of the prodigal son) he runs out to meet that boy.

So the people of Nineveh turned right around. They came back to God and God met them more than halfway. One day London and every other city on earth will be destroyed. I tell you that the world is to perish, and everything in it. God has said that. Call me a Jonah if you will. I am a preacher as he was, and God is going to do this. When the city perishes and when the world perishes, everything and everyone that is sinful will go with it—that is my message.

Do you believe that? If so, then I tell you that whether the time is six weeks, six months, six years, or six centuries, God has lengthened the time to make it a day of repentance. He doesn't want anybody to perish. He just wants them to turn to him and admit their life is what it is and that it needs cleaning up. When you turn to him really, properly, truly, you will find that he meets you right there as a loving, forgiving Father. Jonah preached that; Nineveh proved it to be true. There are still thousands in your city who neither know that it is going to come to an end nor, unless they repent, that they will likewise perish, nor do they seem to know that Jesus died that they might be forgiven. That is what I preach, and I urge anyone who realises the truth of it to show God by their acts that they are sorry for what they have been and done, and to cry mightily to him and find what Nineveh found: that he forgives.

Read Jonah 4

To many people it is a great puzzle as to why God didn't finish the book of Jonah at the end of chapter 3. It would have had a "happily ever after" ending. It would have tied up all the loose ends. Here we have a wonderful, complete story of a man who ran away from God and then decided to go God's way, led a city of two million people to God, and there they all finish up happily together, believing in him. But it doesn't end that way. The Bible is an honest portrait of human nature. If there is something wrong with the personality, people's faults are clearly shown so that we put our faith in no one but Jesus Christ. He is the only person who strides through the pages of scripture without a weakness or a fault.

After that magnificent crusade in this big city, a tremendous success, a thousand times more successful than any evangelistic crusade you and I have ever known, we are given a picture of the main preacher which is quite shattering.

Also, this book gets progressively more difficult to understand. Chapter 1 is easy – a man running away from God. Millions are doing that, so we understand that. Chapter 2 – a drowning man yelling to God to save him. We understand that. We have been in a jam and we have cried to God when we were in deep distress. The episode of the great fish is not all that common so we don't understand that so well, but there have been other people to whom this bizarre experience has happened. Chapter 3 becomes more difficult still to believe – that a great city of that size would respond to one street preacher; it takes a lot of accepting, but we accept it. But when we come to chapter 4, this is really difficult.

If you had a normal childhood (and I did) you would hear a parent say "no buts". "But daddy...." We are just the same with our heavenly Father: "But God...." God says: "no buts". If you underline the word "but" in the book of Jonah you find it is a very interesting word. God said, "Go to Nineveh," *but* Jonah said, "No," and went to Tarsus. Jonah got on board that boat *but* God sent a great tempest," and all the "buts" of this little book are "buts" of Jonah against God and "buts" of God against Jonah: but Jonah did this; but God did that.

Who is going to have the last word? If you are in the kind

of relationship to God where you are just not in line with his will for your life, life is just one "but" after another. You say "But God..." and go your own way. God says, "But no, that is not the way you go." Life is a series of "buts" until we come into line with God's will. Jonah had to learn this the hard way and chapter 4 begins "But Jonah". But Jonah was angry; he was displeased. Now this is the most incredible twist in the story. This is one of those things that convinces me we are dealing with absolute historical truth. No committee writing an invented story, a fictional event, would ever dare to say this, would ever even think of it – after a preacher has led a city of two million people to its knees and led them back to God, that he should lose his temper with God for doing it is one of the most difficult things to understand.

Why was Jonah angry with God? What can possibly explain such an end to the story? It must be true. Nobody could have invented it. Well, look at his anger. When God stops being angry, Jonah starts. It is quite strange, isn't it? God's anger – against the cruelty, the wickedness, the evil of that affluent city with few morals if any – stopped when the city said sorry, but as soon as God's anger stopped, Jonah started.

For the second time in the story he prays, but you notice that he is preaching in his prayer. That is not unknown and we must confess that we sometimes do this. We are not so much praying to God, we are telling him what we think. We have all been guilty of such prayer and have listened to such prayers from others – prayers that were really sermons. "Now Lord, didn't I tell you," says Jonah. He is trying to tell God Jonah's will. We now see something that has not been told us at the beginning of the story. We now hear from Jonah's lips the real reason why he fled to the other end of the Mediterranean Sea instead of going to Nineveh; why instead of going east, which God told him to, he went west.

The reason is a peculiar one that is difficult to understand unless you are fairly close to God. When God first called this man, Jonah said, "No I am not going," and he also told God why he wasn't going. It was because he had guessed what would happen if he did and he was not willing to face the consequences. He is now saying to God that he didn't go because there are five things he knew about him, and that would lead to certain consequences which he was not prepared to face. Now that must have been an honest prayer. When a man says, "God I'm not going to let you run my life. I am not going to go your way because I know certain things about you and I am not prepared to face the consequences," that is honest.

What were these things and what were the consequences he didn't like? First of all he says: "You are a gracious God. You are a generous God. You're constantly giving things to people." Secondly he says, "You're a merciful God. You are giving to people all the time more than they deserve." Thirdly, "You are a God who is slow to anger." Now Jonah was a quick-tempered person, very quickly aroused. He knew God was not like that and he said, "You're a slow-tempered God." Fourthly, "You're a God who abounds in steadfast love or loyalty" – meaning that if you say something I know you will stick to it; that you have this kind of love that sticks to people through thick and thin whatever they do to you.

Fifthly, "I knew that you were the kind of God who can change your mind." When he had said he would do evil to someone as punishment he was the kind of God who could change his mind about it and not do it. This sounds strange coming from a man of God: because you are a God of love, because you give, because you give to people what they don't deserve, I don't want to preach about you. Why should a man of God say that kind of thing? Is there something terribly perverted? Is he mentally sick, or has he a very good reason? Jonah knew before he went to Nineveh that if the people showed the slightest sign of being sorry, God would let them off. There was a strange attitude in this prayer. It is a case of "let me tell you; wasn't I right?" Fancy saying that to God and yet we have said it. You may not have used such blatant words as this but just think over your prayer life. Have you never told God what you thought and that you thought you knew best and that the way he went about things was not the right way and not the way that you thought would work out? The problem now is: why should Jonah be worried about God letting people off? Why should he be angry at such a God? At least there is one good feature – he did talk to God about it. I underline that. If ever you feel that God is being unfair, if ever you feel that the way he is running things is not the way you would run them, why don't you tell him? Much better to talk to him about it than tell someone else. Jonah could have gone away gossiping and saying, "I told God this. I told him so." If ever we have a sense of grievance, of complaint at the way that God has handled our life, the best thing to do is to go straight to God and say, "I don't understand you. I can't accept it. I find it difficult to know why you do these things."

What is the reason? I have read many books on Jonah and I discovered five different reasons are given for this. It shows that people don't understand easily or else they would all give the same answer. But I will give you all five and you can take your pick.

First, there are those who say that Jonah's reason for resenting God letting people off was a personal one. It was connected with his own prestige as a prophet. A prophet is a man who, among other things, predicts the future. Here he was for six weeks predicting that an entire city would be destroyed in just a short time. Then of course, nothing happened. Thirty-ninth day came, nothing happened, the fortieth day came and everybody hadn't slept much the previous night because they didn't know whether God would let them off or not. The fortieth day dawned as every other day dawned, went through, sunset came, and nothing happened. Forty-first day, people were looking considerably relieved. There are those who say that Jonah was angry with God because it just made him look silly. Here he was predicting as if some man dressed in weird clothes got up at Hyde Park Corner to say, "London is going to be destroyed with a nuclear bomb in six weeks' time". In six weeks nothing happens. You do look ridiculous.

There are those who say that Jonah was angry purely because he was resentful that the Ninevites would start laughing at him. When he got back to his own country and they said, "Well how did they get on?" "Well he let them off. Nothing's happened." It just made him look silly. Now that is one reason and I honestly don't think that's deep enough for what Jonah has just said but you can take that if you will – a personal reason connected with his own prestige: a preacher who breathes threats and then nothing happens.

Now the second reason that some people have given is a political one. Israel, the country to which Jonah belonged, was a country that had just managed to prevent being swallowed up as a satellite right on the edge of things and in a very precarious position. Nineveh was the capital of Assyria which was an empire that was growing in military power and swallowing up other countries. Israel was the next country on the list. So some people have said it was purely political.

Shortly after this, Nineveh took Israel and ten out of the twelve tribes of the people of God were swallowed up as quickly as that whale swallowed Jonah. Now was it political? Again it doesn't tie in with what Jonah says here but you can take it if you wish.

A third reason given today is that it was racial. Jonah was a Jew, they were Gentiles. Jonah wanted God all to himself, the Jews wanted God all to themselves, and they resented being sent to preach to Gentiles. That is the most common suggestion today, especially by those who treat Jonah as fiction and as a kind of missionary tract. But there is not a word here about Jew and Gentile so it is speculation.

A fourth reason is psychological: that Jonah was sick and was the first of the long line of people who later became known as the Pharisees – people who are so mentally sick that they resent others getting salvation more easily than they got it; those who dislike seeing sinners saved when they have been working jolly hard to be good religious people all their lives. Now this is a spirit that is not unknown today. It was there in our Lord's Day. Jesus said some things to the Pharisees for which they hated him. He said: "Prostitutes and crooked tax collectors get into the kingdom of heaven before you do." Religious people don't like that, and Jonah was a religious man and he didn't like such wicked people as those in Nineveh getting off so lightly. It is extraordinary but human nature in its perversion is capable of resenting forgiveness coming too easily to someone else.

Is that the reason? Is Jonah like the elder brother in the parable of the prodigal son because he had never broken any commandments, resenting the younger brother who wasted all his life and his money coming back and getting a feast?

Again I find no trace of this in the language, so we are left with one reason, which is the one that seems to me to make sense. It is not that easy to understand but I think you will. Jonah was a man who loved God too much. Can you do that? Yes, in the sense of loving so much that your love becomes jealousy; not envy, jealousy, which is a different thing. He could not bear to see people abuse God's grace. He could not bear to see people take the love of God and throw it back in his face. Now only someone who loves God deeply will understand this.

Let me go a little further. We know quite a lot about Jonah from another book in the Old Testament, 2 Kings. There is an incident there about this very man that gives us the clue to understanding why he said what he did to God at this point. Here is the story in brief. It was in the days of a king called Jeroboam, who lived in a shrinking empire. Part of his kingdom was being nibbled away by the powers around him. Jonah was told by God to go to this king and say that God in his mercy would extend the frontiers again during Jeroboam's reign. Jonah went and told the king, "God says you are going to get it back in your reign." Jonah honestly expected the king to be so grateful for this act of mercy because they had lost the frontiers by their own evildoing, and Jonah expected the king to turn over a new leaf for he was a bad person.

Instead we find that what happened was that Jeroboam, getting back the gifts that God gave him of extra territory, did evil in the sight of the Lord. In other words, Jeroboam traded on God's mercy. His attitude was: if God is like this I can do anything I want; if he is a God of mercy I can play the fool.

Jonah had the awful burden of knowing that he had preached the love of God to someone who then abused it to live an evil life. That is about the hardest thing a Christian has to take. You may have heard of Heinrich Heine, who died in Paris after a lifetime of sin and evil, whose dying words were: "Dieu me pardonnera, c'est son métier" – "God will forgive me, that's his trade." That hurts deeply if you know God.

Jonah had been through it once already and found that human nature, being what it is, is told of the mercy of God, it abuses that mercy and regards it as a blank chequebook for sin. When God said go to Nineveh, Jonah's attitude was: now look God, I've been through all this once; I have seen it in my own country. You are a God who lets people off – and when you do, what do they do? Are they grateful to you? Nothing of the sort. Do they turn over a new leaf? Nothing of the sort. They just plunge further into evil. I am not going through it again. Now do you understand? He was a man of God and he was deeply concerned about God's glory and God's reputation, that people should think rightly of God – and when people took what he preached and used it as an excuse to do wrong, he could not stand it.

Now if you don't understand this reason, may I say very humbly and sincerely, then ask how much you love God because if you love him at all it must hurt you when this kind of thing happens.

Jonah was right. As soon as they found out that God let them off, they were back into evil ways – and this is human nature. If you wonder whether this really is the answer, not only have I given you the story from 2 Kings 14 which gives us this clue that it had happened once already, there is also the anguish that Jonah now felt: He said he would rather die than go through this again. Is that exaggerated language? Then let me remind you that another great prophet of God, Elijah, had exactly the same reaction. One day Elijah went to the top of Mount Carmel because God told him to, and had a demonstration with the pagan priests who claimed that they could light altars by fire from heaven. Archaeologists have now revealed that they used to build tunnels under the altars and a priest crept along and lit the thing from below. Elijah challenged them on the top of a mountain, where everybody could see, to build an altar and do it in the open. He said, "I'll do it with my God." It was a dramatic moment. Elijah had said, "Now you call your god to light your fire. I'll ask mine to light mine. We will see who is God." We know what happened and we know that God lit his altar and there must have been perhaps half a million people watching. Two days later Elijah is alone in the desert saying, "Lord take my life." What on earth was happening? If you study it you will see that what Elijah was saying was: God I don't believe they have really repented; it hasn't gone deep enough; they all said they accepted you but I don't believe it; I am the only one even still who believes in you.

God said: You are not, you know. There are a few thousand who still believe in me. You notice he didn't say half a million or more. He said there were a few thousand, but the point is this: Elijah was depressed because he felt that all the public response to his ministry was hollow and not lasting. May I write very frankly as a minister? At a very much smaller scale I have known the same depression. There may have been a great service, there may have been a grand crowd, there may have been an obvious interest in response and then three days later somebody who was there makes the kind of remark that shows they have not changed one bit.

The depression that comes after that is very real: Lord, did it do anything? Did anyone take a step forward? Did anyone change? An apparent interest, an apparent enthusiasm, but how deep was it? Jonah had the same depression as Elijah and he had to battle it through. His anguish confirms the reason that I gave earlier – that in fact he believed that if God let the people off they wouldn't turn to God. They would turn right back away from him and go back to where they were.

So here is the third confirmation I have that this is in fact the reason. God gently asks Jonah whether he is quite sure he is right: "Do you do well to be angry?" I think the third thing now comes. Jonah picked his way out of the city, not on the west side on the way back home but on the east side, further away from home. He climbed a bare hill, taking with him a few branches that he had broken off trees. He built a little booth, a little shelter for himself from the hot midday sun. He sat in it where he could see the city, to see what happened. He still thinks he is right, and he still is.

What did he expect to see when he sat and watched that city having been forgiven by God? He expected to see in that city everything wrong that had been there before, coming back in. He expected them to stop fasting and start feasting, to pull off the sackcloth and put on their robes again. He expected them to start opening the theatres and circuses again. He expected them to start being cruel to each other again. He expected them to start stealing and plundering again. Then he honestly expected that there would come a day when God would be forced to change his mind again and obliterate that city, and Jonah was absolutely right. We know what Nineveh did. Jonah had predicted accurately the result of being let off by God – they began to sin again. Within a few years they were committing again the horrible crimes that God had been so offended by, and soon Nineveh was back to where it was.

The next preacher God sent to Nineveh said: "Woe to this bloody city all full of lies and booty; no end to the plunder, the crack of whip and rumble of wheel; galloping horse and bounding chariot; horsemen charging, flashing sword and glittering spear; host of slain, heaps of corpses, dead bodies without end. They stumble over the bodies and all for the countless harlotries of the harlot, graceful and of deadly charms who betrays nations with her harlotries and peoples with her charms. Behold, I am against you, says the Lord of hosts, and will lift up your skirts over your face and I will let nations look on your nakedness and kingdoms on your shame. I will throw filth at you and treat you with contempt.... All who look on you will shrink from you and say, 'Wasted is Nineveh, who will bemoan her.' When shall I seek comforters for her?"

That was about 150 years afterwards and here is the final word on this city: "God will stretch out his hand against the north and destroy Assyria and he will make Nineveh a desolation, a dry waste like the desert. Herds shall lie down in the midst of her, all the beasts of the field. The vulture and the hedgehog shall lodge in her capitals. The owl shall hoot in the window, the raven croak on the threshold for her cedarwork will be laid bare. This is the exultant city that dwelt securely, that said to herself, 'I am and there is none else'. What a desolation she has become, a lair for wild beasts. Everyone who passes by her hisses and shakes his fists."

Do you know, you will find the Arabs still do that to the ruins of Nineveh? You can visit them today. You'll find the vulture and the hedgehog there. There came a day, not long after Jonah, where God came to an end of his patience and he obliterated that city completely.

Jonah was right and yet he was wrong. He was right in what he understood of human nature. He was wrong in his understanding of divine nature. That is why he was wrong in refusing to go. That is why he was wrong in trying to tell God, as if he knew best. That is why we are wrong every time we tell God that we think we would have managed things better. Why? However well we understand human nature and can tell God everything we think he needs to know about us, he knows it all already. The mistake we make when we grumble against God is this: we don't understand him well enough. That was Jonah's fault.

So now, briefly, God teaches Jonah that while he knows a lot about man he doesn't know much about God. See how he teaches him. Jonah's little booth built of branches pulled up from the valley below is withering already in the heat of the midday sun. It won't cover him much longer. A plant now grows and shades Jonah, probably the castor oil plant, a quick-growing plant, but God is doing something miraculous here. We are now up to the fifth nature miracle in this little book. The bush grows up and shelters Jonah, and as his own little booth withers in the heat, this lovely cool shade of the tree comes over him. Jonah recognises that God has been helping him and relieving him.

So Jonah thanks God and he is glad about it, and he says, "Thank you God for doing that." Somebody has delightfully said this was God's way of cooling down his hotheaded prophet. So the shade comes over this man. Then the next morning, the very next day, God performs yet another miracle and sends a worm that eats out the sap, the heart of the root of this plant, and it withers. Jonah finally reaches the end of his tether. He has had enough. God, why did you have to do that to a poor little plant – it had done nothing to you. He is angry for the plant's sake. Of course he is a bit sorry he has lost his shade too, but he doesn't say that.

What is really happening? Jonah has got to the point where he lets God know he has had enough. He had been knocked down and picked up so many times now that this was the last straw. He had run away and been fetched back; brought to the city and then it was going to be an awful flop; God had grown the plant over him and then taken it away. He felt battered and wanted to die – the same Jonah who when he was drowning in the waves of the Mediterranean had said: let me live.

Whom God loves he chastises and corrects. He tried to get something across to Jonah, giving the prophet an object lesson. "Jonah you have some pity for this little plant. You didn't make it." It meant something to Jonah. It gave him shade, but that is all. Jonah pitied the plant but could he not see that God had so much pity for the city?

It was not that God is saying, "I will never destroy this city." He had so much pity that he would put it off as long as he could. Jonah did not understand this, but God knew there were thousands of wicked people.

There were 120,000 people who were not old enough to know right from wrong, and their right hand from their left hand. God had pity on them. In that city were animals and God made the animals and pitied them too. Do you see now what Jonah had missed? He understood human nature very well indeed. He was absolutely right in his predictions of what people do when they are let off. But he was absolutely wrong in thinking that God had reached the end of his patience and pity. God had a hundred and fifty years more patience left for Nineveh. By and large most of us do not have the patience with others that God has. I suppose we have all had the experience of trying to help someone. We have had the experience of being able, by God's grace, to lead them to the point where they ask God's forgiveness and thank him for it, then, some weeks or months later, they are back in the very things from which we tried to save them. We brought them back again, patiently, to God and said, "God will have you back." He does, and they ask God's forgiveness and he has pity and compassion on them. But alas there comes a point where we reach the end of our own patience and say, "It's just no use trying to keep going with you." We run out of pity but God doesn't run out of pity when we do. He goes on stretching out the day of opportunity as long as he can. People say to me, "Why doesn't God come and put the world right? Why doesn't he come and put right the wrongs and remove the injustices?" The answer is very simple: out of sheer pity he is lengthening the days so that those who are doing the wrongs may find his mercy. That is why he has waited two thousand years already before winding up the affairs of human history.

Thank God that he leaves places on the map still, that people may have an opportunity to find his mercy – that is why he leaves us here. That is why he puts off the serious day when the whole human race will be called to reckon with him. This is a book not about Jonah, nor about a whale, but about God who is great in his patience. He still has pity for us and is more patient with us than we could ever be with each other. In this little book of Jonah, as in the book of human history, God has the last word. The book is unfinished. God said, "should not I pity Nineveh...?" Did Jonah ever reply? Did he learn the lesson? Did he say he was sorry that he had misunderstood God? Did he go back home content with having fulfilled God's will? I don't know. I know that he got back to Israel. I know that he was buried in a little village called Nazareth, and centuries later a little boy used to play around his tomb, a boy called Jesus. I think God did not want us to know because he wants each one of us to take our Bible and write in our own answer to the question. God might ask us: should not I have pity on London? Should not I have pity on those who are doing these evil things?

You might want them wiped out, but should not he have pity? God did not rush to destroy the evil world. Write your own answer to the question that God poses at the end of Jonah and let God have the last word.

MICAH

MICAH

Read Micah 1

How early should one prepare for Christmas? I suppose that the Virgin Mary was preparing nine months for the first Christmas. But I want to tell you that God prepared for the first Christmas for seven hundred years. I know he was thinking about sending his Son to this world away back in all eternity. But it was about seven hundred years before Christmas that he began to tell people it was going to happen and began to get them ready.

There were two men in particular whom he used to tell that Christmas was coming. One was Isaiah and the other was Micah. Isaiah came and said, "Behold, a virgin shall conceive and bear a son." That told them that somebody was coming; somebody would be born. But it was left to this little prophet Micah to say: "You Bethlehem of Judea are not least in the land of Judah. For out of you shall come a King, a Prince."

I would hazard to guess that most Christians could only quote four texts at the most from this prophecy. You could probably quote the one about Bethlehem and Judea quoted in Matthew, where you probably read it. You could quote the texts about beating swords into ploughshares and spears into pruning hooks, but you probably didn't read that in Micah either because you can find it in Isaiah as well.

There are two other texts that you might know. One says, "Who is a God like you who pardons iniquity?" Another for which Micah is famous is perhaps the greatest thing he ever said: "What does God require of you but to do justly, to love mercy and to walk humbly with your God?"

THE MINOR PROPHETS

In all this, God was using Micah to get people ready for the Nativity. Why was it necessary for God's Son to be born and laid in a manger? The answer lies in Micah. One of the reasons why Christmas fails to have a real, deep impact on people; one of the reasons why they can put up their lights and go to Nativity plays and send cards with these scenes of the Gospel on them and yet, by Boxing day have forgotten all about Jesus; and one of the reasons is that people don't know the Old Testament as they should: they don't know the preparation that lay behind it. They don't know the God who sent Jesus. The Old Testament was Jesus' Bible and the God of the Old Testament was Jesus' Father. So we are going to study Micah.

There was nothing special about Micah. He was a very ordinary country man who lived in the village in the dales of Israel. We don't even know his father's name, which says that he is nobody important. There is nothing about his personality that is different; nothing about his life that is unusual. The only two things that are important about him are when he lived and where he lived. He was the right man, in the right place, at the right time. The first few verses tell you where he lived and when he lived.

He lived through the reigns of three bad kings. He saw the nation in which he lived go down and down, morally and spiritually. He saw bribery, corruption – a society that had been stable and godly, disintegrated before his eyes. He saw the capital cities, for they had a civil war and there were now two capitals; Samaria and Jerusalem. He saw everything evil filling up the streets of these two cities and his heart broke. He saw a culture dying. He knew that life would never be the same again and that his children could never grow up in the nation that he had known as a boy. He felt exactly as I do about England.

He had seen the inroads of evil come and he realised that

it could not go on for much longer. He had seen the nation gradually suffer economically. He saw the nation desperately trying to make alliances with more nations around and say, "That's where our answer lies." The politicians of Israel were saying at this time: let's have a common market with Egypt and we will be saved economically – blinded to the fact that the real reason for their economic collapse was the collapse of their moral principles within. They sought within common markets and alliances the answer to their problems, and Micah saw it all and realised the end was in sight.

He lived at the end of an era, when the nation was so sick that he was going to have to say, "My people's wound is too deep to heal." Sometimes one does wonder if Britain has got to that point. The only way the nation will learn is the hard way.

Where did he live? Imagine that we have taken a knife and cut right through the Holy Land of Israel from the Dead Sea to the Mediterranean Sea, from east to west. If you took a slice right through the nation, you would find that it divided into three areas. There were the hills of Judea. They were really mountains, right down to the Dead Sea, 1600 feet below the level of the Mediterranean. The area is dry because of the side the rain falls on. This is what the Bible calls the wilderness – from Jericho at the bottom to Jerusalem at the top. Then you have the green sides of the hills of Judea where the shepherds were. Jerusalem is at the top; Bethlehem a little lower, and the other towns in the hills. Then there is a valley that runs north and south. Then we have some lower hills: dales or glens, some valleys leading from the high mountains down to the plains. Then you have the coastal plain, maybe twenty miles wide, and the sand dunes and the Mediterranean.

Micah lived in an area between the mountains and the coast. He looked down on the coast because Moresheth, where he lived, was on a little shelf, a thousand feet above sea level. From there he could see the sea, and he could see the plain stretched before him.

So he lived in between and that's very significant. Why? Because this little land is at the crossroads of the world. It joins three continents: Europe, Africa, and Asia. All the invading armies that ever passed from one country to the other came marching down this plain. You could watch them from the hills. In the year 719 BC, just about when Micah wrote, a vast army came down the plain led by Sargon. Their destination was Egypt. As Micah watched that vast army going down the plain, he knew that on their way back they would turn to the right and come up through the hills, to his capital city, Jerusalem. He could see it coming.

So that was his unique position – just as Jesus was born in Nazareth, which overlooked the plain of Esdraelon, and saw the same armies marching backwards and forwards through the same plains, for this links up with that crossroads of Megiddo. So Micah stood on his little hill and looked down and saw the armies march and knew that their days as a nation were numbered.

To Micah, as he stood on that hill watching the armies, there came the message of the Lord. It came in the form of pictures. God often speaks to us through pictures because we understand in pictures much better. Even when we have something explained to us we say, "Oh, I see." God gives visions and dreams. When someone is awake, he gives a vision; when asleep, he gives a dream. When his Spirit is moving then young men see visions and old men dream dreams.

This young man Micah saw visions. His vision was of God visiting the earth. Now what do you think he saw? Do you think he saw three camels with wise men trotting across the desert? Do you think he saw some shepherds sleeping out in the fields watching flocks? Do you think he saw a stable in a manger? No, for this was seven hundred years before that happened. He saw God coming to earth in a very different way. He saw God striding on those mountains of Judea. As God's feet touched the mountains, they flowed, they became melted, and they flowed like wax in the fire – mountains flowing.

I remember once flying low over Vesuvius and I will never forget it. The pilot of the plane in which I was travelling obviously wanted to show us into the crater. We swooped down and into the great hole of that mountain; it was like looking into a boiling caldron. You realise that just below our feet now there is molten rock flowing. It is hard to imagine, isn't it? It feels pretty solid to us. Yet in an area with slate it was molten once, and it flowed up into the Lake District at the same time as the Alps were pushed up by a gigantic up-thrust. The God who made the mountains flow once can make them flow again.

As I looked down into the volcano and saw the molten lava, I could see the path. You could still make out the path that lava once made as it tore down the mountainside and engulfed a little town called Pompeii. I knew that those people were caught in unexpected disaster, roasted to death in a moment. You can still walk the streets of Pompeii. I don't know which house it was, but in one there was a man called Pontius Pilate when Vesuvius erupted. Did you know that? There he was with his wife, now out of office, now in disgrace, living in retirement in Pompeii. One day, the mountain flowed down and Pontius Pilate disappeared in the ash. That is what Micah saw, and he trembled. He realised that God cannot let evil go on in his world; that his wrath must overflow and the very mountains would be like wax in fire, and he trembled for his nation. He could see that capital city Samaria, with its stones tumbling down the hillside; he could see it ruined and ploughed up as a field.

It is strange to read history 2,700 years ago when this was written. But many years ago I stood in Samaria. You look at the great stones of the palaces tumbling down the mountain. You can stand on top of them and look at the rubble and ruin. You can see vines growing where people walked. The people who laugh and say, "God is not like that; God will not do that," should go and stand in Samaria and should look and see: every last word Micah uttered has come true.

God visited the earth in 712 BC. After four years at siege, Samaria fell. It is one of the cities that forgot God and became corrupt. Micah said God will visit the earth. It is too deep to heal.

From Samaria and that dreadful vision that he had, Micah felt very sad. A man who has to announce this kind of thing and doesn't feel it cut his heart must have a heart of granite. Poor Micah tore off his clothes, he says, and he went around his villages howling like a jackal. Have you heard a jackal howl? I have, just once, in Kenya. It has a kind of howl that goes higher and higher, and then it finishes in a series of yelps as if it has been attacked by something. The other noise Micah makes, as he says, which I have never heard, is an ostrich crying. I am told that an ostrich cry at night in the desert makes an eerie, drawn out cry. So this poor young man Micah ran around crying, howling like a jackal, like an ostrich. "Can nothing be done? Is it beyond redemption? Is my nation too far gone?"

From the capital cities, he then turned to the villages around him and he saw the name of every village as a curse upon that village. He has some puns here on the names of the towns around him. Here they are. "So then in Gath where tales are told, breathe not a word." Gath means "telling tales". "You who live in Zaanan" – that means marching: there is no marching for you now. "Beth-ezel", that means hillside:

Beth-ezel, standing on the hillside can give no foothold in her sorrow. "Maroth" means bitterness, the town of bitterness – wait trembling for good, and so on.

Why did he say it all? Because beyond all this curse, doom and tragedy he saw a glimmer of hope. He saw a God who would one day visit the earth in mercy and come for precisely this kind of situation. He could see that there was one town out of all of these towns that God was not going to curse, but bless. Looking at all of these villages he said, "There's one up there in the hills and Bethlehem – you Bethlehem...."

You will never understand Christmas if you only think of Bethlehem and forget all these other towns. It was what was happening in them that made Bethlehem the place of God's promise.

Why was it all happening? Why this disaster? Why this doom? Why this punishment? Just two things are listed that had gone wrong: idolatry and oppression. That was enough to bring disaster on a nation. Can I put those two words in simple, modern English in a paraphrase? Number one, they were treating God as a thing. Number two, they were treating each other as things. God made us to love God as God and to love people as people. When we treat God as a thing, we are not loving him with all our heart and soul and mind and strength. When we are treating people as things, we are not loving our neighbours as ourselves. Love has gone, and that was what was wrong with this nation. That is why he needed Jesus to be born at Bethlehem, for this world by nature does not love God and we do not by nature love each other. Somehow we needed help, forgiveness and salvation, we needed God, and only God could help us.

Time and time again God visited this earth in judgment and still men did not learn the lesson. In 700 BC, God visited the earth. It was picture language, "The mountains flowing with fire," but Samaria and Jerusalem were lost. Again and again God visited Israel and still the nations of the world have not learned the lesson. You see, the Jews are God's barometer of history. God chose this little nation, the Jews and would show all the nations of the earth how they are to behave, with what he did with his people Israel. He would use them as an example for the whole world.

That is why Micah says, "Listen, attention all the peoples of the earth" Look at Israel. All the nations of the earth look at this nation. Has any nation suffered like this nation? Why do you think they have suffered? Because they turned away from the way of God. The nations of the world, UK included, will you not learn from Israel? Micah is calling us to learn now and saying that unless London repudiates those things that brought about the end of Jerusalem and Samaria, then no treaty can save us.

At Christmas, will you forget the tinsel and fairy lights? Will you touch reality? Would you look at yourselves and say, "Why was it needed? Why did God have to visit the earth in the person of his Son? Why? Because the very same things are happening in London today that happened in Samaria and Jerusalem.

One feels a frustration that the people would say, "Dear me, what a depressing preacher. Nothing more cheerful or comforting for us than that, and we'll forget so quickly." What proof do they need that God's word is true? There is proof of every word here to be found in a large building near the centre of London: the British Museum. They have stones from Sennacherib's kingdom – the Assyrians; a picture of Sennacherib the Assyrian sitting on his throne and receiving the spoil of the cities mentioned in Micah 1. You can go to the British Museum and see with your own eyes that Micah's word was true.

Why don't we believe? Why don't we realise that God is angry with a world that doesn't love him and a world in which neighbours are not loved? Why don't we realise the serious side of Christmas? Why don't we realise that God's Word is true? For if God's Word in Micah 1 is true, it is also true in Micah 5. You Bethlehem; you're just a little place, but you are not the least in the cities of Judah. Oh no. Out of you will come the King.

That is what the world is crying out for. That is what your life needs and that is what I need – a King. Someone who will sit on the throne of this old life and rule over it properly; someone who will come and get us out of the mess; someone who has got the power and yet the love to put the situation right. Micah says that God will send such a King. He lived seven hundred years before it happened.

Read Micah 2

I have a book which I bought purely because of the picture on the cover. I saw it while browsing through a bookshop and noticed that a portrait of an ancestor of mine appeared on the cover: John Sinclair of Ulster who I am supposed to resemble. So I bought the book just to see what he had been up to and what kind of ancestor I had.

It turned out to be a very sad book. It is about the Highland Clearances – a story of how the highlanders of Scotland were deserted and betrayed by their own clan chiefs; of the famine and pestilence which followed their eviction from their crofts. The reason for it was that the clan chiefs wanted to replace people with sheep. That is why the highlands of Scotland today are no longer so populated. You will see empty crofts and derelict cottages in the glens of Scotland.

Sinclair was the one who introduced the sheep. He introduced the cheviot sheep from my home county of Northumberland. They did so well that the landlords realised they could make three times as much money by getting rid of the people. I was relieved to find that he was disturbed by the results of his action and began to plead for the rights of the simple crofter; began cooperative schemes so that they could share in the prosperity, but he was ignored. The famine and pestilence, the cholera that struck as women and children were forced to wander around the glens of Scotland – I had no idea there was such a terrible little slice of Scottish history until I read this book. I mention this because a similar situation lies behind Micah 2. As we have noted, he was a country man living three thousand feet above the sea. From the high hills, with the two capitals of Jerusalem and Samaria, the businessmen were coming down and dispossessing the little peasants by fraud, threats and violence, and taking over land so that estates might grow big. It was the world of the takeover bid and Micah was one of those who protested and said it was wrong, and God notices when simple, ordinary folk suffer because of greedy businessmen who just want more and more and more.

That is the picture behind this chapter. God is concerned with social problems as well as personal problems. I believe that God is concerned about the people who have struggled to build up a little family business and get pushed to the wall; causing redundancies and people in their fifties at the prime of their career to lose their self respect. God looks down on such things and he is hurt.

So Micah begins chapter 2 with a terrible word "woe", which is much worse than the word "sin". We don't use the word "woe" much now so it has lost its horror. But in fact it is a word that places a curse on someone. When it is of God, it is a word that will come true. It is opposite of the word "blessed". We remember that Jesus used both words: "Blessed are you poor. Woe to you rich. Blessed are those that mourn. Woe to you who laugh now." Jesus kept using the word "woe". It was to pronounce the curse of God on those who deserved punishment by God.

My wife had a little sermon to me recently, but she took the text out of context. She only quoted half the verse. When I was having a sleepless night she quoted to me Micah 2:1, "Woe to you who lie awake at night". But she didn't complete it: "plotting wickedness", and that I wasn't doing. Night is a time to relax and to sleep, not to lie awake. But if you do lie awake there are many directions in which your thoughts can go. Some count sheep. Some wiser folk consider the Good Shepherd. Others, alas, think of how to fleece the sheep. This is what these people were doing.

Your last thoughts at night will determine your first thoughts in the morning. What you think about last thing at night, you may do the next day. This is one of the laws of our Maker. "As a man thinks in his heart, so is he." So as a man lies awake at night plotting, "How can I get that land? How can I get that house? How can I extend my property? How can I build up my business?" Then the next day he will wake up thinking the same thought and it won't be long before he does it. Micah says: "Woe to you who lie awake at night plotting wickedness. You will get up in the morning and you will do it." If it lies within your power, it will be translated into action. God's curse is on you for this because ruthless greed becomes inhuman. If your hand can do it, if you can smash somebody, you will. Your own fist has become your god. You are worshipping the power of your hands. But a man's injustice will always be reflected by God's justice. You are free to sin but you are not free to escape the penalty of that sin. You are free to disregard God's laws but you cannot break them; you will be broken by them.

Micah says that while you lie awake plotting on your beds, he who neither slumbers nor sleeps is also plotting your future and you cannot stop him doing what he has decided to do. You may regard your hand as your god but it is the hand of God that will decide your ultimate destiny. These are strong words, severe language, but the situation demanded it. They would be hurt where it hurt the most– in their pride. For behind their desire to have bigger and bigger property and estates lies pride. The truth is that God's punishment is very simple: he takes from you what you abuse. That is the principle. Whatever we misuse, God takes from us sooner or later. "The mills of God grind slowly but they grind exceedingly small." Micah tells proud property developers that enemies will take their land. Other people will set their boundaries and the people of God must go where they are sent.

It is an intriguing prophecy because until the days of Sennacherib, the ruler of Assyria, the punishment he devised for the nations was not known. The punishment the Assyrians gave to a nation that they defeated was mass emigration, and to take them from their own land and take them elsewhere. It is a punishment that has occurred frequently since. One thinks, for example, of how people of the Channel Islands were transported by the Germans to Eastern Europe. It is a punishment the dictators had, and the Assyrians had it. Micah knew it would happen.

How do people react to this kind of preaching? They don't like it. It is disturbing, uncomfortable and challenging. The people of Micah's day said (literally, in the Hebrew) "Stop dribbling." The Hebrew word is drip. Stop dribbling, Micah. Don't talk like this. Don't say such things. Disgusting, disgraceful, this kind of preaching; such things won't come our way.

This is the well-known disease we call euphoria: it can never happen to me. All of us suffer from it. "Such things cannot come our way." You hear that someone's house has been burgled and you say, "It couldn't happen to us." Then one day you come home and your goods are scattered all over the floor. The shock is that you never thought it would happen to you. You visit people with disease in hospital and you never think it could happen to you. I remember going to talk to a lady who was a nursing sister on a ward that dealt largely with terminal care. Yet when such a disease struck her, she couldn't believe it had happened. She couldn't even recognise the symptoms. She was suffering from euphoria. This is the world we are living in. It is suffering from euphoria. Preach judgment and the world laughs. Walk up the high street with a poster on your chest, "Prepare to Meet Your God," and you will cause nothing but embarrassment. No one will come to you and say, "How can I prepare?" You will just be regarded as a crank.

So Micah was regarded as a crank and he was told to stop saying such things – these things can't happen to us; we are religious, we are prosperous. Indeed, since trade had improved, there had never been so much money in Israel. Though, alas, the rich got richer and the poor got poorer.

What is Micah's reply to that kind of objection? He said, "Is that the way for you to reply, O house of Jacob?" He points out two things to them: first that it was not him speaking but the Spirit of the Lord telling them of things that will happen to them; secondly they were implying that the Holy Spirit enjoys talking to them roughly. Did they honestly believe that the Spirit of the Lord liked giving words like that? Here comes one of those tender moments: no – the threats are for their good, to get them on the path again.

That is why there is judgment in the Bible. That is why there are some pretty tough passages. That is why there are words that cut right through to our heart. It is for our good to get us on the path again. Praise God for his mercy. It takes a great love to talk to someone roughly to help them back onto the path.

So much for the first part of this chapter – it has followed a pattern of a double contrast between man's injustice and

God's justice; between man's unconcern and God's concern. The same structure is repeated now in the second part of the chapter with the difference that when we move to the second half of the chapter, the emphasis switches from punishment to pardon. There is a greater emphasis on God's concern and God's future mercy but the punishment is still there.

We turn then to vv. 8–9. Man's wickedness shows up even more against God's concern. Now don't be under any misapprehension here—the people about whom Micah was speaking were religious people, in the temple every Sabbath. If you asked them if they were the people of God they would have said, "Of course we are." Yet here is one of the most profound principles of the Bible in the Old and New Testaments: "Inasmuch as you do it to the least of these [his brethren] you do it to me" – to the Lord. Loving the Lord and loving your neighbour belong together. You can't have one really without the other. Those who protest that they love their neighbour should show love to God.

Micah observes that men, women and children were not exempt from the ruthless greed of others (vv. 8–9). You steal the shirt from a man's back. Did you know that Exodus forbade that? The law in Exodus said that you had to leave a man with one covering for his shoulders at night. You could take some of his clothes but you must not take all; you must leave him something to cover his cold shoulders at night. That is the law of God and Micah says: you have taken the very shirt off their back. The women, the widows, one of the most vulnerable groups in society because they haven't a man to stand up for them or to protect their interests – the ruthless developers, no doubt with their lawyers behind them, were taking the very homes away from widows who had no man to protect them.

The children, little children born in freedom to be sons of God were being sold into slavery to pay for the whole affair. It is at this point that God gets so sick of the whole thing that he says: the land will vomit you out. This is his Holy Land and people were doing these things to men and women and children who had no one to care for them. Up, be gone. The land is sick of you. The very soil will vomit you out – strong language again.

But God sometimes feels like being sick. It was Jesus who said that lukewarm Christians made him sick. "Because you are neither hot nor cold, I will spit you out." There is something that makes you sick, that makes the land sick, that makes God sick. It is when the people of God, in ruthless greed, treat his children like this. Micah comments again on the kind of preaching that they enjoyed. They liked preachers, they liked sermons, but what kind of sermons did they like? They liked sermons that speak of happiness rather than holiness; sermons that encourage people to enjoy themselves rather than discipline themselves; sermons that speak of self-indulgence rather than self discipline; of pleasures rather than virtues.

So Micah with a biting piece of sarcasm says, "I know the kind of preacher you want. You want the kind of preacher who will extol the joys of strong drink and wine; that is who you want. Somebody who will say to you, 'You're alright. Go on and enjoy the good things; you are alright.'"

That is the kind of preacher we like because we go home undisturbed, we go home in the same condition in which we came.

Right to the end of chapter 11 it is tough, hard, challenging and disturbing, but God never has the last word in that way. Just as whenever you get stung by a nettle, if you look around you will find somewhere near it a dock leaf to rub into the wound to take the sting away. So whenever in the Bible you find a passage of judgment, look around and somewhere near it you will find the most beautiful passage of God's mercy.

Micah could not end this prophecy in chapter 2 without promising something that God would do in the future in sheer mercy. If man shows this unconcern for God's word of judgment, then God still has a concern for the few. Now there is such an abrupt change to vv. 12–13 that many scholars believe that this passage is misplaced. Moffat, in his translation, actually removes these verses from this chapter and puts them somewhere else in the Bible as if they could not possibly fit. But I want to show you that I believe they fit perfectly. Well let us look at what vv. 12–13 actually say and then we shall see how they fit. Verse 12 is about the sheep and v. 13 is about the shepherd. This is the familiar relationship in which God sees himself in relation to his people – the Shepherd and the sheep. Once you have been a shepherd you understand this relationship so well and you love the picture. In our modern suburban society we tend to have very little experience of shepherding and all these pictures of shepherding in the Bible are lost on us, so we have to make an effort to get into a rural situation to understand the beauty of it. Verse 12 says: "One day I'll bring the sheep home. There is something about bringing sheep home, gathering them off the moors, gathering them up the hills; finding one here and one there, finding a limping sheep down in the hollow. Finding another sheep caught in some barbed wire and another that is weak and ill and bringing them home. The shepherd gathers them together and they come bleating, they come together – a noisy, jostling crowd and you bring them home.

God looked down on that sad land and those greedy people and was going to send them away out of the Holy Land. But one day there would be a few he was going to bring back – a remnant. Do you think God will ever finish with Israel? Never. He has brought them back already to their land, but he is going to bring them back to their Shepherd too. "They will look on him whom they pierced".

In v. 13 it talks about a Shepherd. The literal Hebrew is "he who opens the breach". The breach-maker, the breaker – that is a wonderful title that Jews have given to their Messiah. He is the one who opens the breach, the Shepherd who goes and breaks down the thorn hedge, opens the gate and makes a way through the wall by knocking the stones down; and he is able to lead his sheep home by making a way for them. He is the Shepherd who will break down what is keeping them away.

I sometimes remember unravelling the wool of a sheep from a barbed wire fence and pulling the barbed wire back so the sheep is free to go home. That's what this word means: the breacher and it became the title for the Jewish hope centred in the Christ, the Messiah. When he comes, he will break down the thorn hedge and he will burst open the prison doors, and he will take us home – the breach maker.

"He will lead you back home out of exile and he will go before you and meet you." We have pictures on the Assyrian monuments of Israel being led away from their own land. It is significant that they are driven away from Israel from behind. There are Assyrians with whips from behind. Reluctantly, with many backward glances, they leave the land they have loved and known. If you are taking people from home, you have to drive them from behind. But if you are taking them home, you can lead them from in front.

I remember frequently when I had to take say, a horse and cart loaded with corn down to the mill in the nearest town, you had to drive your horse there all the way. But when you turned for home there was no holding them. This is the picture: the Shepherd will lead you back. He will go on ahead; he will just open the breach for you and that is all that will be needed. You will be driven out of your land but you will be led back into it – a lovely picture.

But how does it fit the chapter? Agreed, it's got a very different tone to everything else. Agreed, it seems to move into another world; vv. 12–14 seem to be like coming out of a thundercloud and into the sunshine. But is that a reason for saying it doesn't fit? Is there not sunshine after the rain?

Apart altogether from the fourfold structure of the first and second half of the chapter, which seems to be a perfect parallel in structure, it seems to suggest the completeness of the chapter. The real reason why it fits is this: the chapter begins with the land being taken away from those who do not deserve to have it, and it finishes with the land being restored to the sheep.

The other thing we have forgotten is something Jesus said. When Jesus came to earth, he didn't come as a land grabber; he was born in a borrowed manger in someone else's stable. He became a refugee and fled to Egypt with no home. Throughout his adult life he had nowhere to lay his head and he was buried in a borrowed tomb, yet he said, "The meek shall inherit the earth." So when you are pushed around and you feel that the little man is being forgotten, when you feel that life is grinding on, and the economic situation like a great juggernaut is crushing humanity beneath it, then just remember that God will one day take it all away from those who grasped it and give it to his flock and lead them home. What a message! The one born in a manger is the one to whom all things have been given. In him all things are yours. What an inheritance.

MICAH

Read Micah 3

Seven hundred years before the Nativity, Micah said that it would be in Bethlehem that Jesus would be born. But the whole prophecy of Micah tells us why it was necessary for Jesus to be born in our world. Chapter 3 is the darkest chapter of the prophecy – the darkest night just before the dawn. With chapters 4–5 we move into hope for the future, but it is against this backcloth of doom and judgment that the glory and the hope become so real.

In every society there are bound to be leaders. This is a natural and God-ordained pattern for human life. One of the most frightening books was *Lord of the Flies* – the story of a planeload of schoolboys travelling to visit their parents overseas, and the plane crashes and the pilot is killed, and the boys are left on a desert island by themselves for many months before rescue. What happens in that little society of schoolboys is what happens in every society. Very quickly, leaders begin to emerge who at first do good for their fellow boys and help them to build a camp, find food and learn how to survive. But it isn't long, a matter of days, before the power, which the leaders wield, goes to their heads and they begin to abuse their position. Before long, various evils begin to invade that little society and it finishes up with murder. It is so realistic a book. The author is saying we have within us, every one of us – even a little schoolboy has within him – the seeds of the evils of our whole society.

That little story is a picture of what has happened to society after society. It was this fact that led Lord Acton to make his famous statement: "Power tends to corrupt and absolute power tends to corrupt absolutely." There will always be leaders; it is God's will that there should be leaders of society. God's pattern for society is neither democracy, in which the people push the leaders around, nor dictatorship in which the leaders push the people around. His pattern for society is to have leaders who lead the people, but who are themselves led by God. God himself holds responsible the leaders of nations and churches for the leadership they exercise; they are responsible to him.

The kind of pattern that emerges in the novel *Lord of the Flies* is the pattern that you could see in France just before the peasants revolted in the French Revolution at the end of the eighteenth century. You can see the same pattern in Germany just before the peasants' war. You can see the same pattern in Russia. If you read the true novel Nikolas and Alexandra, you see the same pattern there: leaders corrupted by power and interested only in exploiting their position for their own power, prestige, or property.

You can see this situation in ancient Israel seven hundred years before Jesus was born. God raised up a peasant boy to speak against evils. Can you imagine a little Yorkshire lad coming down and going into the Houses of Commons and Lords and arraigning the leaders of our nation before God for their crimes? That is what God chose to do with a boy called Micah, and we have his prophecy here in the Bible.

We have to look at the leaders of the nation and what they were doing. It is not a chapter I like to preach from. One of the disciplines I accepted very early in my ministry was the discipline of preaching the *whole* Word of God. May I say to all preachers: accept the discipline of preaching right through the Word of God instead of picking out the texts that appeal to you. It is uncomfortable. We hate doing it, but it is God's Word.

If we are honest preachers, we've got to be able to say at the end of the day what Saint Paul said to the church at Ephesus: I have declared to you the whole counsel of God. I haven't picked out the texts I liked. I haven't just taken the nice pieces; I have not just given you comfort. I have declared the whole counsel of God and therefore your blood is on your head, not mine. You can only say that if you have declared the whole counsel of God.

Let us go into Micah 3. "Listen, you leaders," says Micah, "you are the very people who ought to know the difference between right and wrong." The first requirement in a politician is that he be a man, not of party or of personality, but of principle. Would to God we could get back to the days in which, in a general election, the first concern of the constituency was, "What are the moral principles of this man?" Not, "What party does he belong to?" Not, "Will he safeguard our interests best?" Not, "What will happen to my stocks and shares if the other lot get in?" Not, "Is he an engaging or charming personality? Does he come across on TV?" But: "What does he understand about right and wrong?"

Micah is saying to the political leaders of his nation that they are supposed to know right from wrong. If they don't, how can one blame the nation for following their lead? They were supposed to know. He then accuses the leaders: you hate good and you love evil. That is a perverted government if you like. How did they possibly get from moral leadership to the point where they hated good and loved evil? There is a dangerous halfway house. What was this halfway house? Step number one: to seek to do with the laws of the land what God wants, and therefore, to be concerned with the difference between right and wrong. Step number two, to be more concerned with what the people want and therefore, to become indifferent to right and wrong and to settle things on grounds of expediency rather than grounds of principle. Then comes step number three: for the leaders to give themselves what they want and to hate good and to love evil.

We are now living in a day in which the laws are being discussed, debated and decided upon grounds of expediency: what basically the people want, with little thought for the laws of God, and little thought for what he wants for our nation. Micah charged the leaders, and he accuses them of cannibalism (3:2b–3). they did not literally cut up people and cook and eat them. But what they did was to strip them to the bone, abusing their position to take from them. Instead of looking after the flock, they were fleecing them and then expected God to answer their prayers.

There is a simple sermon here with three points to remember: corruption, complacency and condemnation. It is a staggering thing that the first two go together. The more corrupt you are, the more complacent you become because the deader your conscience becomes, the more you hate good and love evil, the less concerned you are and the more complacent you become, even in your religion.

It is a profound principle which we have already stated and which we need to remember: God can only forgive those who forgive. I can only have mercy on those who show mercy. I can only give my pardon to those who are prepared to pass it on. Jesus laid this principle down very clearly in the parable of two people who owed money, one a large sum, one a smaller sum. He told another story of a king who forgave someone a large debt and that someone went out and refused to forgive another a smaller debt. We say in the Lord's Prayer, "Forgive us our trespasses as we forgive...." How many people have you and I forgiven this week? We have had opportunities to forgive, I am quite sure. "As we forgive...."

Did those leaders really expect God to listen? They are encouraged in their complacency by false prophets. Micah now turns from the politicians to them. The false prophets were to blame for the complacency. They cried: "peace". They were like chaplains to the government, saying that all was well – smoothing it over, saying there was nothing to worry about; that it is just cranks who go around speaking of doom. The false say, "peace". They only do it because they are paid. They have become professionals. Micah is giving them tough meat – hard words. He accuses religious leaders of misleading the people.

We have seen that happen in our society. Even back in the 1970s church members shared with me their deep concern that, in national media, professing Christian scholars and preachers, religious leaders, had been denying the virgin birth, miracles and the resurrection of Jesus Christ. I thanked God for a Roman Catholic cardinal who said: "Jesus is God." In a prayer meeting we thanked God for Cardinal Heenan who said, "What's the point of praying to Jesus if he's not God?" Thank God for such a word, when we get ecclesiastical leaders preaching a new theology and a new morality, of which Billy Graham said: "It's only the old immorality dressed up." We are in a sad and a sorry plight.

Micah taught that political and religious leaders alike should have been the very people who knew the difference between right and wrong. Here we come to his third point of condemnation. What is their punishment? It is that they should live in a mental and spiritual darkness in which they cannot see or hear anything of God – in which the heavens are silent like brass, in which God no longer communicates his will, and in which the men of God who should be giving the Word of God to the people have to admit that they have no message from God. The sermons they had been preaching, they made up. Micah says: you will hang your head in shame and admit you hadn't got a message from God because God was not speaking. There were no visions. You were blind; you were in the dark. You did not know what God wanted to say.

Alas that is the punishment on religious leaders who preach peace when there is no peace. They finish up with nothing but their own opinions to give out from the pulpit week by week, and the people know it is not from God. Now Micah dares to talk about himself and present his credentials to the nation. What right has a young country lad to march into the leaders in Jerusalem and say, "Listen, you leaders"? What credentials does he present? What qualifications has he? What theological degrees does he have?

Micah presents his credentials. He was full of power and the Spirit of God (3:8). He needed no qualifications other than that. He was not a false prophet; he did not come with a message of peace and comfort but with a message of truth. He came in the name of the Lord and in the power of the Lord. When a man has those credentials, you will find one thing inevitably follows. What comes out of his lips is a courageous exposure of evil. To do that without the Spirit of the Lord would be to do something that would rebound very quickly. But a man filled with power and the Spirit of the Lord can say, "I've been sent to tell not of peace, but of punishment, not of comfort, but a call to repentance." Micah comes as a true servant of God. He doesn't mind repeating himself. He knows that novelty is not the important thing. The important thing is to say the truth and to say it again and again until people listen to it and accept it.

In vv. 9–12 Micah repeats the same sermon that he has preached in vv. 1–7. The same three points are made to the same congregation: Listen, you leaders – corruption, complacency, and condemnation. Same outline, same three points. He tells them the root of their trouble. The real problem was that money meant more to them than morality. They were all on the make. Politicians were bribed; they had their price. Prophets "divine for money".

Micah told them what was going to happen to the lovely city of Jerusalem. It was going to be ploughed like a field. We know from historical records that was exactly what happened. When Jerusalem was sacked, the general who

MICAH

sacked it ordered them to take a plough and to plough through the temple. That is why there is no trace of that temple left. Did anybody listen? What did they think of this young lad who marched in from the glens of Israel and said such things to the political and ecclesiastical leaders? What did they think? Did anybody take notice? Yes – one man. One man took notice in the whole nation – the king, Hezekiah.

The king sat on his throne; he had been disturbed and troubled for a long time at the state of his nation. When this country lad came marching in and said, "Listen, you leaders," the king listened. He was humble enough to admit that Micah was right. The king humbled himself. The king then was not a constitutional monarch; he really reigned then. Micah never said one word about the king; it was an appeal. The king took it up and Hezekiah ordered a reform in the nation. He began to alter the laws of Israel again, and he began to apply them again. He began to be concerned with what God wanted of the nation again.

Do you know the result? God postponed the disaster for one hundred years; three generations came and went in peace because the king listened to the prophet. It is all written down there in history. They were able to postpone the collapse of the nation for one hundred years because the king listened. It was only a hundred years later that, alas, the nation slipped back again and the disaster came.

In Jeremiah 26, a century has rolled by from the days when Micah spoke. It had been a temporary reformation and they had slipped back. Now another youngster of seventeen years of age has been called by God to speak to the nation. This time, he is not getting away with it so easily. A young Jeremiah, whose very name has come to mean a pessimist because he prophesied disaster, was arrested and put on trial for his life.

Then Jeremiah [v. 12] spoke in his defence. "The Lord

sent me to prophesy against this temple and this city. He gave me every word of all that I have spoken, but if you stop your sinning and begin obeying the Lord, your God, he will cancel all the punishments he has announced against you. As for me, I am helpless and in your power do with me as you think best, but there is one thing sure. If you kill me, you will be killing an innocent man and the responsibility will lie upon you and upon this city and upon every person living in it. For it is absolutely true that the Lord sent me to speak every word that you have heard from me."

Then the officials and people said to the priest and the false prophets, "This man does not deserve the death sentence for he has spoken to us in the name of the Lord, our God."

Then some of the wise old men stood and spoke to all the people standing around and said, now listen, "The decision is right, for back in the days when Micah, the Moreshite, prophesied in the days of King Hezekiah of Judah, he told the people that God said, This hill shall be ploughed like an open field and this city of Jerusalem raised into heaps of stone. A forest shall grow at the top where the great temple now stands. But did King Hezekiah and the people kill him for saying this? No, they turned from their wickedness and worshipped the Lord and begged the Lord to have mercy upon them. And the Lord held back the terrible punishment he had pronounced against them. If we kill Jeremiah for giving us the messages of God, who knows what God will do to us."

Isn't that interesting? Micah's message saved a nation for one hundred years. One young man full of power and the Spirit of God did that. We have a wonderful God, able to take nobodies, able to choose someone whom the world counts foolish, and cause the wisdom of the world to look silly as a result.

If it can happen to the nation of Israel, God's chosen

people, it can happen to Britain. Why should we have any right to expect it not to? Why should we expect the laws of God to operate on every other nation, but not ours? I do not believe that our national leadership has yet reached the depths to which those leaders had sunk seven hundred years before Christ, but I firmly believe we are on our way.

Back in the 1970s I spoke at a time when it was my doubtful privilege to stand in Westminster Hall (in those days a freezing place, no heating, no chairs to sit on, people wandering in and out, an amplifier that didn't work, a lovely choir that found difficulty in singing, with its back against a window, with sun streaming in so that people couldn't even look at them). It was the most adverse circumstances I think I had ever spoken in, but what hurt deeper was the sense of deadness in the "mother of parliaments". MPs strolled in, chatted to their friends, and strolled out again, as if it was a bus station. The gentleman who had arranged this, one of the godliest men in our land, said to me before the occasion began, with a tone of sadness and a look of deep hurt in his face, "David, this house is in the hands of Satan."

I said, "What makes you say that?"

He replied, "I never thought I would have to be handling legislation such as comes on my desk now."

While I spoke about a virgin who conceived by the Holy Ghost and had a baby of the Holy Ghost before her marriage, there was a woman MP pleading in the House of Commons for free contraceptives for all unmarried people on demand. With divorce virtually by consent and abortion virtually on demand, these are the laws we were passing even then. We were not asking, "What does God think?" We were asking, "What's going to keep the people reasonably peaceful?" The false prophets cry: "Peace." You can almost date when the rot set in. It was the Profumo Affair that marked the rot and it was then that our government lost respect. It was no accident that it was at the same time that a bishop went into an English court to defend the book *Lady Chatterley's Lover* and it was no coincidence that that was the only year in English history when the Bible was not the best-selling volume in our bookshops. Lady Chatterley beat it to the top of charts. We have put our feet already on a slippery slope and another Micah is needed.

God has raised up David Gardner, a clergyman whom I met in the House of Commons. God gave him a message for our nation which he published as the booklet *A Warning to our Nation*. Her Majesty the Queen sent for David Gardner. I learned of how the Queen talked to him about our nation. David said, "I have no doubt whatever that the Queen is born again." But she doesn't reign in this country; she has no power in this land. Yes, the Queen was concerned, but she can do nothing about it because the speech she makes in Parliament is written for her. That is one of the tragedies of our situation, I believe. Yes, voices are being raised. Prophets are being heard again in our land. God is speaking. Will our leaders listen, as they listened to Micah, as Hezekiah and the wise old men of those days said: we must put this right before our nation collapses? Will people listen today?

I apply this study to our nation in the name of the Lord. I apply this study to our world because the Bible looks into the future and sees a day in which this corruption of leadership reaches its logical conclusion. The world is in the grip of a world dictator who hates good and loves evil—Antichrist himself. His power over the world will be supported by a false prophet who will cry, "Peace and security." The world will come under a totalitarian regime that will acknowledge no God other than itself. The Bible predicts that – a world in which leadership worldwide is totally corrupted.

Micah saw beyond this. He saw beyond the immediate crisis. He saw beyond the disaster coming to his capital city.

He saw that in the last days, the mountain of the house of the Lord will be established and all nations would flow to it and come and say, "This God will be our God," and then they would learn war no more. He saw something else: that God would choose a little village called "Bethlehem."

Micah said in the name of God: "And you Bethlehem, you're not just a little village in Judah. You are not least among the princes of Judah; out of you shall come a governor – a king. And the government shall be upon his shoulder." One day, the kingdoms of this world will become the kingdoms of our Lord and Saviour. One day, the government will be in his hands and he is coming to bring peace and righteousness of a lasting kind. Then we will be ashamed in that day – that we let it all happen, that we let it go on, and that we did not pray for our leaders as we should, and that we did not say "God save them".

There used to be a weekly meeting of Members of Parliament for prayer. There used to be a meeting for Bible study every week taken by the Reverend Dick Lucas. Neither meeting was taking place by a certain point in the 1970s. The only thing that the Christian fellowship in the Houses of Parliament was still doing was holding an annual carol service. Pray for those who have openly declared themselves as belonging to Christ and are willing to meet.

Read Micah 4

Micah saw in a vision the capital city ruined, wrecked and decayed, but he put to his eye the telescope of faith. God showed him a vision on the horizon of time, at the very end of human history, and he was able to see. Prophecy is a miracle. The one thing that you and I cannot see is the future. It is beyond the reach of our minds. We can discuss the past; we can look at the present. But no one on earth can tell me what is going to happen next year. However, prophecy is a miracle of prediction, for God knows the future as well as we know the past. God enabled Micah by the miracle of prophecy. Filled with the Spirit of God, Micah was enabled by him to see what was going to happen in the future.

I want to go through his vision now and put it into modern language if I can, so you can get it. The vision centred on a little mountain we would call a hill. But as Micah saw through the telescope of prophecy, he saw that that little mountain had become the most famous mountain in the whole world. At the end of history, everybody is talking about one little mountain that you would not have looked at, that you would never have travelled a mile to see. Yet in the vision, he sees pilgrims, tourists, politicians and leaders coming from all the nations to this little mountain. Every race is there. Every culture is represented; the costumes are all different. He can see people of all nations coming because it is the most renowned in all the world. Why? There is one thing makes this little mountain different from all the others: it is the mountain of God; the mountain of the Lord.

At the end of history, everybody will be talking about Mount Zion. In the vision Micah realises that at last the world has come to its senses and is wanting to know what God thinks. At last the world has realised that there is only one God – the God of Israel. At last the world is coming humbly and saying: we have failed; God, what do you say? What a vision that is and what hope there is in it. At last, the world is ready to seek God's advice and not only to seek it, but to take it: tell us what to do and we will do it. That is what God has been waiting for since he made the world and he has never had it, except for one man. "I come to do your will".

Micah sees that at the end of history there will be a true summit meeting, but the summit will be Mount Zion. What a vision. No longer will men make their own laws. It is extraordinary that we think that democracy is going to bring peace and prosperity. The laws that will put this world right will not be made by debate but by decree. It is not the House of Commons or the House of Lords that will bring peace and prosperity; it is the house of the Lord. That is what Micah is seeing, and that when people let one person rule the world, the Lord himself, then we will have decrees that will bring justice and fair dealing between the nations. Disputes will be settled.

This is our longing; our dream. Micah sees a future in which the Lord, in Mount Zion, is decreeing what is right and what is fair, and the nations will come for arbitration. They will not settle their disputes by war because war never settled anything. When I read of how hundreds of thousands of men volunteered in the First World War to go and fight the war to end wars, I am depressed because the war did not end war; neither did the Second World War. War settles nothing. When will we learn that only God can settle an issue with absolute justice and fairness so that the nations see that is right, and we all accept it.

So there is a picture of nations going to arbitration before God, accepting his will, going to Mount Zion to stop war, and going there because God is there – the God of Israel is the only God who exists – and having him bring peace. Do you know what can happen then? Some of the loveliest words in the Bible now. They can beat their swords into ploughshares. All that is spent on armaments can be spent to produce food. Their spears that would pierce hearts and cut human beings into bits would be made into pruning hooks, to tend the vine and the fruit tree to help to feed hungry people. What a vision! But you can't have the second without the first. When will mankind learn that we can't have peace and prosperity until we're prepared to go to God and say, "God, tell us what to do and we'll do it?"

So because of this running down of armaments, because

we can now close the military academies, because we can now stop our young men becoming soldiers, sailors and airmen, a picture of prosperity follows. Every man will sit quietly in his own home, under his own fig tree, every man living quietly without fear. Here is a picture of a world free from fear.

If this picture is true and if Micah is right, and this is the way to world peace, can you not see how far off course our race has gone? You have here a picture of peace in which there is still private property – "Each man in his own home, under his own fig tree." How wrong can you be to think that communising the situation is going to bring peace and prosperity. It is not God's way.

There are still nations in the ideal world and therefore, those who want to see one international culture and community are barking up the wrong tree. God likes variety. He wants nations to live together. Why do you think he made the nations? Why do you think he made different cultures? Why do you think he made different colours of skin? He doesn't want us all the same. So here we have an ideal picture that includes nations.

But far more serious than that, we have been looking in the wrong direction. Do you realise that every headquarters of world peace has been built in the wrong place? We built the League of Nations in Geneva, Switzerland; it was the wrong place. We built the United Nations building in New York; it is the wrong place. There is only one building and only one place: the temple of the Lord in Jerusalem. How wide of the mark can you get? But the biggest mistake we have made is this: we have thought that we can have peace and prosperity without God.

Somebody could at this point say, "Hold on preacher. You're just an idealist like everybody else." Do you know what my proof is? "The mouth of the Lord of hosts has spoken" – I have no other guarantee that we can have the world we would all love to see. Praise God, that is enough for me.

It was enough for Micah. The rule of the Lord our God would be forever. We are pinning all our hopes on him. People were turning to idols. Instead of looking to the God of Israel, people look to gods they have constructed to get them out of their mess. But even though the nations turn to their idols and put their trust in other things and other people, God's people look to God.

Christians are the only people on earth who know, absolutely certainly, that there is one day going to be true peace. Others may dream and hope, but we know. You see God never says anything he doesn't mean. We have proved that in our own experience. In our own limited way, we have claimed the promises of God and found that he meant them. We never found that he let us down – not once. Therefore, if the mouth of the Lord has spoken, we will follow him. We pin all our hopes for the future on God; we do not pin them on man, because what is man? The proud creature who has failed over thousands of years to bring peace. In four thousand years, up to today, we have had only three hundred years free from war. In those three hundred years, we have had cold wars. So we do not look to man, but we look to God.

One thing more: this is the God of Israel. You can't have God without his people. Here we run into one of the most difficult things in our modern situation. The fact is that God has chosen to work for peace and prosperity through his chosen people. We cannot have God without the Jews. "How odd of God to choose the Jews, but odder still for those who choose the Jewish God and spurn the Jews." God never has gone back on his promise or calling of Israel. He never does. Once he has called a person, he continues. He called Israel and he has not gone back on his promise. They have been badly treated because they are his people. I was talking to a Jew and asking: "Why do you think it is that you've been hated more than any other nation?"

The reply was very simple: "Because the human race is in rebellion against God and we remind people of God." I think that's a very discerning comment. They have been badly treated and their sufferings are only to be explained because they are God's people. Why has Israel suffered more than any other nation in world history? Because God was punishing them. We stand in awe when we see what God let happen to his own people. He has allowed it to happen because they, of all people, were chosen among all the nations of the earth. They are the chosen people and he chose them to be his people and to show the world what he was like. But as Micah says in his earlier prophecies, when the Jew, who has let money speak more than morality in their affairs, then God allows them to be punished. When the Jews lose their holy vocation, to be the channel of God's grace to a lost world, then God cannot but treat them seriously. This is the reason behind all their sufferings. For two thousand years and more, they have been scattered among the nations – sick – but in Micah's telescope he sees not only all the nations coming to Mount Zion, but he sees that in that coming day, God will bring his people back and make them strong in their own land.

We have lived to see this. In 1948, we lived to see it in our lifetime. 2,700 years ago it was predicted and we have lived to see it – doesn't that make you excited? They are back in their own land, stronger than ever. Yes, it is God's doing and it is marvellous in our eyes, but something else is predicted of Israel that has not yet come true, alas. That is why they are not yet fulfilling their divine vocation. The something is this: that God will bring them back in that day and be their king. They have come back as a democracy, a republic. They have come back to make their own laws, not God's laws. In Israel today you find a secular state. God is not yet their king in their own land. But the Bible predicts that God will one day take away the ungodliness of Jacob and restore them not only physically to their land but spiritually to their king, and I look forward to that happening.

When could it happen? What would cause Israel as a nation to turn back to God? In reality there is only one thing that is needed to convince a Jew: it is to meet Jesus. I remember a Jewess coming to me after one Sunday evening service I preached at, near Ely, in a little chapel. She came afterwards and said, "Do you mean Jesus is the messiah we're looking for and that he's alive now?"

"Yes," I said. Suddenly she knew more than I did about him. She had met Jesus and her understanding of Jesus was deeper than anything I have. She had the one thing that would unlock it all. A Saul on the road to Damascus had it all, he had it all there, and then he met Jesus, and the whole thing fitted and clicked into place.

I believe that the Jews will turn as a nation to God again when they look at him whom they have pierced. In other words, I believe that this prophecy will come true when Jesus steps back into their land and they see him again. When his feet touch the Mount of Olives, next door to Mount Zion, I believe that then the Jews themselves will see their king and accept him. What a thrilling moment that is – not only for them but for the whole world. What will that make possible if the casting off of the Jews has meant so much to us Gentiles?

The tragedy is that God offered them the king. He was born king of the Jews; they knew that. "Where is he that is born king of the Jews?" said the wise men. As Jesus died, Pilate put above his head, "This is the king of the Jews."

Do you remember what the angel said to Mary?

"Don't be frightened Mary," said the angel, "for God has

decided to bless you wonderfully. Very soon now, you will become pregnant and have a baby boy and you are to name him, Jesus. He shall be very great and shall be called the Son of God, and the Lord God shall give him the throne of his ancestor David and he shall reign over Israel forever. His kingdom shall have no end."

It will come. One day the nation will receive their king. What a vision and what a future! Nobody else would do. You see, it is David's throne and the prediction in Micah is: "You will then have royal might and power as you did before." When did they have it before? The answer is in King David's time. What they need is a son of David to restore royal might. At the moment, Israel hasn't got royal might. It has might, but not royal might. One day it will have royal might.

Christians will reign with Jesus when he comes, but the Jews are a vital part of the plan. I believe in a millennium. I believe that Christ must be king on earth to demonstrate his power before the new heaven and the new earth are ushered in. It is the only time I can see when Micah's vision will come true. What a vision for the future, the last days of history.

It is with some sadness, therefore, that I turn to the last few verses of the chapter. The last vision in this chapter of Micah is terrible. It is a vision that is nearer to the time in which he lives. The telescope is zooming back now from the distant horizon of time to the immediate years ahead. We might summarise his theme: "In the future I see every man living quietly without fear but now you scream in terror. In the future I see a king in Jerusalem, but now where is your king? In the future I see wise men coming to God and accepting his decree, but now where are your wise men? They are gone. In the future I see every man sitting under his own fig tree, but now I see that you will have to leave this city and go into a far land. I see trouble long before I see the vision."

One of the most remarkable predictions Micah made was that they would go into exile in Babylon – and Babylon was not even a nation when he said that. People argue that this must have been written centuries later, because how could Micah know that Babylon would be the nation that would take Israel into captivity? The answer is: God knew. It is a miracle again – of prediction in just one word, because Babylon was just a tiny little district in the mighty Assyrian empire when Micah said this. But he said, "You'll go into Babylon." God knew it would become one of the greatest pagan empires.

Then Micah says that he sees the nations coming to Israel before that ideal world, and coming not to seek God but to try to wipe out Israel. He sees the nations uniting and coming against them and gloating over them, eager for their blood, anxious to destroy them. I believe that the world will come against this little nation. It may well happen in our lifetime that we see the nations of the world coming to wipe out the Jews once and for all – but they won't do it. They don't understand God's plan. He is going to draw nations in antagonism against Israel, that he may bring their power to an end and show their pride to be futile; so that his people may be seen to be victorious and his people will treat their attackers like sheaves on a threshing floor.

We saw that happen on a lesser scale in the Six-Day War. That is nothing to what is going to happen at the end of history. God promises victory to Israel. Do you know we are living in these events? Until the twentieth century, people read Micah and they were reading something which they did not know would happen. Not only do we have the promise of God to base our hope upon, we have the fulfilment of part of that promise already, and we look for the rest.

So one day the united nations come against Israel, and God breaks the power and pride of human armies through his people and gives them a crushing victory, but it will be God's victory, not theirs. That is why the spoils of it must be offered to the Lord and not taken for Israel. They must not touch a thing that is delivered into their hands on that day. Then, beyond that, we see a total change of picture. We see the nations acknowledging that God is supreme and coming to Mount Zion in humility and saying: "Tell us what to do and we'll do it." Peace and prosperity will come.

God has said it and to make sure that you believe it, God said it twice. He not only said it to a country lad called Micah, he said it to a town courtier called Isaiah. If you read Isaiah 2, you will find the identical prediction. "It shall come to pass in the last days that the mountain of the Lord shall be established above all the mountains and nations shall flow to it." You can read it twice in God's Word. Do you believe it?

Many years after Micah had made this prediction of Jerusalem – that it would be ploughed up and left for weeds to grow over it – two rabbis walked through ruined Jerusalem. It was exactly as Micah had said. The buildings had been pulled down; the brambles and thorns were growing over the temple area. The whole place was laid waste. In fact, it had literally been ploughed up with a plough, and the furrows marked the temple courts. One rabbi began to weep and the other rabbi said, "Why are you weeping?" He replied, "There is no hope. Our nation is finished."

The other rabbi drew from his robe the scroll of Micah and he read the last few verses of chapter 3, predicting the ruin and desolation of Jerusalem. Then, after reading it, he said to the weeping brother, "You see how literally God has done this." Then turning back to the scroll, he read 4:1–4. Then he said, "Let us rejoice, my brother. The same God who brought this judgment promises that blessing. The marks of the ploughshare assure me that Jerusalem will one day be rebuilt."

Happy are those who are able to take God at his Word and believe that one day, through his people Israel coming to their king, peace and prosperity will come to the nations.

Read Micah 5

A friend of mine, a well-known preacher, was preaching in Edinburgh one weekend and was due to fly back to London a few days later. During his prayers on the morning of his departure, he had a premonition. As a result of it, he did not fly from Edinburgh to London but took the train, a longer journey. The aeroplane in which he was due to fly crashed at London Airport. It was simply a premonition. Stronger than that are predictions about the future. One of the best known predictors of the future is a Mrs Jeane Dixon in the United States, who predicted, for example, President Kennedy's assassination. She was right in that one; she was completely wrong about the subsequent events and the following election. Premonitions and predictions tend to be a bit slaphappy. Some of them happen, some of them don't. We tend to hear about the ones that do come off. We don't hear about the others because that would be bad business for those who commercialise predictions.

But when we come to prophecies we are dealing with something entirely different. With prophecies we are dealing with the words of the only person in the universe who knows exactly what is going to happen in the future. He is the Lord himself and thank him that he does not tell us everything about the future. If he told us everything that was going to happen in the next twelve months, I doubt if we could cope. If we were going to have some wild success, we would become so impatient that we would not be prepared to wait for it. If we were going to face some great tragedy, then we would probably grieve over it. It is a wise providence that has veiled the future from us, but God, in his mercy, has drawn aside the curtain and shown us some things about the future which are absolutely certain to happen. He has shown us just enough for us to prepare for that future.

So when we deal with the prophecies of the Bible, we are not dealing with premonitions, which tend to be vague and groundless; sometimes something happens, sometimes it doesn't. We are dealing with clear predictions, prophecies from God who alone knows about the future. We can be absolutely certain that they will be fulfilled. Micah is one of those prophets of Israel who drew aside the veil and told us what was going to happen in the future. Some of the things he told us have actually come true and are now history; others are yet to be. Micah 5 is one of these chapters.

Micah, by the gift of prophecy, which is a telescope into the future among other things, looks into the future, and events that are in fact separated by many years as we count time appear in his eye as a vision of things that happen together. It is one of the most difficult things in prophecy to unravel that there may be centuries between separate visions. Indeed you can have things a thousand years apart mentioned in the same book, in the same chapter, and in the same verse. This is why it is very important to look deep into God's word when he is predicting the future.

Let me give you two examples of verses in the Old Testament which compress at least two thousand years into one verse and bring together two events – one of which has already happened to us and one of which has not happened yet. Take the first, "And it will come to pass in the last days that I will pour out my Spirit upon all flesh". Peter quoted that on the day of Pentecost as having been fulfilled, but the verse went on to talk about the sun being switched off, the moon being turned to blood, and signs in the heavens above. Those events have not happened. They are still future to us and they were in the same prophecy.

Take another example: Jesus' first sermon took as its text the first verse or two of Isaiah 61, "The Spirit of the Lord is upon me," and then he listed all the wonderful things he was going to do: lame walking, blind seeing – to preach the acceptable year of the Lord. Then he stopped and he didn't quote the rest of the sentence, which is, "And the day of vengeance of our God". The simple fact is that through the telescope of prophecy, Isaiah saw two things together, which we now know were widely separated in time. The Spirit of the Lord coming upon the Lord Jesus and proclaiming the year in which God will accept people by grace, and the day of vengeance of our God, which is something yet in the future.

Now Micah is exactly the same. Looking ahead with the telescope of faith he can see events which we now know cover more than two thousand years stretched out before him. But as he looks he sees them all condensed into one picture. We must try to sort it out. Prophecy has been called history written beforehand. Here we have a miracle because no man is able to write history books before the events. Only the Lord can do that. It is a miracle to write history before it happens.

Here is this young man, filled with the Spirit of the Lord, predicting what is going to happen – to the letter. Do you know that in the Old Testament, you can find the complete earthly ministry of Christ and every major event that occurred in it? The events are scattered over the whole of the Old Testament, but it is written there beforehand—every detail. The little detail that we are going to look at now is this: seven hundred years before Jesus was born, Micah said exactly where it would happen. That is a miracle – to write history so long before it happens.

If I try to express this symbolically, Micah saw, as it were, a deep valley through which Israel would pass in the near future; that was the first thing he saw. Then he saw something wonderful – a peak, though not a very big one. Beyond the peak he saw a very long plain in which nothing was happening. Then in the distance, he saw a whole range of mountains – peak after peak, wonderful event after wonderful event.

Now in v. 1 we have the valley described; in v. 2 that first peak, the first wonderful thing that God was going to do. In v. 3 we have the plain, and in vv. 4–15 the distant mountain range. We are between vv. 3 and 4. The intriguing thing is that every event predicted in Micah 5 is in exactly the right order. Here is a miracle: thousands of years of history written before it took place. If someone asks me how I know it will happen, my answer is that 1–3 happened to the letter and that is good enough for me. I am prepared to take 4–15 on trust. So many of the predictions that the prophets have made in the past have come true that we have the confidence to believe the rest. So here we live in the middle of chapter 5. We can look back and see these things. We look back, not now through prophecy but through history. We can read the record of these three events. We know them to be true, but we still look to that mountain range, much nearer. They are looming very high above us now, but we look forward.

Let us look at vv. 1–3. They have all happened. We are looking into the past now. Where Micah looked forward, we look backwards. We are going to look at three things that he predicted would happen, which have all come true to the detail. Now let's take the first, "mobilise" – v. 1. "The enemy lays siege to Jerusalem. With a rod, they shall strike the judge of Israel on the face." Micah can see Jerusalem in a siege, the enemy, thousands of them, surrounding the capital. When Micah said this, there was no sign of an enemy anywhere near Jerusalem, nor did it come true for another hundred years. But a hundred years later it all came true and the Babylonians came around Jerusalem. The story of that siege is one of the most dreadful descriptions of human suffering but now comes the little detail that marks the truth. The judge of Israel, the supreme judge in those days, was the king. Every case could be taken right up through the local magistrates right to the king. Micah saw in the vision, in this deep valley through which they were going to go through, that the king would be struck and injured on the face, maltreated, humiliated in the sight of all. The king, struck on the face – what would you think if you saw someone go up to Queen Elizabeth and strike her on the face in front of everybody, and people helpless to do anything about it? How would you feel?

What Micah had foreseen did happen and is recorded in 2 Kings 25. The Babylonian troops surrounding the city captured the king in the plains of Jericho and all his men scattered and he was taken to Riblah, where he was tried and sentenced before the king of Babylon. He was forced to watch as his sons were killed before his eyes. Then his eyes were put out, and he was bound with chains and taken away to Babylon. The king was struck on the face. Do you see that blinded king taken away in chains? What Micah saw happened to the letter one hundred years afterwards—that is 5:1. The valley mentioned is the deep, dark valley that they were going to pass through, and it happened about six hundred years before Jesus was born.

But now (in 5:2), looking forward, Micah sees something new. We have come to the best-known verse in Micah, the one quoted in Matthew, which has made a little village mean more to us than maybe any other village we have ever heard about: "And you, Bethlehem....." What a lovely sound that word has – have you ever noticed? It is a beautiful word that seems to bring a smile to people's faces, a word that seems to bring peace into our hearts, a word that is associated with joy – Bethlehem. You just say that word to somebody and see what feelings it kindles. The funny thing is that Bethlehem has nothing about it. It is a tiny little village, utterly insignificant. It was so small that it was nearly not counted at all, because in the records of Judea they only listed as communities of any significance those with a thousand families or more. Bethlehem, of Judea, only just scraped on to the list because it had a few over one thousand families. Literally, the Hebrew here says: "And you Bethlehem, you are not the least among the thousands of Judea." You may be the bottom of the list, but you are not least. You may have just scraped into significance, may have just crept over the line and people notice you. This little village of ordinary working people, wasn't it like God to make something of a village like that?

If you and I had been in charge of the arrangements for the arrival upon earth of the King of kings, we would never have chosen Bethlehem. That is the mistake the wise men made. When the wise men came saying, "Where is he that is born king of the Jews?" they went straight for the biggest city and they went straight to the palace. That is where you and I would go if we had heard that a prince had been born. But God chose Bethlehem, which literally means "house of bread", where people work with their hands for their daily bread, an ordinary unnoticed village. It was so ordinary that there were other towns called "Bethlehem" which were more important. Therefore, Bethlehem had to have an extra name: "Bethlehem Ephrathah." There was a Bethlehem in Galilee; there was another one across the Jordan. So if you said, "Bethlehem" in the early days, everybody thought of the one in Galilee. Once a year the entire attention of the world centres on that little village in the Holy Land, and the bells of Bethlehem ring out to the whole world.

People from all over the world make pilgrimages to that little village. Bethlehem had its great day; Bethlehem had its moment. It produced David, a little shepherd boy who used to sit out on the hills practising throwing stones with his sling and playing his guitar. It was that boy who was chosen to be the most beloved king they had ever had, and in whose days peace and prosperity extended the borders of Israel greater than they had ever known. It was the golden age of Israel's history. But after David left Bethlehem and made Jerusalem his city, Bethlehem Ephrathah faded back into insignificance and was forgotten again. It lost its fame and Jerusalem overshadowed it from then on. The city of David now became Jerusalem. That was his capital.

But now, three hundred years after King David's reign, Micah, looking through his telescope, could see that little village doing it again. Bethlehem Ephrathah was not the least among the thousands. It was going to be the birthplace of the King. Ever since, Bethlehem has been to us one of the most sacred spots on earth, one of the loveliest places ever to hear about or to visit.

It was this very prophecy that put the wise men on to the right track – on the road to Bethlehem. For seven hundred years the Jews turned their attention to the little village again, believing that another king like David would come from that city. Since it was David's city, they realised too that, as the prophets had foretold, it would be another king from the line of David. This little village was the centre of their hopes for nigh on seven hundred years, and one night in the darkness the cry of a newborn baby was heard.

Something a man had seen seven hundred years before came true. Mary laid him in a manger and called him "Jesus". "O Bethlehem" – it was this very prophecy that led to the slaughter of those innocent babies in that village so that every other mother with a little baby boy in her arms saw Herod's soldiers come and kill those babies. This prophecy brought both joy and sorrow, but it was Micah who was given the privilege of naming the village. Jesus fulfilled Micah 5:2 to the letter. He was born in Bethlehem. He nearly wasn't. He wasn't even living there; his mother wasn't there. It was a Roman emperor hundreds of miles away who said to one of his subordinates, "I think we'll tax those people." The subordinate said, "But that's going to be a difficult job. They're scattered around; there are no lists. How are we going to make sure they all pay?" "Well, send them back to the town of their family; let them all gather." That decision in Rome brought a pregnant girl to Bethlehem, and Jesus was born.

Even the tax laws of the emperor were ordained by God to fulfil this prophecy to the letter. Jesus came and was born, but not as a resident. Maybe that is why they missed him; maybe that's why they never thought he was the king, because he didn't belong to Bethlehem; he didn't live there. Yet God, in a wonderful way, fulfilled the prophecy without forcing people to believe that it had been fulfilled.

Later in his life, when he was thirty-three years of age, somebody said to Jesus, "You can't be the messiah because the messiah has to be born in Bethlehem and you are from Nazareth," and Jesus said nothing. He never forces people to believe in prophecy. He waits for them to have faith. Later, when it got out that Jesus had been born in Bethlehem, later when the Christians preached the Christmas narrative, do know what happened? The Jews made a determined attempt to explain away Micah's prophecy. Some of the extraordinary lengths to which they went to explain it away really take your breath away.

In the year AD 70, Bethlehem was sacked by Titus, and it became an Arab township with no Jewish families in Bethlehem to have baby kings any more. Everything points to Jesus. Jesus was born in Bethlehem of Judea of the line of David. Micah saw it seven hundred years before that.

What is the most extraordinary detail of the whole prediction? As in v. 1 there is something in the tail end of the verse that is quite extraordinary, so in v. 2 there is something extraordinary: "It will be the birthplace of my king, who has always existed." What an extraordinary thing to say. I am quite sure that Micah didn't even understand what he said when he said it. Fancy saying that someone's going to be born who always existed. What a puzzling prediction, but we know that it is true that someone was born who was always alive. Of no one else can that be said. "In the beginning was the Word, and the Word was with God, and the Word was God" (John 1); "And the word became flesh...." (John 1:14a) – Micah's prophecy cannot be understood until you believe that Jesus was the pre-existent Son of God, but Micah saw it and he spoke it.

Now v. 3. Beyond this little peak, Micah sees something else extraordinary. He sees beyond the birth of Jesus, born to be King of Israel, and then he sees God abandoning his people for a long time so that God and Israel are no longer together. Israel is away from her own land and away from her own God for a long time. What a remarkable thing to see. It is all there in this verse. Yet we now know that that period is two thousand years long, and Micah saw it. He saw that God and Israel would part company after the birth of the King in Bethlehem. Micah does not describe any event to take place in that two thousand years. It is a blank in Israel's history. They have been wandering around the face of the earth. They have gone to country after country and it has been a blank in the purpose of God for that people. We know what happened in that period. Why do we know? Because we fill it in. The amazing thing to me is that here I am, a Gentile, communicating with you. Here I am, taking a Jewish book, written by Jewish people and speaking about Jewish things. I am not a Jew by birth, by blood, but I am a son of Abraham according to Romans. My Saviour is a Jew still and always will be. He is still a human being and he has still got a human body and he is still circumcised and he is still a Jew. Isn't that extraordinary? Micah did not see this side of it. He saw that the Jews would be out of the picture and that God's purpose would not be fulfilled through them. What he did not see, but what other prophets like Isaiah did see, is that God would bring the Gentiles in. After Christmas people think of the wise men who came, and call it the "Epiphany" – the appearance of the light of God to the Gentiles. Praise God that he has included us Gentiles. For this whole period that Micah saw, it has been the Gentiles who have had to take the God of the Jews to the world.

Notice again the end of the verse, which again is a key to the whole thing. It is a prophecy that people for two thousand years never thought would be fulfilled – that at the end of this period the exiles will come back. They will rejoin their brethren in their own land. It is exciting to go to Israel today. You see Jews from America, Russia, Yemen, the Far East. They have been living separately with separate cultures, separate languages. They assimilated to other peoples and now they are meeting their brethren in their own land. It is an extraordinary ferment of culture: the music, the art; they are bringing the riches of the cultures of the nation and it is mingling again. The language which was dead for two thousand years, which no one even knew how to pronounce, has come to life again and they speak Hebrew again. Micah saw it and we live to see it.

So here are vv. 1–3 and they have all come true to the letter. Do you know what people say to me sometimes? Sometimes ministers have said this to me and certainly others have said it to me: "You take the Bible too literally." Do you blame me? They say: "Why do you take the book of Revelation so literally, as if it is describing events?

Why, when the Bible talks about Adam, do you think he was literally a man?" The answer is proof after proof after proof that when God says something is going to happen, he means it literally.

Here in Micah 5:1-3 everything came true literally, therefore, I am prepared to take the rest of the chapter literally. God means what he says. Thank God he means it literally. Jesus is coming back literally. The kingdoms of this world are going to become the kingdom of our Saviour literally. There is going to be peace and justice on earth literally. There is going to be a new heaven and a new earth literally. Praise God for the literal truth. So when I read vv. 4–15 I take them literally, simply as they stand in their basic meaning.

I can sum them up very quickly. It describes the period when the king of Israel becomes the King of Israel. It describes the period when the King born at Bethlehem is finally acknowledged by the Jews. Micah says that will be a day of rebirth for the nation, a spiritual rebirth as when a woman with travail brings new life. It will be a rebirth; think of that – when Israel is born again.

Look what happens now – four things, one after another. Number one is *peace*: and he will be our peace. Do you know the reason we haven't got any peace in the world? The reason is that we haven't got him in the world as he wants to be in the world. He will be our peace. Why? Because he is a ruler who cares; he is a shepherd-king. All the great leaders of Israel were shepherds: Moses was, David was. If you are really going to be a great king, you must learn to be a great carer, and shepherding is always God's preparation for reigning. Those who shepherd well will reign.

Jesus is a shepherd-king. He will stand and feed his flock – words that we know from Isaiah 2 and Handel's *Messiah*. He will feed his flock; he will be a shepherd. He will care for them, protect them, and he will be our *peace*. Do you know that if you saw Jesus physically standing with you now, in all his power and glory, you wouldn't be afraid of anything? He would be your peace. You would have nothing to worry about. By faith you can see him standing with you, and he is your peace. He will feed his flock.

When he comes back as King to Israel, that war-torn land where you never know when death will come over the hedge, where farmers plough the fields with rifles hanging over their shoulders, that land will be at peace and they will remain there undisturbed. It matters not who invades. I do not know who the Assyrian mentioned here is, but when the land is invaded he will raise up enough leaders and princes to cure the crisis—seven leaders, eight leaders. Seven's the perfect number so he will throw in one extra – eight. There will be enough people to cope with the crisis.

Secondly: *purpose*. For the first time, Israel will fulfil her vocation to the nations of the world. What is that vocation? It is to be like the gentle dew or showers of blessing. When you live in a dry land like the Middle East, and the dew comes down at night, and you see the green grass grow, and when the showers come and the grain swells, how you praise God for the dew and the rain and that is how the Jews are meant to be to the world. So literally, if a Jewish family moved into the house next door to you, you would say, "Praise the Lord; there's a shower of blessing come to our street." That is what they were meant to be. Instead, there is suspicion, dislike, and resentment. But one day, they will be like showers; gentle, but not soft to those who resent or resist. They will be like a lion, and the nations will be like helpless sheep. This is the choice you have: you can either have the Jews as a gentle dew and a shower of blessing, or you must face them as a lion.

Thirdly: *purity*. Shall I tell you what has been the greatest weakness of the Jewish race through the long years of their history? That they have copied others, that they have assimilated themselves to others, that they have adopted the practices that heathens have. So God says: in that day, Israel, when Jesus born in Bethlehem becomes your King, I will do away with everything else you have trusted in to save you, everything else you have copied from other nations, everything you have depended on instead of depending on me; your weapons.

There is one hymn that is sung every November 11th in Britain which I don't think the nation has a right to sing. It seems to me hypocritical to sing *O God, our help in ages past*, which goes on: "Sufficient is thine arm alone and our defence is sure." As long as we have any nuclear missiles we cannot sing that song. But that song is a song of Israel, not a song for other nations to sing. In the day when Jesus is King of Israel they will scrap all their weapons, all their missiles, all their jet aircraft; every defence will go and they will be able to sing that: "Sufficient is thine arm alone and our defence is sure." Think of all the money that little country is having to spend to defend itself at the moment, but that will go. Other things will go too. Do you know that the Jews have, from time to time, adopted trust in occult powers? They have known witchcraft, they have known spiritist mediums. They have had their horoscopes; they didn't read tea leaves in those days, they read clouds and they had cloud readers who would come and look at the clouds, and see things in the clouds, and read the fortune of Israel from the clouds. Micah says: I see a day in which all your witchcraft is gone, in which you don't have cloud readers, fortune tellers, any more; I see a day in which all occult powers and black magic have disappeared.

During their history, Israel alas adopted idolatrous worship. You can read all about it in the Old Testament: Baal worship, foul fertility cults with obscene monuments called "Ashtoreth" and other things. In that day, when Jesus is King, there will be none of that. "No longer will you worship what you have made with your own hands." You see whatever you make with your hands is a creature, not the creator. All that will be gone. Everything that was pulling Israel down when Micah lived will be gone; he can see those mountains rising above sub-swamps . He can see the pure worship of the Lord at last.

The final thing he sees is that God's rule, for the first time in world history, will be established by the immediate punishment of disobedience. The nations that will not obey God in that day will not get away with it any more, they will be punished immediately by the Lord. At the moment, as we live today, when nations disobey God they can get away with it for quite a long time. There is a bill to be paid in the long run, but in that day God will take vengeance immediately on those who disobey him.

So the future is unveiled so we can see what is going to happen. There are two different reactions that you can have when you know the future: one is fatalism and the other is freedom.

Fatalism says, "Well if God has got it all worked out, if it is all fixed, all decided, there is nothing I need to do, nothing I can do. It is all set." The Bible is not a book of fatalism. Yes, God has decided certain things and they will certainly happen but the Bible is not fatalistic. It is rather a book of freedom, a book in which God is free to decide what he wants to do. Thank God that he has freewill. Some people talk about human freewill in such a way that they deny the Maker freewill. They think that he must do what we decide; that we must be free. I say he must be free; he is free. He is the only really free person. So when God has decided to wind up history in a certain way nothing will stop him winding up history in that way. Thank God I can be sure of how history is going to end. I don't run around worrying if people are going to press the wrong button and bring our human race to a dreadful holocaust of an ending by some human folly. I don't worry about that because God is going to wind up history his way. He is in charge. God is free, but here is the other side: God, in his mercy, has left us free. On the basis of unveiling the future, he would say: now it is up to you to relate yourselves to that future. It is within the capacity of your decision to become part of that future or not.

Later in Micah we shall see the lovely news that he is the God who pardons. In other words, your future can be changed. The world's future can't be changed, but yours can be. God has decided how he will bring time to a triumphant conclusion in Christ. It is his purpose to sum up all things in his Son and no one can thwart that purpose. History is fixed, but your future is not. Your future depends on how you respond to that future. Whether you are part of it or not depends on you.

Here are three questions for you. Number one: what do you think of the people of Israel? Do you look forward to being joined with them? One day, the two flocks will come into one fold, and Jew and Gentile together will worship God. Do you look forward to all that God has got to do for them as a nation? Do you long for and look for their rebirth?

Question number two: what do you think about the God of Israel? I meet people who say, "I don't like the God of the Old Testament. He's a God of vengeance; he's a God who punishes. He's a God of war. I prefer the God of Jesus." Let me tell you that the God of Jesus was the God of the Old Testament. The only God that ever existed is the God of Israel. What do you think of the God of the Old Testament? Because he is the God that we worship. Have you got some sentimental Santa Claus, grandfather kind of picture of God and think you have picked it up from the New Testament? Then just remember that the God and Father of our Lord Jesus is the God of Abraham, and of Isaac, and of Jacob. What do you think of the God of Israel?

Last question: what have you done with the King of Israel? We know what Israel did with their own King and we know what they have done with him for two thousand years, but what have *you* done with him? Are you any better? You can't have the kingdom without the King.

Read Micah 6

We live in the present. I suppose that is a pretty obvious statement to make but the present is only a tiny fraction of our existence. Most of our life is in the past or the future and here we are in this tiny fragment of time called "the present". It is in this tiny fragment that everything significant happens and we make all our major decisions. The one thing that is quite certain is that none of us can alter the past.

The present is part of a process that stretches right through. What we do in the present moment has a cause in the past and a consequence in the future. If we are to understand what we are at the moment and why we react as we do, we have to understand the past from which we have come and through which we have lived, and then we will see what the future is going to hold, too. To get away from this little bit of philosophising back to the Bible, the prophet Micah in chapter 6 is looking at the present in which Israel is living. He is concerned there solely with the moment of time in which he lives, seven hundred years BC. He is going to look back into the past and try and find the cause for the people's condition in the present. Then he is going to look into the future and find the consequence of their behaviour in the present.

Let us look first at the conditions in Micah's day. He

was looking at a nation where the standards were in sharp decline, where the rich got richer and the poor got poorer; honesty, loyalty, a fair day's work for a fair day's pay, were memories of the grandparents. He was looking at a society in which everybody was on the make, in which everybody was trying to get more and more, no matter how many people they hurt in doing so. He was looking at a society in which money talked more than morality.

What was the cause for that in the past? It doesn't just happen suddenly. What Britain is today didn't happen suddenly. What we see in our nation has not just happened out of the blue, arbitrarily. There is a cause in the past, and there is also, alas, a consequence in the future.

Verses 1–5 pose the question of who is to blame for the state of the nation. Let a case be heard in court. Let the evidence be presented. Micah now imagines a large court in which God and his people confront one another to find out who is to blame for what has happened. Into this court the witnesses are going to come. They are unusual witnesses – the mountains and the hills of the Middle East. The mountains of Judah, who have watched all this, know what has gone in the valleys. Let them be the witnesses and let the case be put. Let the land itself bear testimony as to what has actually happened to cause this dreadful state of affairs. Now the first thing that happens is that God invites his people to state their case against him first. This is the most astonishing thing to me. What a reasonable God we have, who is not only willing to talk but willing to listen, a God who's saying: come let us reason together; I will let you put your case first then I will put mine. Let us be absolutely fair. If you think I am to blame then you state your case, produce your evidence. Call on these mountains. It is a tremendous challenge, but what a fair God.

Alas, God knows that people are only too ready to blame

him when things go wrong. It is one of the signs of our fallen nature that when we pay the penalty for our own sins and the selfishness of our human race, we blame God. A typical example is war. What causes war? Human selfishness causes war. Yet when war comes we say, "God, why did you do it?" We blame God for letting it happen. It could have been avoided if we had obeyed the laws of God. God knows perfectly well that when things go wrong, when people are not happy and comfortable and healthy, they blame God and say it is he who is to blame.

God is saying: state your case; bring your evidence; call your witnesses. The simple fact is that no such case could ever stand. We say these things in the heat of the moment; we say them under the pressure of events, but when we begin to look at the evidence and look around for witnesses, we can't find any. God cannot be accused of causing our problems. We must never make him the scapegoat for our responsibility.

Between verses 1 and 2 there is apparently a silence, for no case is stated. Nobody dare get up and say, "Well God, here is the evidence. You did this, you did that, and you did the other and here are the witnesses to prove it." So Micah moves on. God asks ringing questions to which there is no answer.

Question number one is: "What have I done that makes you turn away from me?" What a question. Yet God is asking every person on earth who does not love him, who does not worship him, who does not adore him, this question. It is people who are in the dock now and God becomes the prosecutor. He is firing the deadly questions. He asks the second question, "Why is your patience with me exhausted?" You know, one of the very frequent sins, which we don't always recognise, is that we become impatient with God. We want everything quickly.

Why can we not wait on the Lord? After all, God took

centuries to do so many of the things that he did. Why is your patience exhausted? Why can't you wait? You know again there is no answer. So God reminds his people that he cut the chains of their slavery. He brought them out of Egypt, sent Moses to set them free, sent Aaron to speak for them and sent Miriam to teach them to sing and dance. You know, funnily enough, with perverted human nature, someone who gives us love can so easily become the object of our dislike. Someone who gives us charity becomes someone we don't like. Isn't it strange?

The real crime of people is sheer ingratitude. They had faced the king of Moab; Balak wanted to curse them through the prophet Balaam. What did God do? He controlled Balaam's mouth so he could only bless them. Trace back everything that happened in their history – and find that everything in it was for their good, by God's grace. That is God's case against them.

So I apply that to my own heart and to your heart very simply: if ever we are tempted to complain against God, if ever we are tempted to grumble at the way he deals with us, if ever we are tempted to blame him for something for which he is not responsible, then God would say to us: "I saved you. I rescued you. At every point in your life I have done things for your good. It is your crime, and the crime is ingratitude. It is your fault in not responding to my love." That is God's case and it is virtually unanswerable. He claims that his crime is kindness. Is that a crime? Surely the crime is in those hearts that have received all his kindness and still fight, grumble, and say "Why?"

We have to assume that there is a gap between verses 5 and 6, and that something happened in that gap; that the people of Judah, as they listened to Micah, began to have pangs of conscience, began to remember the goodness of God, began to remember how he had established them in the land, and rescued them from slavery, and they began to feel a little uncomfortable. Then they began to feel guilty and then they began to be concerned. How can we put this right? How can we get into God's good books again? How can we please him after this? How can we get right with God?

That is the most important question for every man and woman on earth. For we are all in this position: that all of us have shown ingratitude to God for his goodness, every one of us. The most important question is this: how can I please God? How can I be in a right relationship with him? How can I give him what he wants from me? How can I undo the ingratitude of the past? Micah answers it and reaches the peak of his prophecy, one of the noblest statements that has ever been made, one of the greatest definitions of religion that could possibly ever be written or read in v. 8 – what a statement. But he answers it negatively before he answers it positively. It is always necessary in answering a question to say what the answer is not, as well as what it is, so that people are utterly clear in their minds. So Micah first of all tells us what not to do. The answer that natural man gives is this: God likes religion, so the more religion I give him the more he likes it. If I want to please him then he wants more and more religion. Now that is the answer that our heart would give. We honestly think that that is what God wants: attend more meetings; do more in church. Our instinctive answer is "more religion". The way they thought in those days was to think in terms of bringing offerings and sacrifices. So they thought: it's going to take an awful lot to show gratitude again, to get on God's right side again, so we will bring yearling calves. We will bring thousands of rams, ten thousand rivers of oil. If he is still not satisfied we'll even bring our little children, our elder son, and sacrifice him. Surely that will do the trick? Do you know that a society that lives in bribery and corruption very quickly gets the idea that God has his price;

that in fact you can buy God. That you can please him the way you please other people: lots of presents.

Think of a husband and he has done something wrong and is a bit unpopular with his wife – you see him going home with arms full of chrysanthemums. It is the instinctive reaction, and because we can get away with it at a human level from time to time we think that that is how we can get away with it with God. Alas, there are parents who think if you buy children expensive toys you can buy their love. That happens in an affluent society. That is not the way to get God's love; that is not the way to please him. You can offer him the most costly present of all. It may sound appalling to you to think of offering your eldest son as a sacrifice; Abraham was ready to do it with Isaac. God told him not to at the last moment. God made it clear he didn't want that. But in the times of King Ahaz, just about Micah's time, they had picked up the idea from pagan sources that God was pleased with human sacrifice. Do you know that archaeologists have uncovered in the Middle East little earthen jars and inside the skeletons of babies, buried under the altars of pagan temples? People thought that this would please God and that somehow such a costly gift would satisfy and overcome the past mistakes, and help him to forget the ingratitude, but it doesn't work that way.

That is the negative answer: God will never be satisfied with more and more religion. Nor does he want from you all your money and all the things that money can buy.

What does God really want? Just three things: "To do justly, to love mercy, and to walk humbly with your God." That is the fundamental requirement of God. If you are going to please God now, and if I am going to, it won't be the number of meetings we have attended, it won't even be the amount of money we have spent on his work. It will be whether I have done justly, and loved mercy, and walked humbly with God. Let us look at this simple definition. It is lovely; it is poetry. Yet I hope the poetry of it won't dull your senses to its meaning.

First of all, Micah is saying nothing new; it has all been said before and he is conscious that he is not saying anything original. God had been telling them for centuries what he wanted. If you read through the entire five books of Moses you can summarise them in three phrases: to do justly, to love mercy, and to walk humbly with God. Even in Micah's day it had all been said clearly by three other prophets. Amos said, "Do justly" – that is the summary of his whole prophecy. Hosea said "Love mercy", and that is a summary of his whole prophecy. Isaiah had said "Walk humbly", and that is a summary of Isaiah's life from the day when he saw the Lord high and lifted up, and he was humbled and said, "Woe is me".

Micah simply took what had been said before in so many different ways and put it in one illuminating, golden text: "What does God require from you? To do justly, to love mercy, and to walk humbly." I see in those three phrases a kind of growing depth of spirituality. The first is the easiest: to do justly, though it is hard enough. It is even harder for our human nature to go on to the second and to love mercy. The tragedy is that if we manage the first two we become proud of it and we think we are really getting somewhere, so the third becomes the most difficult of all: to walk humbly with your God. You see, if you do justly and love mercy you are like God, but you must never think you are like God. You must remember that he is God, and to walk humbly must follow.

Here then are the three simple requirements. You see, God is not so much concerned with what we give to him but how we live before him. He is not so much concerned with what he wants *from* us, it is what he wants *in* us that is far more important. It is so much easier to give to him than to live

MICAH

for him. It is so much easier to have something taken from us by him than to have something done in us by him. But God makes it utterly clear: for you to be fair, for you to go beyond justice and to give what people do not deserve – to love mercy. When you have achieved it, to think of yourself as nothing before God. We know that if we made a resolution to do these three things we would never make it. Nor did the people of Judah, for we pass to the third, rather sad section of this chapter, vv. 9–16. Only God would put v. 9 after v. 8. If we had been writing the prophet Micah's prophecy we would have finished with v. 8. It is the climax, the peak. We have reached the heights of this prophecy. Now this is the greatest statement perhaps in the Old Testament about what God requires.

We have reached it, and suddenly Micah comes sliding down into a dark valley. Why? He just wants the people of Israel to know quite clearly that they won't make it. You can make resolutions but you can't keep them. It is beyond human nature to do justly, to love mercy, and to walk humbly with God. So he goes straight on and points out that you cannot even do the first of these three things, never mind loving mercy and walking humbly with God. Look at the simple matter of being fair and just. Could God be happy with the state of society, with the dishonesty, unfairness and injustice in it? Micah now slates the people of those days. He deals with the little crooks first, the traders who have scales – they have filed a little bit of metal off one of the pans, and they have a bag of weights that are not quite accurate.

I knew a person who used to throw sweets on the scales, and used to throw them good and hard – and when the needle went over, whip the pan off quickly. He was noted for this. That is what Micah is talking about. Then he goes onto the big timers and he was referring to the equivalent of violence, extortion, mugging, blackmail and so on. Then he says even of the general citizens that lying has become so common that people don't know when they are telling the truth any longer. It has become common to be deceitful, to lie, and to tell an untruth. Micah is talking of a society in which dishonesty has become the norm.

So he was pointing out that there were small time crooks, big time crooks – everybody was in it. Nobody was really concerned about basic justice, a fair day's work for a fair day's pay. There is an indictment. They could not even be just, never mind merciful or humble. God asked three things from them and they could not even manage the first.

I believe that this is a comment on our economic situation today. The message, in effect is: if this is how you are going to get your money then I will see that your money will not keep its value. You will save and it will mean nothing; you will try to use it but you will find it won't buy what you want it to buy. For money is simply trust. The currency note in my pocket is simply a promise written on a piece of paper. It is dependent on mutual trust, and in a society of mistrust money cannot hold its value.

Do you honestly think God will let you enjoy an affluence gained dishonestly? Never. You will plant vineyards but you won't get juice to make wine. You will sow corn but you won't reap it. You will save money but it will become worthless. In this kind of society even money can't hold it's own. In a sense, the punishment fits the crime because money is not a bad thing in itself. Love of money is.

Micah points out that God's people had followed the example of Ahab, one of the most evil kings of Israel. Ahab had a lovely big estate and he loved walking around in it at night and saying, "Mine, mine, mine, these vineyards, these fields." There was only one snag: his boundary at one point had a little dent in it. There was a little vineyard which belonged to someone else and it rather spoiled his fence. It belonged to a man called Naboth. The king, rich though he was, was a baby in his heart. That night he sulked, he turned his face to the wall, and Jezebel his queen said, "What's the matter darling?"

"Well it's that fence. I'd love to complete that hedge along there and there's a little vineyard just spoiling it."

"What, you're going to let a little man hang on to his vineyard. Who's king in this land? We'll deal with him."

They murdered Naboth just to get a little vineyard, just to complete his hedge, so that he could walk right around his boundary. That was Ahab.

So God says through Micah: you're doing just this; therefore I'm going to make you, my people, the laughing stock of the nations.

It all happened and it all came true and it is a terrible warning to us. What does God want from you? Lots of money? No. Lots of meetings? No. Does he want some big costly sacrifice from you? No. What does he want from you? Just three things, "To do justly, to love mercy, and to walk humbly with your God."

This chapter is unsatisfying, isn't it? This chapter leaves you sort of in midair. It is unresolved; they don't live happily ever after. It has a kind of unfinished tone, like an unfinished symphony. The Old Testament doesn't solve the problem which can be stated so simply. This is what God requires of us, those three things, and we are unable to give him what he requires. That is the problem.

The Old Testament makes it absolutely clear how we are to live. There is no doubt whatever, and we did not need the Old Testament to make it any clearer. It is there. We know all that; we know what God wants from us today. We know equally well that by nature we are unjust, unmerciful and proud, and that is the problem. We know that we can't resolve it. So what is going to happen? Do we just face a future like

Israel faced in Micah's prophecy: doom? Is there no way through this? Praise God, there is. The New Testament has got it. Micah saw that sacrifices will be no use because they are no substitute for right living. Supposing you could find a sacrifice of a life that had been lived right. Just think this through.

God says that if you give him your eldest son he will still not be satisfied. But what will satisfy him is that he gives his only Son. Isn't that tremendous?

Now why should the sacrifice of the life of Jesus be any more acceptable than yearling calves or thousands of rams? It is because it was the first sacrifice that had lived in this way. Jesus did justly, loved mercy and walked humbly with God. For the first time a life had been lived on earth that gave God what he wanted—the only life that has ever done so. Jesus – for thirty-three years on our planet, in our flesh, walked around in our society with people just as crooked as ourselves, and Jesus did absolutely justly. Every time they tried to make him act unjustly he found a way to be fair; not a word escaped his lips that wasn't fair. Not an act or judgment that he made was unfair. He loved mercy. He loved to say to a woman taken in adultery, "Neither do I condemn you. Go and sin no more." He loved mercy. He walked humbly because the words that he spoke were just the words that the Father told him to say.

So he offered God the Father what was wanted. God accepted that sacrifice and can forgive sin. That is how it has been resolved. Praise God I can stand before him though I have not acted justly, not loved mercy, and not walked humbly, but I can say: "Lord, I present to you his sacrifice, his life, as a substitute for mine."

But somebody could say, "Well, that sounds too simple, too easy. That means I can go on acting unjustly, I can go on being unmerciful, I can go on being proud." Never. For

Christ is to become my substitute not only in his death but in my life. He is not only to die in my place; he is to live in my place. It becomes gloriously possible to give God what he wants. If I will let Christ be my substitute in life as well as in death, to live in my life instead of me, then you will see me doing justly, loving mercy and walking humbly – because it won't be me at all, it will be Christ going on giving the Father what he wants. That is why the Old Testament is incomplete without the New. That is why you are left with this unresolved problem: this is what God wants but I can't give it to him. Through Christ's death on the cross and life in my heart I can at last give God what he wants.

Read Micah 7

Have you noticed how little we now know about Micah? We know where he lived, when he lived and that is about all. You can't tell me now whether he was young or old, whether he was married or single, whether he was tall or short, handsome or plain. You can't tell me whether he was generally a happy man or a sad man. You don't know anything about his temperament or his temptations. We do know that he was country rather than town. We know that he was poor rather than rich. We know that he was blunt rather than subtle but that is about all.

The point is that the man doesn't matter – not that much. The only part of Micah that really mattered was his mouth. We have been studying this book not to learn about the man but to learn about the message that he brought. For the one thing Micah did was to pass the message on. That is why he is remembered and that is why you know his name. One day when we get to heaven you can look around for Micah and then you will have all the other questions answered. But the message we have got to know very well indeed.

Now I want to remind you that the message he passed on

passed through three stages: pictures, prophecies, passages. Micah says the word of the Lord came to him in visions. Now that means in pictures – which he saw very clearly, probably with his eyes, but which were visions that came through his eyes to his mind during the day when he was wide awake and fully conscious. The Lord plants pictures in our minds two ways. Either when we are asleep, which we call dreams, or when we are awake, which we call visions. When the Holy Spirit comes on people they dream dreams and see visions. But Micah says: the Word of the Lord came to me in visions; I could see things clearly.

What we have been studying first of all came as it were in a series of slides on a screen to Micah and he is simply describing what he saw. He could see the future; he could see his own nation hundreds of years into the future. He could see Bethlehem, and he could see a King being born in Bethlehem, but it all came as pictures. Now what Micah did, the supreme thing he did for us, was to translate the pictures into prophecies, to translate what he saw into what he said. Believe me, that is a very difficult thing to do. To translate words into pictures is one thing. But Micah's task was the opposite: to take a picture, which only he had seen, and put it into words so that in other people's minds he could create the same picture. That was what a prophet invariably was: a man who painted a picture in people's minds through words. How could he do it? The answer is: the Holy Spirit again. As the Holy Spirit gave him the picture, the Holy Spirit enabled him to do this very difficult thing and help other people to see the pictures, using words only. In this age of visual media it has become even more difficult for us to translate pictures into words and to use the medium of language to paint a picture in people's minds. That is why radio is a much better medium than television, because when you listen to radio or listen to a radio play, your mind translates the words into pictures. Whereas watching television your imagination is not used. Therefore imagination is one of those gifts we are now in danger of losing. But Micah translated pictures into words – that people's imagination could then be filled with the Spirit of God and truth, and see what was going to happen in the future. But we don't hear these words now.

We don't have Micah standing with us. We now have Micah's prophecies in the form of passages. So it has reached a third stage: pictures, which he saw; prophecies, which people heard; and now passages, which we read.

It is still the Word of God, still the living word, but one change has taken place between the prophecy and the passage. From the spoken to the written word this is what has happened: prophecies that were spread over many years have now been condensed into seven chapters. Things that Micah said at different times in his lifetime are now together and side-by-side. So we have studied what may have taken Micah forty years, for he lived through the reigns of three kings and prophesied all the way. Therefore we get a rather distorted view and we can't possibly get everything out of Micah. You will have to go back and back to this book over your lifetime and still you will find new thoughts in it as I do every time I read it.

Let us get into chapter 7. There are four pictures here: Number one, a picture of the nation as it was in Micah's day; number two, a picture of Micah as he was in his day; number three, a picture of the nation as it was to be in the future; number four, a picture of God himself. Whether these four pictures all came to Micah at one and the same time or whether they were spread out, the remarkable thing is that when they are put together in a passage in the Bible they make sense. Each one leads on to the next; each one explains the previous one. You can see the thread of God's thoughts on which the pearls of this prophecy are strung.

Now let us look at these four pictures. In chapter 7, of all the chapters in Micah, the prophet comes nearest to letting you see inside his own heart. I think at the end of this chapter you will begin to feel that you know Micah. For more than any other chapter he includes autobiography here. For the first time in this little book Micah talks about himself in detail. He shares with us the great personal tragedy of his life. He has never mentioned it thus far, but in this chapter he mentions a personal tragedy that would be enough to stop a man preaching, yet he went on, and we shall see that as we go through.

Let us look at the first picture. He begins with a terrible statement: "Woe is me." I don't know if that conveys anything to you at all. Probably not and I'll tell you why: it is an expression you have never used. Nowadays we would just write, "Ugh!" It is a groan, a feeling of abject misery, "Oh!"

Have you ever felt like that? Have you ever felt lost, lonely and just hopeless? Ever felt like giving in? Ever felt that you just were neither worthy nor adequate to carry on? Then you know what this phrase means "Woe is me" means. It means someone has come to the end of himself – really down, depressed and hopeless. There is nothing to be done; we can't do a thing. It has just got on top of us. We live in a world in which more and more people are feeling, "Woe is me. Stop the world I want to get off; it's gone too far; it's too much for me; it's all caving in on me. It's hopeless. We can march. We can protest, but it just goes on and the situation gets worse." Do you ever feel like this?

There are people who feel that way about our nation – that they can't stop the rot, that it is hopeless and has gone too far. "Woe is me," and Micah shows us that his heart feels the situation is hopeless. What has got him down? The fact that when he looks out on the world he can't find a good person. He was not the first prophet to be depressed by this. Elijah is an outstanding example of a man who said, "Lord I'm the only one left who still thinks about you." He wasn't saying it in a boastful way; he just felt so depressed.

Micah, with typical country man's expressions and a picture from his own country life says that it is like going out in the winter to look for some fruit. The harvest is over. You look for just one fig or one grape and there isn't one. He feels like that in his nation. He looks for one good, honest, fair-minded person. The word he uses for "good" is very interesting. The nearest English equivalent is "loyal".

He has looked everywhere in society. He has looked at the top, at the men in power. He looks at the governor; he looks at the judge. He sees that they are corrupt; that they will do anything for money, and that therefore the rich man can decide and money is talking right at the top of society. So a man who has no money has no hope of getting justice, of getting wrongs righted, and this depresses. I have lived in a land where this kind of situation applies. Thank God it doesn't yet in Britain, but believe me if you think that it could not happen to British justice then think again.

No wonder Micah is down. Then he says that if there is a God in heaven it can't go on much longer. Your day is coming; your punishment is coming and it is you who will be afraid then of the court. It is you who will be afraid of the law then, not us. He is speaking for the downtrodden peasant of Israel. He is speaking for those who didn't stand a chance of being heard because of the corruption in the land.

Then he turns from high society and the remote figures who run it, to the situation in his own immediate neighbourhood. "Don't trust anyone." What a thing to have to say. That is Micah's advice in the present situation. Don't trust a soul. Don't trust your best friend; you can no longer do so. Don't trust her who lies in your bosom – that is sad, when you have got to the stage where you cannot trust your own wife.

Family life is broken up through lack of loyalty. Son turns against father, daughter-in-law against mother-in-law, husband against wife – there is no longer trust within the family circle. No longer loyalty, no longer love, no longer integrity within the family. He then makes this simple statement of society in his day: a man's enemies will be in his own home. Are you beginning to sense what the tragedy of Micah's life might be? For that very phrase was quoted by the Lord Jesus Christ and he said this will happen to Christians too. What happened to Micah will happen to Christians, and that is that the enemies of the Christian may be those within his or her own family.

Alas, I know as I speak this is true. Jesus said, "Don't think that I came to bring peace I came to bring a sword, to set parent against child, brother against sister, for a man's enemies will be those of his own household" – quoted from Micah. If you are going to stand for God in a world that does not like God, if you are going to follow Christ in a world that does not follow Christ, you may well find that your greatest enemy is in your own home.

Here we are beginning to realise what it cost Micah to be a prophet. He could not have written that paragraph unless it was true of his own experience. He could not have said it like that unless the poor man had found it to be true. Fancy a man having to go out and preach against a nation, coming back home, and finding that his own family is not behind him in his ministry. That is a tragedy, and a very heavy burden to bear. We come now to a different picture in vv. 7–10.

Now you would think that this was enough to put a man in a mental hospital with a complete nervous breakdown. You would think that with all these pressures on him, a whole nation against him, not one good man to back him up or to help him, not one man of integrity to say to him, "That's true what you say," and to come home and find that even his own family and home is against him, would be enough to send a man around the bend, wouldn't you? But no, he may be depressed but he is not in despair. He may be knocked down but he is not knocked out. He may have fallen but he will rise again. He may be in darkness but he will live to see the light, and that is the next picture. Why? Because there is one person in the whole universe that Micah can trust. There may be no good man around, but there is a good God above. He is looking to one person. He can't trust his nation; he can't trust his family. He looks to the Lord for his help. This is the answer to depression. This is the answer to the situation getting you down. This is the answer to the pressures of life becoming so heavy that you feel like giving up. The answer is: there's still one person I can trust; there is still one person of integrity; there is still one person who will save me. I may be down but I will be up again because of him. What a lovely thought that is. That is how Micah kept going. That is how you will keep going.

Self-pity is the quickest way to spiral down in depression. Every normal depression begins with self-pity in some form or another – feeling sorry for yourself. Micah does not feel sorry for himself. "Woe is me" yes, but he says, "as for me I look to the Lord." As my grandfather used to keep saying, "When the outlook's bad, try the up-look." I look to the Lord who is going to help me. This very text comes in Bunyan's *The Pilgrim's Progress.* Pilgrim goes into a dark valley and he is attacked by Apollyon, the devil. The battle is very fierce. Christian falls to the ground and Apollyon jumps after him to kill him and thrusts the sword into him to finish him off. Christian remembers the sword of the Spirit, which is the Word of God, and Christian quotes Micah 7. He says, "I may have fallen but I will rise again." Now that is what lifts people up again. You may be down, you may find that life gets you down, you may be depressed, you may feel that there is nobody else but you – in the office or the shop, or where you work – nobody but you, you can't find someone, but look up. He is going to lift you up again. He is going to shine his light into your darkness, and as with Micah you will see his goodness.

Notice that Micah does not think that he, Micah, is perfect. It would be very easy for some people to say, "There isn't a good man left; only me," and give the impression that they think they are perfect. Micah never thought that. Indeed, he regarded his present sufferings as God's chastisement for his sin. His understanding was: look, I have sinned; I have done wrong and the Lord is punishing me for doing wrong. I do not know in what way Micah had sinned. Yet Micah is not saying: I am perfect and you are all bad. Rather: in going through this pressure, God is dealing with me too. I will patiently bear this punishment of my sin because I know that after he has dealt with me he will pick me up again.

That is an insight into a Christian suffering under pressure. It may be that God wants to deal with you too. So he lets you go through it and he picks you up again afterwards. So Micah, with no pride in his heart is saying: if God wants to deal with me by taking me through a deep valley then that is all right but he will pick me up again afterwards and that is the main thing; I will patiently wait for the Lord. He knows that God will pick him up.

In v. 10, notice: I see "her" [not "them"] trampled down like mud in the street." The more I read this the more I come to a conclusion that I have not seen in any commentary or heard anywhere else but I am sure it's right. Micah's greatest burden in life was his own wife. I cannot begin to imagine what that burden would be like, for I have a wife who as soon as I get home from speaking at a meeting, asks the first question, "How did you get on?" But to have a wife who did not back you up, who was not part of your ministry, who was not glad you were speaking the Word of God – what a burden.

It must have been a terrible burden to go up to Jerusalem and speak fearlessly in the public streets against the governors, the rulers and the judges, and then come home and have a nagging wife say, "Hmm, you've been making a fool of yourself again I hear. You should hear what the neighbours think about you." Then, the more foolish you look, the more she begins to laugh instead of to nag and make fun of you. Do you notice she says, "Where is that God of yours" – not of "ours", but "of yours". His wife did not share his faith – what a burden, and the poor man was called to be a preacher.

I knew of one sad case like this where a minister of the gospel used to go to church and preach the good news of God while his wife sat on the vicarage lawn and knitted. The burden for that man to have to preach to others while his own wife was not with him. Micah had to do it. He had no choice. People could throw it in his face; his wife threw it in his face, "This God of yours..." – taunting him all the time. Micah had to go on proclaiming the truth against that. Can you imagine it? I think the most painful thing that Micah ever had to face was that God showed him a picture of the future of his wife. He saw his wife's body lying in the street and people trampling on it.

To know that God would deal with her that way, and to know that this was where all her taunting and ridicule was going to lead her. Praise God for a man like Micah who can cope with a situation like that and look to the Lord. This is the personal side of Micah's life, and I want to say this: having listened to many men who have preached, who have taught the Word of God, and those who have done so privately by passing on the messages of God one-to-one, it is those who have suffered in some way who have a dimension to the message that others don't have. You see, if you are going to pass the Word of God on to someone else it will be at cost to yourself.

Verse 11 is a complete contrast. It is a picture of a glorious future, of peace and prosperity. At first sight there seems to be no connection whatever between verses 10 and 11, but there is. What Micah is conveying is this: God is punishing me at the moment but he is going to lift me up again in the future. What he will do to me he will do to his people. He is punishing Israel and he is going to punish them, but he is going to lift them up again.

Thank God that he doesn't leave us down. He chastises his people, yes, but he always brings them back again.

What Micah expects to happen for himself will happen to the nation too. He sees a picture now of his nation with the cities rebuilt larger than ever, with the fields restocked, and the fertile areas of Bashan and Gilead full of cattle. He can see the boundaries extended. He can see so many things happening. As he looks into the future he can see the nations of the world coming with a very changed attitude to God's people.

There are certain steps described. They will first of all be amazed. We have almost reached that stage already. Aren't the nations of the world amazed at what Israel has done in modern times? It is an amazing feat. But then it says they will move on from amazement to awe. When they see God's people go on and on against all human opposition, against all odds, it will change to awe. The awe will change to anxiety as they begin to be afraid. There is something more here than just a nation; there is God here. Something supernatural is happening. The anxiety will give way to agony as they come trembling before God and admit that their attitude to Israel has revealed their attitude to the God of Israel. Nations will come crawling like worms and snakes out of their holes, and come trembling to this people of God.

It will be a miracle. God will do again the miracles he did when he brought his people out of slavery in Egypt. It will require miracles, and we are going to see miracles happen in the Middle East. I believe that. People will be in awe and wonder: God acting in history for his people. What a future! So Micah, believing that not only will he be lifted up again, believes that the nation will be restored again, and so we come to the great climax of Micah's prophecy for up to v. 17 we are left with a huge question: if the nation was so far gone that there wasn't a good man in it, how could such a godless nation ever have such a glorious future? They don't deserve it. There is no reason why they should have it. Why? How can such a thing be?

How can you get from vv. 1–5 through to vv. 11–17? How can a nation that has been as far gone as this get to that state? There is only one possible answer: forgiveness. If God was not a God of grace and forgiveness there would be no hope for the future. If God would forgive this nation then he will forgive you and me.

So Micah says: who is a God like you, pardoning iniquity and passing over transgression from the remnant of his inheritance? There is no other god worshipped in the world who would do this kind of thing.

Now Micah is playing on his own name. The name "Micah" means "like God". When his parents called him that, they hoped their little boy would grow up to be like God, and he did. But Micah says: I have never heard of a God called Micah because there is no god like God. Now you can search all the religions of the world and you will never see a god called "Micah". There is no god like God. So, playing on his name, Micah is saying: there's no god called 'Micah' because there's no god like God; who is a God like you who pardons, who forgives, who takes a nation that hasn't a godly man in it, and yet promises them a future like that? What a God; a God who forgives."

That is the God we meet to worship, otherwise there would be no hope of us ever having a future. Think of the glorious future Jesus has painted for us. "I go to prepare a place for you." How can David Pawson look forward to a place like that? There is only one answer, "Who is a God like you who pardons iniquity?"

So Micah comes to the great climax. You know some people think that Micah 6:8 is the climax of his prophecy. "What does the Lord require of you but to do justly, to love mercy, and to walk humbly with your God?" That's a great statement, it is a peak, but it is not the peak of his prophecy because the simple fact is that there isn't one of us who is able to do justly, or to love mercy, or to walk humbly. By nature we are unfair, hard and proud people. So it is not very good news. The climax is this: when you have done unjustly, been unmerciful and walked proudly, you can still come to the God who forgives.

Why? Because here is a picture of God. God can get angry but he is not a God who can stay angry. That is what Micah teaches us. He is angry with sin, and sin makes him angry, but he will not be angry forever. There is soon a feeling of mercy and compassion for the sinner. That is why God loves to forgive. Of course forgiveness has to be received. Of course it is not automatic. Of course it does not mean that all the world is going to heaven, but it does mean that those who are willing to come to a God who forgives and to say, "God be merciful to me a sinner" have a glorious future.

I care not how bad they are, I care not how many sins they have committed, the moment they come to God and say, "God be merciful", his anger evaporates like the morning dew and he has compassion. That is Micah's peak prophecy. What does God do with your sins? He gets rid of them. He tramples them under his feet. He puts them in a place beyond recovery, beyond reach. The furthest place on earth that Micah could think of was in the bottom of the sea – where they put radioactive waste in sealed canisters. He has taken my sins and he has put them at the bottom of the ocean, buried in the deepest sea. You will never get further from your sins than that on earth. Have you noticed the hyperbole, the language that the psalmists use again and again? How far is the east from the west? That is how far he has removed your sins from you; buried in the deepest sea.

How do you know? How can Micah be so sure? How can he be so confident that God will forgive? The answer is in the last verse: he made a promise. Once he has made a promise you can be absolutely sure. He made a promise to Jacob, whose name was changed to Israel; father of twelve sons who became the twelve tribes of Israel, and God made a promise to Jacob.

Maybe that promise was made 1300 years earlier, but the Lord made it. Thirteen hundred years is nothing. God made a promise to our father Abraham and you made that promise. You see, to Micah it doesn't matter that the promise was made 1300 years previously. It was a promise. We may forget promises, but God doesn't. We are now some 2,700 years later than Micah, but we can read Micah and say, "God you promised it and we hold you to your promise. You promised it and therefore you are going to bury our sins in the deepest sea. You gave us your Word." Not because we are just interested in lectures on history; not because we are supposed to read the Bible because we are Christians, but simply because we can hold it in front of God's face and say: "God, you gave us your Word that you would forgive and we claim the promise of Micah on that one."

NAHUM

NAHUM

Read Nahum

Jonah and Nahum, interestingly enough, both describe God as slow to anger, but the difference is that with Nahum time had run out. Once aroused you cannot turn God's wrath away – once you have reached that point of boiling over. It is frequently called in the Bible the day of his wrath. While his wrath is simmering it can be turned away but when it boils over, nothing can stop it, and for different nations and for different individuals it has boiled over at different times, and for the whole world there is a day of wrath coming, when people would rather be swallowed in an earthquake than look at the anger on the face of God and his son Jesus. That is in Revelation chapter 6.

So God is now filled with wrath. He is boiling over. Though the King of Nineveh tried to pray and fast again, he was trying to copy what happened with Jonah, but it did not work this time and God would not accept it. So there comes a time when it is too late to change. The last verse of Nahum is: there is no remedy for your wound; your injury is past healing. Now funnily enough this is described as good news – but not for the Assyrians, it is good news for Israel. Because, you see, Nahum was born when the ten tribes were occupied. He was born in occupied territory, under Assyrian rule in the Holy Land. Can you imagine that? Born and bred and brought up under the Assyrians, and so his prophecy of the doom of Nineveh is good news and we get this lovely phrase: how beautiful are the feet of those who bring good tidings, running over the mountains. Now feet are not very beautiful, are they? Do you ever like photographs of your feet taken? It is bad enough having your face photographed, but your feet? No. There is only one situation in which feet are beautiful and that is feet that have run with good news! You could kiss the feet of someone who had brought you news that in your land which has been occupied your whole life by cruel enemies, freedom is about to come. It is great news. In fact, Nahum says everyone who hears the news about you will clap their hands! For who has not felt their endless cruelty? It is a vivid prophecy.

Now once again there is a question that we must ask: does God control history as well as nature? Nahum asks you this. The Bible is theistic in outlook; the Bible says it is God who draws the atlas of history. Paul on Mars Hill at Athens said to the Greeks that God allots a nation its room in time and space, and so it is God who allows a nation to rise and get an empire; it is God who brings it to an end. I believe God brought the British Empire – the empire in which the sun never set – to an end. When we washed our hands of the Jewish people in 1947 and said we want nothing more to do with the Jews, God said then you can't look after anybody else, and within five years the empire had gone. That is my understanding of history. God not only controls all of nature he controls all of history, and it is he who raises up princes and brings them down; it is he who allows the nation to expand and then crashes it. Christians in Germany, two years before the wall came down in Berlin, were announcing in the name of Jesus that God was bringing that wall down. So, you see, they believed that God is in charge of history and therefore history is predictable, and part of the prophets' task was to predict history and to write history before it happened, and here is Nahum saying Nineveh is finished, which seems unbelievable when you look at the power and the might of Nineveh, and yet it happened within a very short space of time.

NAHUM

Nahum is almost all prediction so let us just analyse Nahum's little prophecy. It is only three chapters and they divide very easily between the chapters. Their concern was the fall of Nineveh. First of all there is the proclamation of who is going to be touched by God. The divine intervention means disaster for God's enemies, and deliverance for his friends. When God intervenes it always has this dual character. When God steps into history and acts, it means disaster for all his enemies, those who defy him and who trust themselves. Those are the enemies of God – they trust in their own strength and they defy God, and when God acts it is they who face disaster. That is because, as Nahum makes quite clear, one side of God's character is that he is a jealous God. Now he is not envious. God does not envy anybody anything, because it is all his anyway. I love Psalm 50 where it says: God says if I was hungry I wouldn't tell you. You know, that's a lovely little insight into God's sufficiency. It goes on: the cattle on a thousand hills are mine, the silver and gold are mine.

But God is jealous and that is different. You might be envious about what somebody else has, but you are jealous about what you have which somebody wants to take from you. Do you understand? You may be envious about someone else's wife, but you would be jealous about your own, and God is jealous for his name; he is jealous for his reputation; he is jealous for his people; he is jealous for his world. God says it is his name, his reputation, his world, and he is not having people behaving like this in his world. That is jealousy, and jealousy leads to vengeance – that is another word of Nahum's. We need to remember that God is a God of vengeance because he is a God of jealousy; he is not a God of malicious revenge, he is a God of vengeance. That is why you are exhorted in the Bible never to repay evil with evil, just leave it to God. Vengeance is mine, says the Lord.

I wonder when you last heard a sermon on God's jealousy or his vengeance, but that is part of his character because he is a holy God and Nahum concentrates almost exclusively on God's jealousy and on his vengeance against those who defy him and trust themselves. But those who have trusted God all through the Assyrian atrocities, and believe that God will one day sort it all out, are going to be delivered. So it is good news.

The first chapter is an acrostic poem. This means that each verse begins with the next letter of the alphabet. If you could read it in Hebrew it is a very skilfully constructed poem, easily remembered because each statement begins with the next letter. An acrostic is a way of helping people to remember what has been said. Nahum did not do it so the Ninevites could remember it but so that his people in Israel could remember it easily. It was good news for them. Store it in your heart, learn it off by heart, repeat it to yourself, tell it to your children, Nineveh is finished because God is jealous for his name.

That is chapter 1. And he alternates through the chapter: a statement to Nineveh; a statement to Israel – bad news for Nineveh; good news for Israel. It is marvellous literary work. These prophets could put words together by the inspiration of the Holy Spirit in a memorable way.

Then we come to chapter 2, and if chapter one is a proclamation that Nineveh will fall, chapter 2 is a description of how it will happen, and it is absolutely astonishing in its detail. I was watching television when the first CBN reporter in Baghdad said the first bombs were falling. Did you see that memorable thing? The marvel of television – you see a war actually start now. It was the first time that has ever happened. Millions around the world actually saw hostilities begin. But Nahum saw them begin before they even happened, and describes them like a television reporter, as if he is seeing it unroll in front of him, and yet it has not happened yet. But it is so vivid in detail. It is full of poetic feelings. It is a memorable description.

Nahum's message is clear: Nineveh, you are finished; you are already surrounded by enemy armies. Sound the alarm, man the ramparts, muster to your defences full force and keep a sharp watch for the enemy attack to begin, for the land of the people of God lies empty and broken after your attacks but the Lord will restore their honour and power again. Shields flash red in the sunlight, the attack begins, see their scarlet uniforms, see their glittering chariots moving forward side by side, pulled by prancing steeds; your own chariots race recklessly along the streets and through the squares, darting like lightning, gleaming like torches. The king shouts for his officers! They stumble in their haste, rushing to the walls to set up their defences, but too late, the river gates are open, the enemy has entered, the palace is in panic. So it goes on. That is hot stuff, isn't it?

The fascinating thing is that the people who came to destroy Nineveh wore scarlet uniforms and there was no army in Nahum's day that wore scarlet uniforms. He even saw the colour of their uniforms and he saw how they got in through the river gates. They drained the river and came in through the sluice gates, they got into Nineveh and he saw it all happening. Read Nahum – it is a vivid description. Listen to the poetry: woe to Nineveh, city of blood full of lies crammed with plunder! Listen, I hear the crack of the whips as the chariots rush forward against her. Wheels rumbling, horses hooves pounding and chariots clattering as they bump wildly through the streets; see the flashing swords and glittering spears in the uraised hands of the cavalry. The dead are lying in the streets, bodies, heaps of bodies everywhere. Men stumble over them, scramble to their feet and fall again. All this because Nineveh sold herself to the enemies of God. What vivid writing. Can you imagine the guy preaching this? He is seeing it all happen vividly. That is chapter 2 and he describes first of all a day of looting. He sees the city looted, everything of value taken away, all the treasures gone, and then he says: I see a den of lions, but the lions are weak and dying. Do you remember when somebody called Britain a toothless lion? That is what Nahum is calling Nineveh. Now that is very significant because the lion was the emblem of Assyria; they regarded themselves as lions. But here they have become toothless lions, or paper tigers. They are no longer a threat to anyone, they are in terror themselves. There is a kind of poetic justice in this.

Then, in chapter 3, Nahum moves from description to explanation. Why? You see, first of all he proclaims that God is going to intervene on behalf of his friends and against his enemies, but then comes the description. How will this happen? By an invasion of a greater force coming into the city and taking over this den of lions. What is the explanation of why this is happening? The answer is: because of the sheer inhumanity of Assyria.

You see they did not know the ten commandments, so God does not judge them for breaking the ten commandments. When God sends a prophet to pronounce against people who are not the people of God, he doesn't throw the ten commandments at them. In Amos he throws at them inhumanity – that everybody knows that they should be kind rather than cruel. Those who have never heard of the ten commandments know it is wrong to be barbaric and cruel and to torture people. Everybody knows that. So God judges people by what they know. That is a principle that goes right through scripture. If a person does not know the ten commandments they will not be judged for breaking the ten commandments. If a person has never heard of Christ they will not be judged for not having heard of Christ, but everybody has some knowledge of God through creation outside them and conscience inside them, and God will judge everybody by what their own conscience knew and we all know inhumanity is wrong, don't we?

It did not take Christians to write the United Nations document, the Declaration of Human Rights. We know human rights, and it was because they rode over human rights that this was happening to them – that they conquered by force. That was how they expanded. It was like a blitzkrieg and they had chariots and they just rode over a country, slaughtered all the inhabitants and took it by force! God can give you more territory without you taking it by force. There is a right way to expand and a wrong way. But the other thing that he mentions particularly is that they were corrupted by finance. That is singled out: that when they became wealthy that corrupted them, and bribery became common, and it was these two things that Nahum said they knew were wrong for which God is destroying their city. I find those two things remarkable because our world is not a stranger to either and people know it is wrong. Thank God we live in a country where bribery is not too bad yet, but it is getting worse. When you go to a country and you can't get a driving licence or a passport without bribing everybody on the way into the office, you are glad to get back here. Those who travel know this. But that is what happened here: they conquered by force and they were corrupted by finance, and so, says Nahum, woe to this bloody city! As we have seen, the word "woe", unfortunately, has lost its meaning for us. It is a curse, a terrible word you should never use. I am afraid most often in our country we hear a parent say "Woe betide you if you do that again." Never say that to a child for you are cursing that child.

If you go to the Sea of Galilee, you say "Oh what a beautiful place." It is so beautiful that everybody loves it.

It is totally different from what it was in the time of Jesus' earthly ministry. There were 250,000 people living around the shores of Galilee, and in those days it was highly urbanised. Capernaum was a big fishing town; so was Bethsaida, and Chorazin. Where are these towns? Why is it that if you go there today you have to stay in Tiberias, which is the only town on the shores of Galilee? I will tell you why. It is because Jesus cursed all the other towns. He said: Woe to you Capernaum, woe to you Bethsaida, woe to you Chorazin, it is the mighty works that have been done in you; if they had been done in Tyre and Sidon they would have repented long ago. The only town he did not curse was Tiberias. The result is that Tiberias is still there but the others you can hardly find – just a few stones.

Woe to that bloody city – that is a terrible curse and Nahum pronounced it. What happened to Nineveh, less than a decade later, after Nahum pronounced that, all happened to the last detail and it has never been inhabited again. Let me paint a picture of it today. There is the great palace – there are owls and hedgehogs and wild beasts. That is all you can find there today. Nineveh has gone, never to be inhabited again. It was lost for centuries. Nobody knew where it was and in fact people doubted its existence until 1820, when an Englishman called Layard was tramping through the area and staying in the town on the west bank of the Tigris and he looked opposite and saw a pile of rubble. They did not know what it was, and he went over and after digging around he thought: I think I have found Nineveh – and he had. What happened to Nahum? He didn't go back home actually. You will find his tomb on the west bank of the Tigris today, and if you go they will point to the tomb and say that is where Nahum lies. So his tomb is on the opposite bank to that, and is still there, revered by the Arabs as one of the prophets.

Secondly, moving now from his activity to his integrity:

God is consistent. He is always the same. He does not change in character – a unique combination of justice and mercy. If you go to either of those too much and forget the other, you will get an unbalanced view of God. If you only think of God's justice you get too hard a view of God; if you only think of his mercy you get too soft a view of God, and in the one case there will be fear but no love, and in the other case there will be love but no fear. We need both, and the prophets really do balance wonderfully.

HABAKKUK

HABAKKUK

In the Old Testament we encounter prophets –they are all kinds of people from different backgrounds – different types who found themselves getting into a prophetic ministry. On those models we build our own understanding, because the only difference between the Old and the New Testament as regards the prophetic ministry is that in the New Testament there are going to be many more.

It is with this in mind that we are going to study the prophet Habakkuk. I am dying to meet him because as I have studied his work and got into his heart, I have felt very close to him. I believe by the end of this chapter you will feel you know him, and that when you spot him in glory you will say, "Why, that's Habakkuk" – and you will look forward to going over and shaking his hand.

So we start with a bit of introduction and then get into the first five verses. It is a very short book, only three little chapters, and therefore it has been described as one of the Minor Prophets. I do not like that term. To God all prophets are important, whether they speak a little or a lot. Even if God only gave you three words for somebody else, that is prophecy. You don't need to do it at length for fifty years as some of them did, or twenty-five years as Jeremiah did. There are some prophets in the Old Testament who only speak once, and then as far as we know, they disappear; but they have given a message from God. That is all a prophet is: someone who has heard a message and passes it on to the right people. It is such a simple ministry. You don't need to be theologically educated. You don't need to be a public speaker. In fact, God seems to entrust this ministry to those who don't have a gift of oratory. It is exciting to hear ordinary folk, who would never be able to get up into a pulpit and preach a sermon, hear from God and pass on a word from God.

Let us go back to Moses for example. Moses was a pretty major prophet. He said an awful lot that he heard from God, but we are told that Moses was scared to pass it on, at least when the message was for Pharaoh. Moses said, "I couldn't do that—I'm no speaker." God said: "All right Moses. You will not be the prophet to Pharaoh; Aaron will be your prophet." Now that is an interesting use of the term. Aaron's job as the prophet to Moses was very simple. All he had to do was to listen to what Moses said and if Moses said, "Let my people go," Aaron had to take that message – go to Pharaoh and say, "God says, 'let my people go.'" He didn't have to sit down and study it for hours. He didn't have to say, "Now how can I make this attractive to Pharaoh?" He didn't have to say, "Now I'll try and get three points out of that – "my people", let my people, "let my people go," and then find a good introduction, a good conclusion and some good illustrations to liven it up, and then go to Pharaoh and say, "Pharaoh, I've got a word from the Lord for you – my introduction, point one, point two...." That was not what Aaron had to do. To be a good prophet, the only thing Aaron had to do was to listen carefully to Moses and then speak carefully to Pharaoh, that's all.

That is a ministry within your reach. There is only one qualification you are going to need, and I will tell you what that is later. It is not only open to you – do you realise that God is longing to talk? He is wanting to talk to people today, but his frustration is that he can't get enough people to listen and then speak. He is looking for messengers, and Habakkuk was one of them. He was simply a man who heard something from God and passed it on. He was an ordinary man who never even intended to be a prophet. He did not expect it.

Now when you first read the book it strikes you that there are one or two unusual features about this as a prophecy. When you read chapter 1 you find that this man did most of his talking to God, not to people. We tend to think of a prophet as someone getting up in a public square and addressing the multitudes and haranguing the throngs, but in fact this man talked to God, and we are going to learn quite a lot from that. That is where it begins. A prophet is someone who is on speaking terms with God.

The second thing, when you read chapter 2 you notice something unusual about it. You find that when he delivered his message to the people he didn't speak it, and God has a multitude of ways of passing on the message. He wrote it. Have you ever considered that a prophetic ministry can consist of writing? In fact, Habakkuk had to write it up in great big letters on a poster on a hoarding so large that somebody running past could get the message.

It might be that somebody in advertising could become a prophet of God and put some things up on church notice boards. I have seen some snappy things put up. There was a vicar in Liverpool, for example, a little dynamo, a lovely man. He has a wooden fence alongside a motorway, so he goes out periodically with a pot of paint and a big brush. One Easter I remember he wrote up: "Jesus is dying to meet you", and then the authorities made him take that down. At Christmas he put up: "Santa Claus never died for anybody" in great big letters, and you know everybody going past that fence was getting the message. He was hearing something from God, and putting it up in big letters. Habakkuk did that. Have you got a garden fence? You may laugh, but somebody might take that seriously, because that is what Habakkuk did.

Then you read the chapter 3, and you find that it has to

be set to music. We should explore the connection between the prophetic ministry and music. There is a profound connection, which many Christian musicians have not yet seen – in fact very few have seen. We have seen the use of music in worship and in evangelism but very few have yet seen the prophetic ministry of music, and how to use their instruments and lyrics for a prophetic ministry to tell people what God is feeling and what God is saying now today. I am trying to encourage poets to get into a prophetic ministry, artists to get into a prophetic ministry – but that is another unusual feature of Habakkuk: he sets your feet a-dancing by the end. He doesn't begin there, far from it. He doesn't feel like dancing much at the beginning, but by the end he has really got you into it.

The book is unique and full of interest. It is a difficult one to translate. The translators tell me it is one of the hardest to get from Hebrew into English. There is one verse (3:9) where there are over one hundred possible different readings. Can you imagine a translator's job when he has to choose between them?

The Hebrew word "Habakkuk" either means a vegetable, which doesn't help me much—fancy calling your little child a vegetable; or else it means an embrace – well, that is a bit better. What kind of a job did he have? I don't know. Not a clue. One of God's nobodies, and God loves to use nobodies and confound the somebodies with them. He loves to take people who are nobody and really show the somebodies what he can do. That is why he took a little parlourmaid, Gladys Aylward, and took her out to China to show what he can do with a nobody. If you feel you are a nobody, you are probably well qualified for a prophetic ministry.

Then how did he get started? What are we looking for as we study this little book? Well we could say we are going to be looking at the different aspects of the prophetic ministry.

HABAKKUK

We shall look at prophetic prayer in chapter 1, at prophetic preaching in chapter 2 and prophetic praise in chapter 3. You see, the prophetic ministry can be a whole lot of things. It is related to so much, but I think my main interest in studying this is to ask not "How did the prophet get hold of his message" but, "How did God get hold of the prophet?" That is more interesting and more important, and I see that there was an amazing interchange between the Almighty and this nobody, whereby God first of all got hold of his mind. He made him think; he blew his mind. In fact, God said, "What I'm going to tell you, I haven't told you before because you wouldn't believe it anyway." He stretched his mind. He made him think about what was happening in his nation.

The second part of him that God got hold of was his will. God had to force him almost to do something about it. It is all very well to stay up in the thinking realm. I am afraid many people's interest in prophecy stays there. They read prophetic books, they buy all the latest sensational Christian literature on the end of the world and get the latest programme and timetable and all the details, because they are interested. God is saying, "What are you going to do about that? I don't want prophetic minds that are just wanting to explore the end of the world. I want prophetic wills that are going to act upon what you know." Then I see God pressing further to the citadel of this man, pressing on for his heart, touching his emotions, and if there is one thing God needs to do with many Christians, it is to get down to the heart. It is only eighteen inches from the head to the heart, but oh, what a long journey it is. He needs prophets who feel, prophets who can share his heart, prophets who know his anger, prophets who know his agony, prophets who share his joy and share his grief. We are going to see that by the end of these three chapters God has Habakkuk's mind, will and heart, and he has got a prophet.

There is only one helpful clue to the background that I want to deal with, and then we will go into the book itself. We can work out when this man was a prophet. Even if we don't know who he was, what he was, we can tell you when. If you think of somewhere around the year 600 BC, you are just about on, and that tells us quite a lot. He was a contemporary of Jeremiah, of Nahum and one or two others, yet, as far as we know, he did not have any contact with them.

The prophets seem to have been rather lonely people; they didn't have a lot to do with each other, almost as if they had to be loners with God. It tells us what kind of a background there was, what was happening in his situation, and the astonishing thing is that if you read what was happening in 600 BC it is like reading tomorrow's newspaper. I believe Habakkuk's message is absolutely right for our country. Around 600 BC what was happening internationally around that region of the then known world was this: the world was divided between two superpowers – to the west there was Egypt, to the east Assyria, and there had been a major struggle between these two powers, which was now quietening down and it looked as if it was going to be resolved. But on the international scene something else was happening which was complicating that picture and just beginning to raise questions: a new world superpower was emerging on the eastern side – Babylon. No one had yet really realised what it was going to mean, but people were beginning to talk and ask.

In the modern era the new power that is arising on the east is Islam. Since 1973 Islam is resurgent; it is militant, and all of us have the feeling that somehow this power is going to affect our lives deeply.

What was happening within the nation around 600 BC? Let me give you a bit of history. There had been a good king about twenty years previously, a boy king, called Josiah or

Josias. He had rediscovered in an old cupboard in the temple when they spring-cleaned, the book of God's law. When he read it he was horrified, and realised that unless there was a change, his nation over which he reigned was doomed. He really tried to reform the nation. He tried very hard to clean up their morals, to clean up their religious life, and he did it through the law. He imposed that reform on society, and he tried to make people good by legislation and it doesn't work. You can attain a certain temporary improvement in public behaviour, but you can't change people. It will not be permanent, and it will slip.

I fear that there are many Christians in our country today who are hoping that somehow the politicians and the police between them will clean up public morals. I beg you, read a little history. I hear Christians talking like this, "Why don't they clean up Britain? Why don't they pass stricter laws? Why don't the police do their job? Why don't the politicians wake up?" Let me say that more than an Act of Parliament is needed, and however much you press for the change of law, unless there is a change of heart accompanying it then the fate that came to Josiah's reform will come to any reform in this country.

I want to underline that. Let's take, for example, abortion. One baby every six minutes is being thrown into the incinerator, and that was a baby that God knew personally; that he was looking forward to enjoying, whose potential he knew, whose personality he knew. How does he feel about that? Well we have pressed for law changes. Even if we achieved a change in the law, that will not be enough because the change of heart would not be there. In a democracy, the law can only apply what the majority of people actually want.

So Josiah made the mistake of thinking that if he changed the law and imposed that, that this would straighten the situation out. Josiah was exactly the same age as Jeremiah

– they were contemporaries, and Jeremiah would have nothing to do with Josiah's reform. Have you ever noticed that? Because Jeremiah knew it was no use, and therefore he didn't support it. He just told the people that it was no use and why. Jeremiah was after a change of heart. He was after renewal, not reform. The result was, of course, that as soon as Josiah died the reform collapsed. In fact he was killed meddling in the great superpowers' struggle. He went to Armageddon and there he was killed by the Egyptians.

He was followed by a king, Jehoiakim, who was a pleasure-lover, who built himself a bigger palace, who was concerned not with the welfare of his people but with his own status; and because the ruler at the top was like this, everybody followed him. Everybody became concerned not with morals, but with status. An age of materialism set in, and everybody was after what they could get – an improved standard of living, more pleasure, more comfort, more things. Whenever that happens, you know the result: as material prosperity rises, moral character declines. It always happens.

In Habakkuk's day it had really happened, and the nation was in a sorry state. For one thing, the law was paralysed. It seemed as if law and order could not be maintained. People flouted the law if they could, and in fact, we are now in our country in a situation where crime actually pays. Did you know that? Most crimes are not now solved, so in fact, you have more than a fifty-fifty chance of getting away with it; it pays. This had all kinds of effects in society for Habakkuk's day. There was exploitation; might was right; if you were strong you got away with it, and the people who couldn't defend themselves were trampled down. But the one thing that became characteristic of society in his day, which he talks about most was that it became a violent society. You could not walk the streets at night. Mugging was common. Robbery in broad daylight was common. Violence was the feature of his society. Whenever God withdraws his Spirit from any country, any nation, any society, the one thing that will appear is violence. Read Genesis 6, where God was just grieved that he ever made man. He got sick of the whole business and he withdrew his Spirit from them and said, "My Spirit isn't going to struggle with you forever." Do you know what happened? Almost the next verse: "Violence filled the earth."

There are places in London where you cannot walk alone at night. This is happening here, and it is spreading. That is what Habakkuk found in his nation. Does all this sound strangely familiar? It is familiar because it's part of real life.

How do you really feel about the state of our nation? How deeply does it upset you? How burdened are you? How concerned are you, or do you try to keep it out of your mind as much as possible? Do you find in your religion, in your spiritual activity, a kind of recharging centre that enables you to go right into that world and to face it, or do you find your spiritual activity an escape from that world so that you can forget its pressures?

Habakkuk was a man who felt this so deeply that his spirit cried out about it, and he cried out not to the people, but first of all to God. That is how his prophetic ministry began. The frustration he felt, the burden he felt, the anger he felt, the anxiety he felt, the insecurity he felt – he cried out to God. He says, "God, how long? How long are you going to let this go on?" That is when his prophetic ministry was born.

Just an angry, frustrated man giving God an earful – that is how it began. Let us look at his prayer. He dares to criticise God. He dares to shout at God: what do you think you are doing? Why are you tolerating all this? Why are you doing nothing about it?

As I mentioned earlier, the prophet is on speaking terms with God. That means that he is prepared to tell God whatever is in his heart, and if there is one virtue in Habakkuk's prayer it is that it was an honest prayer. I want to encourage you to be honest with God. Tell him exactly how you feel – about him too. He can take it. Argue with God, yes, argue with him. I warn you that you will not win the argument. Habakkuk didn't, but he argued. Do you know, I almost feel that God is longing for a prayer that will be bold enough really to tell him what we think of him; really to challenge him; really to call on him and to cry to him. I think God responds to someone who hammers at him. He really does. He can take it, and he would rather you did that than give him polite prayers that are not really honest.

I had a lovely letter recently from Zimbabwe from an elderly lady who had been listening to some tapes of messages of mine. She wrote this letter. She said, "Twenty years ago I had a very nasty car accident, and it left me completely crippled and in real pain. I could struggle around on sticks, but then three years ago the doctor told me I would be completely helpless and I would need to be looked after, and he said I would be in a wheelchair. I was just so angry." She was alone—she had no one to look after her. She went home and she determined to end it all. So she got together all her drugs and all her pills, and it was midnight, and before she ended it all she decided to tell God exactly what she thought of him. She said, "I cursed God for three hours. I told him exactly what I thought." She said, "Every promise in the Bible I could remember I threw in his face and said, 'It's not true, it's not true. You don't mean it.'" For three hours she cursed God, from midnight until three am. Then she went to get the pills and whether she tripped and fell or whether she fainted, she doesn't know, but she fell across the bed unconscious.

When she woke up, it was so bright that she was sure she had died and was facing God and facing his glory. She was scared stiff, remembering that her last part of life had been cursing God for three hours. She was frightened, and then she realised that she could feel her hands, and she felt the rest of her body and it was pretty solid. She realised that it was the sunlight streaming in through the bedroom window, and so she thought, "Well, but I feel so different. Why?" She stood up and realized she had no more pain, so she ran around the bedroom and realised she could run. So she ran out of the house and she ran down to the shops, and she told everybody at the shops. Then she ran to a doctor and she ran into the surgery, and he said, "My, you're looking lively this morning!"

She said, "The Lord has healed me," and the doctor said, "Hallelujah!"

She wrote to me three years later, to tell me that she was without pain, running around at eighty-four. It was the result of cursing God for three hours. Isn't God amazing?

You see, you don't need to be correct in your prayer, you need to be real, and Habakkuk says, "God, how long are you going to let this go on? How long are you going to let our nation slide like this? How long are you going to make me watch injustice? How much longer do I have to cry to you? How much longer do I have to pray? How long, how long, how long? All I can see is violence everywhere. Lord, what are you doing? Why do you tolerate wrong?" That is his exact phrase: "Why are you tolerating it?"

That is real prayer, isn't it? God can take it right on the chin, and God can give as good as he gets – even better. But God responded to that man because he was a man who was really burdened for his country, who was angry about it, who was frustrated; who couldn't understand why God did nothing about it. The real truth was, as we shall see, that in fact God is usually much more tolerant than his people. Have you ever noticed that? God is much more patient than

I am. Martin Luther once said, "If I'd been God, I'd have kicked the whole world to pieces centuries ago." Have you ever felt like that?

We are so intolerant that we say, "Lord, why don't you do something about all this? Why don't you stop the crime? Why don't you stop all these dreadful things happening?" Sometimes I think the Lord wants to say: I had to tolerate quite a lot in you, you know, and if I had acted as soon as you went wrong you wouldn't even be praying to me now.

Habakkuk was honest. His prayer was intercessory prayer. He was praying for the nation – burdened by it. One of the hopeful signs in our day is the growth in intercession for the nation. Have you noticed that?

It was importunate prayer, in that it was hammering at God, and we can refer to the teaching of Jesus. In parable after parable he said: go on hammering at the door of heaven; you will get it; go on asking and you will receive; go on knocking and the door will be opened; go on seeking and you will find.

There is a truth there that we need to know, and Habakkuk had kept on, but above all he was offering what I want to call interrogatory prayer. Do you know what I mean by that? I mean asking God questions: Why God? How long God? What are you going to do about it God?" – and believing you will get an answer. The phrase "answered prayer" needs a little understanding. Too often it means, if somebody says, "You know, my prayer was answered," they mean they got a result. That is not what the Bible means by answered prayer. By "answered prayer" in the Bible it means: when you get a reply. It is not the result that answers your prayer; it is the reply, and interrogatory prayer expects a reply.

Habakkuk was asking questions. God replied, and the reply made Habakkuk into a prophet. Have you ever tried asking God questions and going on asking until you get a reply? The reply could make you a prophet, because what God says will be the message that he wants passed on.

Read Habakkuk to 2:3
For three years I was an RAF chaplain. What happened was, when a new intake of men came in to the RAF, the Church of England grabbed about eighty percent of them, the Roman Catholics got quite a portion of what was left, and the ragtag and bobtail came to me. So I was chaplain to Methodists, Baptists, Presbyterians, Congregational, Salvation Army, Brethren, Quakers, Muslims, Hindus, agnostics, atheists— the lot. Whenever a man arrived with his new card for the chaplain to sign, and I noticed in the top right-hand corner that he had registered as an atheist, there were three things I always had to say to him. First of all I said, "Look, I want to shake your hand. You have got more faith than I have. I really believe that it takes more faith to believe that nothing turned into something by chance, and that something became all that there is now, again by chance." So I used to congratulate him on his faith.

The second thing was that as his chaplain I promised him that if he died in active service under my care, which was a possibility in that theatre, I promised him that I would bury him without a single prayer, without any hymns, without any reading from the Bible. I promised: "I will announce to the mourners that you are dead – finished, and there is no God and no heaven, nothing at all." It is amazing how many atheists get shaken by that, you know. It is all right living as one, but dying as one is a very different matter.

But the third thing I used to say to them was this: "Now sit down and tell me what kind of a God you don't believe in," and usually at the end of that I could say, "Let's shake on it. I don't believe in that kind of a God either." Never condemn an atheist until you find out what kind of a God he was told to believe in. It is not whether you believe in God that matters, it is what kind of a God you do or don't believe in – that is what matters. I don't really care whether you say, "I believe in God." My question would be, "What kind of a God do you believe in?"

There were two men on the bridge of a ship crossing the Atlantic on a beautiful moonlit night, stars out, calm sea, and somebody said to the captain: "You know, it's easy to believe in God on a night like this."

The captain replied, "Yes, I believe in a God on a night like this – a God who's as cold as that sea and as far away as those stars."

The majority of the people of this land are now operating without a God framework, without an awareness of God. The real problem is not atheism. There are very few atheists, and when I meet a genuine one I find he is quite easy to talk to. He has thought things through; he is prepared to argue.

There are other positions which are more dangerous. Some belong to a philosophy called agnosticism, which simply means "I don't know", and I have the feeling that nowadays it also means "I don't care either".

There is a philosophy around which is the most dangerous of all to our faith and it is called "deism". Deism believes in God, but has no relationship to him. Deism says, "There is a God somewhere. There is an old man upstairs somewhere who made all this; who created it all, but who no longer controls it; who has nothing to do with it now. He is a long way away, and we have got to live without him. We have got to get on to the best of our ability with life as it is. God may exist, but he is not part of the scene.

Years ago, that deism was applied to nature and people said: God may have made nature, but now it carries on without him. It carries on according to rigid laws of cause and effect, which scientists can discover and then manipulate but

God is no longer involved in what he has created. Therefore miracles cannot happen because nature operates without God and God cannot do anything in nature; he is away up there. Charles Darwin was a deist. He believed in God, he mentions God on the last page of his book *Origin of Species*, but it is a God who made it all and wound it all up and then left it to operate without him.

In our day, the deism that has gripped people inside as well as outside church has not only ruled God out of nature, even though God made nature, but rules God out of history. It says that God may have started the whole of history off, but now history operates without him. God is not involved. History operates according to social laws, political laws, economic laws. Therefore the task of the politician is not to seek God, but to find out the economic laws that will cure inflation and unemployment, and to manipulate those laws so that we can bring prosperity back. Our government in this country is more concerned with the economic laws than the spiritual and moral laws, yet our prosperity does not depend on the economic laws; it depends on the spiritual and moral ones. But if you are a deist, then you may believe in God; you may like some of our politicians, go to church on Sunday; you may say prayers; you may sing hymns, but God is still away up there, not involved in what is happening down here. Society has to get along without him.

That philosophy is more dangerous than atheism and agnosticism. The philosophy of the Bible is called "theism" and theism says, "God not only exists; God not only created all as it is, but God is in full control of it all." He is directly involved with every aspect of life. His intentions and his emotions are the primary factors in what happens.

If you study nature and come to the conclusion there are certain laws of nature, those laws are nothing other than God's habits, and God can change his habits any time he wishes. If you discover economic laws in society you are only discovering God's habits. Thank God he has habits otherwise we wouldn't be able to survive in a world when we would not know what temperature water boiled at or anything. God has habits and he sticks to them, but he can also override them at any time he wishes – that is the philosophy of theism.

Now of the four philosophies I've mentioned: atheism, agnosticism, deism and theism, it is theism that has the big problems. If you are a theist, you have got the questions, because if I dare to say, "God is running England at this time, God is running the world right now, God is responsible for everything that you read about in your daily newspaper" I have got real problems, real questions. I then have to try to understand what God is doing. As I read the news headlines, I have got ask, "Why did God let that happen?"

If you are a real theist you have the kind of problems that Habakkuk had. "God, if you're really in charge, if you're really controlling this nation's affairs, why do you tolerate what is happening? Why do you let it go on?" Now you have no problem if God is staying up in heaven and has left us to get on with it by ourselves; but if God is actually in charge, if you're a theist (and if you believe in the Bible you've got to be a theist because that's the biblical outlook), nothing happens except by divine permission or authority.

Well here are two texts. One is from Amos: "Did I not bring Israel up from Egypt?" None of us have problems with that because there is God redeeming his people. But what follows is: "Did I not bring Israel from Egypt? ... And did I not bring the Philistines from Crete?" When did you last hear a preacher mention that? We have all heard from preachers who bring the Israelites over the Jordan and into the Promised Land, but when did they mention that at the same time, into the same land, God brought the Philistines from Crete? What on earth do you think you're doing, God? You bring your people into the land flowing with milk and honey, and at the same time you bring the Philistines from Crete into the same place, and they are going to have three hundred years of problems as a result. But that is the God of the Bible. He is not just the God of his own people; he is the God of all peoples. He is, as Jeremiah calls him, the God of all nations, the God of all mankind; is anything too hard for the Lord? I want you to get a really big view of God: the God of all the nations; the theistic God of the Bible; the God who is in control of Britain, and Israel and all nations. This is the God we are worshipping.

Then we look at a text from the New Testament, just so that you don't think that once we move into the Christian portion of the Bible we leave this concept behind. Many Christians seem to think that now God isn't even interested in Israel anymore, just the church. Forget it. This is what Paul says at Athens, preaching on Mars Hill: "From one man he made every nation of men that they should inhabit the whole earth, and he determined the times set for them and the exact places where they should live." Now that is a God who decides how much room in time and space every nation has – that is the God of all mankind. It is against that background that we have the problems of asking why God does not do some of the things you would expect him to, and why he does do some of the things you would not expect him to do.

The theist has these problems, and Habakkuk is a theist. So his problem was: God, why are you doing nothing about the state of our nation? It is declining morally as it prospers materially. This troubles Habakkuk. How much longer can you cope with letting this happen? That is the cry of many a heart in England that is really sensing what is happening. "God, how much longer can you be patient with our country? We've had freedom from invasion for nearly a thousand years. How much longer can we expect to escape what almost every other country in the world has experienced? Lord, how much longer are you going to watch the foundations of our society destroyed?"

Do you know what the foundation of our society is? When King Alfred wrote the first English laws, he set at their head the Ten Commandments, and then he developed them into English law, and that has been for all these centuries the foundation of our social life, our security, all that we take for granted. You can sum up the Ten Commandments in one word – respect: respect for God, respect for his name, respect for his day, respect for your parents, respect for life, respect for marriage, respect for reputation, respect for property. When the foundations are destroyed it's the respect that goes.

If I pick out three illustrations, just three examples almost from random, this will help you to understand. Take respect for property: that is written into a healthy society. "Thou shall not steal." The bill for shoplifting is huge. Respect for marriage. The effect of divorce is appalling. The result will be terrible. There are parts of inner cities where over half the children do not know normal family life and will never have two parents to look to in the house. The one that is missing is dad. How will they ever come to understand God as Father if they have never known one?

Respect for life: it is almost too easy to raise the abortion thing, and we are almost becoming immune to it but, as I have said, it means that one human every six minutes is being murdered. We have already murdered more children now than lives lost during World War II.

I want to tell you something else. Some of you will remember the debate on capital punishment and the humanists pulled the wool over our eyes and we thought that abolishing capital punishment was motivated by a high evaluation of human life. It was nothing of the kind. It was motivated by a low evaluation, and it is no coincidence that the abolition of capital punishment led within a few years to widespread abortion. Both were due to the same movement. If you abolish capital punishment, it means you are devaluing the life of the victim and murder becomes no more serious than theft, but to God it is in a different category altogether. When we devalue human life – when we no longer regard a life as so sacred that if a man takes that life wilfully then he deserves to lose his own; as soon as we have devalued that then it happens all down the line and you must be aware that infanticide and euthanasia are already on our doorstep.

In the light of all this we ask: God, how long can you cope with this? How much longer are you going to let us get away with it? How much longer can you stand the stench of England in your nostrils? Why aren't you dealing with it? Why aren't you doing something about it? You're in charge; you're in control of history! Why are you letting it go on?" Habakkuk is crying out just like that and God comes back at Habakkuk and is glad he is arguing with him.

Let us see what God says to Habakkuk. What condescension of God to enter into an argument with this man, to respond to his implied rebuke and criticism, but God can take it and God in his grace will respond to someone who will stand up to him in honesty and reality. God says five things by way of rebuke to Habakkuk. First, Habakkuk's eyes may be opened, but they are not wide open enough so he is missing the real meaning. Habakkuk should not just be looking at one nation; he should be watching the nations. Then he would see what God is doing.

If you have tunnel vision—if you only look at your nation, your people, your denomination, those immediately concerned with you, then you will miss what God is doing. God paints on a big canvas. God is the God of all mankind, and to understand what he is going to do with your nation, your people, you need to understand what he is doing with all the nations. Habakkuk, watch the nations – not just the nation but the nations. It is alas true of Christians in our nation, as in any other, that we can get preoccupied with looking at our own nation and lose the world view. The world view will give us God's perspective on where we are in his purposes.

The second thing is this: Habakkuk is in for a big surprise. He needs to get ready to be amazed, to be shattered. So often we have God tied in a little box and we expect his answers to fit in with our petty thinking, but get ready to be surprised if you ask God questions.

Third rebuke to Habakkuk: God has planned to do something about the state of his nation in his lifetime, so he is to stop telling God he is doing nothing. God is going to do something and Habakkuk will see it.

Rebuke number four: "I have not told you what I'm going to do because you wouldn't believe it anyway." Poor old Habakkuk. What a rebuke, and so often God cannot share his secrets with us because we would not believe it. He cannot tell us what he is going to do as he wants to for, as Amos says, God does nothing without revealing it first to his prophets. He always gives warning; he always gives notice to his people if they are listening and if they can believe it, but when he knows that they are not going to believe it, he doesn't say.

The fifth rebuke is: I have already started doing it and you have missed it. I am raising up the Babylonians. God was under no illusions about the Babylonians. He told Habakkuk: I know exactly what they are like; they are ruthless; they are cruel. God uses picture after picture of beasts and birds of prey, wolves, leopards and eagles. He is saying: I know what they do; I know they come charging into a country. They laugh at fortified cities. They build a ramp. They come in.

I know what they do. They plunder property. They deport people. They are a ruthless, cruel nation.

God makes two statements about them which are pretty tough. One: he knows that they are a law to themselves. They acknowledge no authority other than their own. They are the very embodiment of lawlessness, which is to be totally a law to yourself. Babylon has always been that. Babel always was that. Babylon, throughout the Bible from beginning to the book of Revelation, stands for men who are a law to themselves – who acknowledge no law above theirs. The other thing that God says about them is that they are guilty men whose own strength is their god. Babylon wasn't the last nation to be like that.

Habakkuk is absolutely shattered at this answer. He has been crying out to God: why don't you do something? Now when God says this is what he is doing, the prophet's response is: but God, you can't do that! Isn't it amazing how fickle we are when we argue with God? We first of all say, "God you're doing nothing," and then when he tells us what he is doing, we say, "But God, you can't do that." Our little minds – we have already decided the answer to our own prayers in so many cases. We have already settled how God should act in response. We know what he should do – so we think. Then when he does what he thinks, we complain again, and Habakkuk plunges into a second argument with God.

It is pathetic and yet when you look into your own heart, it is so like your own prayers. "God, I pray and I pray. Give me more patience," and so the Lord puts you in a really tough situation that day, to give you more patience. How do you think he is going to give it to you without letting you get into a real problem? You know, somebody told me actually they had prayed for more patience and then the next day they had forgotten to set the alarm, so they got up late. They had to rush breakfast. They ran to the station and saw the train just pulling out. They got to the office behind time. Everything seemed to go wrong. "And I just prayed for more patience, and look what God did to me the next day." This was the person's reaction.

But God knows what he is doing. After all, he is God, and if there is one thing Habakkuk needs to remember in these early arguments with the Almighty it is: God is God. He is not the chief butler who we can just call and say, "Do this." He is God. It is not our place to tell him what to do; it is his place to tell us what he is going to do. Poor old Habakkuk has not learned this and so he plunges into this second phase of the argument.

Now he is arguing from the opposite point of view: God, you shouldn't be doing this. And he builds up his argument very carefully. Let me spell it out so that you have got it. He starts from three premises, two of which are true and the third is false, but he doesn't realise that. Often we argue with God from a mixture of true and false premises.

Premise number one: If you are an everlasting God, then you couldn't exterminate your people. Now that is a good argument and it is true. If God is everlasting, and puts his hand on a nation or a people, then the everlasting God must ensure that those people survive. That is the reason that Israel has survived to this day, because it is an everlasting God who put his hand on them. That is the secret for their return to the atlas after an absence of nearly two thousand years. Habakkuk is saying: "You can't bring the Babylonians. They have wiped out nation after nation. You are an everlasting God and we are your people. You couldn't let them wipe us out. Now that is a good argument.

The second argument he uses is this: that a righteous God must punish. That is true. A righteous God must discipline, and so Habakkuk accepts that God needs to discipline the nation of Israel.

Now comes his third argument, which is false: "O God, you are of purer eyes than to behold iniquity." That is not true. I have heard it quoted in many prayers; I have heard it quoted by many preachers, and they have all quoted it as if it is true, but it is not true. It is something Habakkuk is saying to twist God's arm.

Let us get the meaning of it first. It does not mean (as I used to think) that God was so pure that in fact, when he saw something evil he had to shut his eyes or turn his head away from it. The word "behold" in Hebrew means "to gaze, to stand and look at something" without doing anything about it. "O God, you are too pure not to have a go. You are too pure to watch something going on and not get in there and stop it." Now we are not that pure, it is true. I am afraid there are things that we can watch going on without doing anything about it, but Habakkuk is saying: God, I do not believe that you could stand and watch the Babylonians come and destroy our country and do nothing about it. I just don't believe you could bring yourself to do it. You are too pure. You couldn't do that. Lord, I challenge you; I defy you. You're going to bring the Babylonians – you couldn't. It is not in your nature to do that. You couldn't stand by and watch that happen to this land. In fact, the truth was that God could stand by and watch, and that in fact he did.

We have got to come to terms with a God who is so patient that he can stand by and watch and not act immediately. Praise God that he is that patient. Praise God that he is that tolerant, but Habakkuk is trying to paint God as less tolerant than he actually is, and he is trying to twist his arm. So he then goes on to say: therefore from my three premises, there are two things that I want to tell you, God. First, in saying you will use the Babylonians, you are using an immoral means, and I don't believe a moral God can do that. Secondly, I believe that you are actually going to produce an immoral end by using them. Do you know one of the most difficult things for God's people to understand is that God can use people who are not his people to teach his people a lesson? Do you find that easy?

People say they find difficulty understanding one of Jesus' parables in Luke 16, the parable of the unjust steward. How could the Lord use a crook, a criminal, to teach a lesson to his people? Where is the problem? It is no problem, that parable, and it is a very simple, straightforward lesson. That crook had two values right in his life. First, he valued people more than things, and second, he valued the future more than the present, and he acted on both those values. As Jesus said, "The children of darkness are often wiser in their generation than children of light," therefore we can learn a great deal from the children of darkness; we don't have a monopoly on shrewdness.

We can't bear the thought that God would use somebody who is not even part of his people and somebody who is morally worse than we are to correct us. Some Christians can have this attitude when they are stopped for speeding by a policeman, "He's not even a believer!" We don't say this, we just sort of feel it inside. "I'm nearer to God than he is, and why should he stop me for speeding? I'm sure I live a better life than he does. I'm sure I'm nearer to the Lord than he is," but the Lord has sent that policeman along to you as a minister. That is the word used in Romans 13 of the government and the authorities – they are ministers of God. So next time you are stopped say, "I'm sorry, Reverend. You're a minister of God to me, and you've stopped me behaving dangerously to other people. Thank you." That is a different attitude, isn't it?

Lord, you're going to bring the Babylonians? Don't you realise they are ten times worse than we are? How could you watch the wicked destroy those more righteous than themselves? – says Habakkuk. How could you do it? I know we are bad and I admit we deserve punishment, but how could you use them to punish us? It's not moral. The end will not be moral any more than the means.

I will tell you what will result, says Habakkuk. Don't you realise that it is like a fisherman with a net with great hooks? They simply outfish the waters. They don't leave anything behind. Where the Babylonians have fished, there are no fish left, and they even worship their nets. They live in luxury and they simply take everything. Wherever the Babylonians go, there is nothing left and the sea of nations is empty. So Habakkuk is saying: God, you really don't know what you are doing.

Then comes the little bit at the beginning of chapter 2. Habakkuk, in his failure to understand God – in his argument with God – says that he is going to get up on the walls and watch. It is as though he is daring God to bring the Babylonians – calling his bluff. Now the commentaries I have read have so spiritualised 2:1 that Habakkuk got into a really holy mood and wanted to be near heaven and climbed up a tower and was going to pray. In fact, v. 1 is full of "I": "I will stand at my watch and station myself on the ramparts. I will look to see what he will say to me. In other words: let's really see: right, God, I've given you an argument – let's see if you can cope with that one; you dare to bring the Babylonians. I can see Habakkuk standing up there with his arms folded on the ramparts watching the horizon: you're going to bring the Babylonians, are you? I dare you. It is a defiant attitude. It is a man who cannot accept that God knows what he's doing. It is a man standing, arguing with God. My explanation of what God is communicating to this angry man is that Habakkuk is in the wrong place. Why is he up there watching from the ramparts? Why is he not down there, telling the people the Babylonians are coming? Did the prophet think that God revealed this to him so that he could satisfy his curiosity or win an argument? Had he been told they were coming so that he could get up on the top of the wall and defy God to do it? God had told Habakkuk so that he could do something about it. It was a time for action, not argument. God had told the prophet's mind what he was going to do, but now wanted his will. He wanted him to do something about it. If God tells the prophet what he is going to do, it is in order that the prophet may do something.

There was a remarkable prophecy that came from Russia, from the godly monk Seraphin in 1911.

An evil will shortly take Russia, and wherever this evil comes, rivers of blood will flow. This evil will take the whole world and wherever it goes, rivers of blood will flow because of it. It is not the Russian soul, but it is an imposition on the Russian soul. It is not an ideology or a philosophy, but a spirit from Hell. In the last days, Germany will be divided in two. France will be just nothing. Italy will be judged by natural disasters. Britain will lose her empire and all her colonies and will come to almost total ruin, but will be saved by praying women. America will feed the world, but will finally collapse. Russia and China will destroy each other. Finally Russia will be free, and from her believers will go forth and turn many from the nations to God.

That was said in 1911 and it was brought out from Russia by a nun, Mother Barbara, who lived on the Mount of Olives. Isn't that an astonishing word? But why do you think God would tell us this? In order that we might say, "We know what's going to happen. We've got the secrets. We know it all," or in order that we might argue with God and say, "God, we don't agree with this. We don't think this is the right way to do it. We don't think this is the answer, that you should evangelise the world with believers from Russia." By the way, isn't that an exciting thought? God is really getting his church ready where people are learning to live very close to Jesus.

It may not suit our preconceived notions, but why should God reveal these things to us? So that we can be in the know? So that we can have something better than the astrologer can produce? No, it is so that we might do something about it. "Habakkuk, get back down into those streets and write the message up in big letters."

Secondly, Habakkuk has the time wrong and thought God was going to wait some time. There was a time appointed for the Babylonian invasion and it would not be delayed a single day. If it lingered, that was not because God had forgotten or changed his mind but because there was a time.

You know, one of the things that I think we get most wrong is that our timing is so short and God's is so long. God takes not only the larger view, being the God of all mankind; he takes the longer view, because he is the God of all history. A thousand years is like a day to him, and to him it has only been a couple of days since Jesus was crucified.

This is my simple burden for you: God knows what he is doing. I don't know how much longer he can be tolerant of what is happening in this land. When you consider all that God has done for our country – all that he has invested among us. He brought us the gospel of Jesus within thirty years of Jesus dying on the cross and rising again, and we have had it ever since. The first martyr for the faith was a Roman soldier called Albinus, St Aubin. He was one of those who brought us the truth to set us free. God has put a church or a chapel building within walking distance of 97% of the population of this land, and given us more clergy than doctors per head of population, and given us so many versions of the Bible in English we hardly know which one to use. How do you think he feels now? There was a day when this country was the major exporter of the truth, and sent more men and money overseas to bring the good news of Jesus than any other nation in the world. That has now passed over the Atlantic to America. I believe the signs are already on the wall that God is going to deliver us into the hands of our enemies unless we hear.

So my last word is this: God did not send the renewal to us for our sake. He did it because he still loves this country and because he still wants to have mercy on it. He did it because he wanted to turn the church inside out, that he might turn the world upside down, or rather right way up. He did it so that he would have a body of people whose prime concern would not be their own prayer, their own healing, their own body, but whose prime concern would be to get up there and write it in big letters for the nation to see – that God is still rich in mercy and longs to save us before it is too late. Unless the renewal movement hears that and does that, then we shall finish where the Welsh revival finished, with repetitive singing, and all over the country the renewal shows the danger of that. While we sing our little choruses, a nation that God has loved goes down the drain.

Read Habakkuk 2:4–end

One of the names used for some prophets in the Old Testament is "seer"– a prophet not only who hears and speaks but sees. This is not a full definition; it is only a description. A prophet is someone who sees things from God's point of view. I am afraid that kind of vision is extremely rare nowadays.

The 1970s was called by a philosopher the "me decade", when we all saw things from our point of view. That outlook has got right into Christians. We are told not to be conformed to this world, but we are always doing it. That was the decade in which we all wanted to know how this would affect *me*. Even in renewal our main question can be: I want this blessing – what is in it for me?

But the prophet is the person who sees things from God's point of view. He doesn't think that God is there to meet my needs; I am here to bring God what he wants. It is a totally different point of view. Since God is seeking in these days a prophetic people in England, he is looking for men and women and young people who will say: "God, let me see things from your point of view; let me hear what you are thinking; let me feel what you are feeling in your heart. Share with me the secrets of the intentions of your will. But Lord, you have made me sit in heavenly places with Christ Jesus, then let me see things from there, please. Give me your perspective; let me see things your way. That is what the renewal was all about, to create a prophetic people who would not be preoccupied with their own needs and their own problems and their own desires, but who would be so preoccupied with God that they would see things from his point of view. They would be a prophetic people who saw.

Where that vision is missing then the people perish, or as the NIV puts it much better and more truly to the Hebrew: Where there is no revelation the people cast off restraint. Where people do not see things from God's point of view, then they live carelessly. That is one of God's statements and analysis of history, which I think should be written over our country right now: where there is no revelation, the people cast off restraint. Where they do not see things from God's point of view but only from theirs, even in religion, then they will live carelessly.

Habakkuk began his prayer life with God by being very honest about how he saw things. He said, "How long, Lord, are you going to make me go on looking at this scene?" He then told God what he saw: violence; a law that was paralysed; increasing disorder in society – he saw all that and he told God what he saw. Before he could be a prophet,

God had to change his outlook until Habakkuk saw what God saw and looked from God's point of view.

In chapters 1 and 2 we see gradually how Habakkuk was changed around, and how God was telling the prophet that he was looking at things the wrong way. Habakkuk says, "I'm going to stand on my watch and I am going to look to see. What he expected to see was his outlook, but God replied. Then God said: "Habakkuk, see...." Then 2:4 begins with that little word, "See" or "Behold". It is a very important word in scripture. There is an awful lot of it, and it means: get God's point of view, have a good look.

Now when you look at things from God's point of view, two things will happen to your outlook. My grandfather, if he was asked by a child to sign an autograph book, used to write: "When the outlook is bad, try the up-look." But we are going to try the "down-look", even when the outlook is bad. The two dimensions that come into your viewpoint are these: first of all, you will get a larger view in space and secondly, you will get a longer view in time, because that is how God sees things.

The first point we have already covered. Habakkuk had tunnel vision and he told the Lord what he saw in his nation. God let Habakkuk know that he should be watching the nations instead of just looking at his little patch – Israel; get a bigger view, get a larger view in space and see that God is the God of the nations. Then he would begin to understand what God was doing with his nation, when he saw the context.

In our day when mass media brings the world to us, when we have instant communication of anything that happens around the world, of all people we Christians should not have tunnel vision. We should get the larger view constantly. We should see God as God of all the nations. The prophet Isaiah, when he began his ministry, had a vision. It was a very limited one. It was of himself and his own people. He saw the holiness of God and he said, "Woe is me. I'm a man of filthy speech and I dwell in the midst of a people of filthy speech." That was the vision that got him going, but Isaiah had to get a bit bigger vision than that if he was going to be God's prophet. In Isaiah 40 he got the larger vision and that is why the chapters after Isaiah 40 are usually so much deeper and more helpful to us than the chapters before – because he got the larger vision and he saw the bigness of God, who names the stars, and to whom the nations are a drop in the bucket – just the dust on his scales. Getting the larger view, then all those amazing chapters that come after chapter 40 were possible.

In 1972 I took our church through the book of Daniel. Through that book, we were trying to get the larger view of God's purposes with the nations. There were two things that were said then to which I want to draw your attention. The first was when I said: "The next world power will be the Arabs and their oil." In 1973 they discovered that power and they flexed their muscles and then we were living under that cloud. To understand what's happening here, you need to be watching the Middle East very carefully; get the larger view. The other thing I dared to say in 1972 was this – when the Shah [of Persia] celebrated the 2,500th anniversary of his empire [and our own royal family went to celebrate it with him] – "the Shah will be overthrown and lose the throne of Persia because he gave himself the title on that celebration, 'King of kings'." That only belongs to Jesus. I did not know that seven years would pass before he would lose his throne. Suddenly, everything would be gone. He died far from home, having been in exile in many countries. But you see, you get the longer view. That was just seven years to fulfilment, but that is the blink of an eye to God.

Just as you need the larger view in space, of a God who is God of all nations and to whom the nations are a drop in the bucket and you are like grasshoppers, so you need the longer view in which God takes his time. After all, he has all eternity to fulfil his purposes. That is usually the answer to our questions about apparent injustice: get the longer view. Take Psalm 73, which is primarily about God's judgment of individuals. Here the psalmist is nearly thrown off balance; his faith nearly collapses. He says, "God, I can't cope with it. The wicked are healthy and wealthy. They even die peacefully in bed and here am I – I have cleansed my heart in vain. I have tried to live a good life and they get away with it and I am suffering and I am having troubles and I am in pain." On the short view, life is totally unjust and unfair.

Then the psalmist says: "Then I went into the sanctuary of God and I understood their end. I saw where ultimately they were heading and I saw you put them on a very slippery slope and they will not be able to stop sliding down it until they are in utter ruin." He got the longer view. If your view is confined to this life only, then life is terribly unjust. Where is a moral God, if you look at this life only? Because wicked people get away with it right to their deathbed. When they are dead, people look on their corpse and say, "Look at that face; aren't they in peace?" It is nothing more than the physical relaxation of the face muscles on death. But the psalmist got the long view. "Whom have I in heaven besides you on earth? I have got you and you will receive me afterward into glory." He has the long view now, and now he sees. Oh God, thank you; you are a just God. Everything is going to be right because, God, you are right.

When you get that long view, instead of saying, "Oh dear, isn't life unfair to me, all these problems," you say, "This momentary light affliction works an exceeding weight of glory." You are getting the longer view. The "Me Decade" lived on the short-term view – the instant. Everything we want instantly. But God is not an instant God. "The mills of

God grind slowly, but they grind exceeding small."

This was Habakkuk's problem. He had a problem about a righteous God allowing the Babylonians to come and wipe out the Israelites. He couldn't cope with that because he did not have a long enough view. He said: God, you couldn't stand and watch that happening; you're too pure to let that happen – but God could stand and watch it happen because he takes the longer-term view.

Twenty-one civilisations have risen and fallen in history. It has taken time for them to rise, time for them to plateau, and time for them to fall. But God's moral laws have operated on every civilisation that has arisen. The graph of their rise and their plateau and their fall is identical in every case. If you want to know where western civilisation is, it is now well down the slope. There is nothing now can save western civilisation. It is another civilisation that is on the way out. I find it rather difficult just to think about that and realise I am part of a dying civilisation. My children grew up in a dying civilisation and there is nothing can stop it.

God's laws cannot be broken. You have never broken a single one of the Ten Commandments; they will break you, but you will never break them. History is *his* story and just as individuals may appear to get away with it, right to their deathbed – there may appear to be no God of righteousness as you look around at individual lives – if you get the longer view then their story is his story. They have not broken a single commandment. The truth is that no individual gets away with a single thing because God is God. Because he doesn't send his bills in every Friday that does not mean that anybody has got away with anything, nor do nations get away with anything. They may think they have done, but God's laws cannot be broken by nations or individuals.

It is against that backcloth that God is now going to tell Habakkuk to get a longer view of Babylon. He was going to show the prophet the future of the nation.

He was going to show Habakkuk where it is going to end: the downfall of Babylon. We need to know this. The last book in the Bible, the book of Revelation, spends more than a chapter on the downfall of Babylon. We need to see the ultimate end of human civilisation without God, the ultimate disaster in the long term, for that is how God always operates. He is not an instant God with instant solutions. He is the eternal God and his long-term purposes will be revealed and fulfilled. It is only because we want him to clear everything up by next Tuesday that we cannot see his purposes.

Habakkuk's questions were summed up in one. At the end of 1:13 he said, "Why are you silent while the wicked swallow up those more righteous than themselves?" Within that question there are two questions: why do you let the wicked get away with it? and why do you let that happen to the righteous?

Now most of chapter 2 is the long view about the wicked. It is about Babylon. There is only one little phrase about what will happen to the righteous, yet that is the most important phrase of the lot. We shall return to it because it is the one phrase from this chapter that is quoted by almost every apostle in the New Testament: "The righteous will live by faith." What a statement! That is all that God needs to say about the righteous, but what about the wicked?

God now allows Habakkuk to see what the Babylonians are like. Look at the pride and the greed of this nation – these are the two fundamental things that a righteous God cannot stand in people. They are two deadly sins: to be self-sufficient and never satisfied. You don't need to know the Ten Commandments to know that these are offensive to God. One of the principles of God's judgment is that he is so fair, so just, that he never punishes someone for the light they did not have. That is so important that you must get hold of it because you will be asked by people: "Well, what about those who have never heard? What about those who have never heard of Jesus? What about those who have never heard about the Ten Commandments?"

The answer is, they will not be judged by the standard of Jesus if they have never heard of him. They will not be judged by the Ten Commandments if they have never heard the Ten Commandments. God is fair but because a person has not heard about Jesus or about the Jewish commandments and laws, that does not mean that they don't have any light, far from it. I have noticed recently, going through the Old Testament prophets, that they said almost as much about other nations as about Israel. Have you ever noticed that? Isaiah 14–24, Jeremiah 46–51, Ezekiel 23–35, most of Nahum, some of Zephaniah, all of Jonah, all of Daniel – all of this was directed not to the people of God, it was prophetic ministry to all kinds of nations.

When the other nations were judged by God through the prophet, it was not by the Ten Commandments. For most of them, they are condemned on one ground: inhumanity. I have told you that the instinctive feel of every human being, very early in life is, "It's not fair." "In that case," says God, "You know what's fair and I judge you by that." This sense of humanity and justice is common to the whole human race. God will judge the nations that have never heard about Jesus by their humanity, by their justice because they know what is not fair. If you read Amos 1–2 you find that again and again, Amos brings up against other nations their inhumanity:

"For three sins of Damascus and for four I will not turn back my wrath because she thrashed Gilead with sledges having iron teeth. For three sins of Damascus and for four, I will not turn back my wrath because she sold whole communities of captives. For three sins of Edom and for four, I will not turn back because he pursued his brother with a sword, stifling all compassion. For three sins of Ammon and for four, I will not turn back my wrath because he ripped open the pregnant women in order to extend his borders." This is not the Ten Commandments; this is common humanity.

Babylon, in Habakkuk 2, is judged for her inhumanity. You do not even need to know the Bible to know when someone is being inhuman and cruel. You don't need to know about Jesus to know when there is injustice. We know when a thing is not fair and when people are being treated badly. At least we all know when we are being treated badly, don't we? We are a bit blind as to when somebody else is. But God would say: you all know when you are being treated unjustly; every one of you knows that – therefore, I judge your attitude to other people on that basis; and Babylon, you are greedy and you are proud; you are self-sufficient. The proud Babylonians were as greedy as the grave, which gets everything in the end. They were just swallowing up nation after nation after nation, plundering the towns, capturing the people, getting everything they could. That was all they cared about.

God revealed to Habakkuk that he saw all that. Habakkuk thought they were wicked and so did God. So one day there would be a song about Babylon, sung by Babylon's victims. It is a taunt song of a number of verses beginning with the word "woe". Do you realise that Handel's, "Hallelujah Chorus" which we all think is marvellous, comes out of the book of Revelation, in which it is first sung over the downfall of Babylon? Have you thought of the downfall of Babylon? That is where Handel got it from, when at last the human civilisation without God collapses and the smoke of her cities is seen by the ships at sea. All those who were captured by the harlot's commercialism see their wealth gone, and see all the proud achievements of men in business, art and science, and all the rest, gone. Then God's people who have suffered under Babylon will sing the "Hallelujah Chorus". "Hallelujah, the Lord God, omnipotent, reigns." That is the context, but we love to rip hallelujahs out of context, don't we?

As we have already noted, when God says "woe", that is God cursing. We are beginning to realise the power of curses again. We are beginning to realise that there are witches in England putting pins in effigies. We are beginning to realise that there are curses.

I was talking to a man the other day and he told me that he fell in love with his wife and only, almost too late really, discovered that her mother was a witch in England. On their wedding day she cursed him with cancer. She didn't approve of him and that was her wedding present to that couple. She cursed him and said, "I curse you with cancer for marrying my daughter." Later they talked to the mother about the love of Jesus, and the curse is kept away by the Holy Spirit in both of them.

God tells Habakkuk that one day all those who have been trodden down under Babylon's heel will sing, will taunt Babylon and say, "Woe to you." There are five things that they will say "Woe" about. They are all stated first as a principle, then as a practice. First as "Woe" to him who does something, and then more personally: and you have done it. The principle is that God says: "Curses be on him who does this and Babylon, you have done it. Woe to him who does it and you have done it." What a terrible song to sing.

The first portion in this song is 2:6–8. It is about ruthless plundering of other people. "Woe to those who grab things from other people, who plunder". In our Millmead Centre in Guildford there were some lovely paintings with quite a story behind them; fourteen paintings of the Old Testament prophets. They were done by a professor called Spiro. He was in the Berlin Academy of Art in the 1930s and he spent those years copying the grand masters owned by his fellow Jews. If there was a Jewish wealthy family in Berlin, who had a Rubens painting, he copied it and then the Rubens copy was put in the home and the real Rubens was smuggled to America. Many of the paintings the Nazis plundered were in fact copies by Professor Spiro, but the Nazis plundered works of art like that.

When he realised he had very little time to live, he escaped to America just before the war and got there penniless, but Einstein asked him to paint his portrait to make him well known. From then on, he became one of the most famous artists in America. His paintings appeared in *Time* magazine regularly. Then when he realised he only had a year or two left, he decided to study the fourteen prophets of the Old Testament and so to study them that he felt what they felt. Then he painted a portrait of each of the prophets, and in each of the paintings the mouth is open and you can hear the prophet talking. They are amazing paintings. After he died, they went on exhibition all over America. His widow wrote and told us she would like to give them to us and have them in our church if we would look after them, and so they were flown over from the USA. There's something very deep about them. But I thought of all the plundering the Nazis did, taking this, that, and the other, and God says, "Woe to him who plunders, he will be plundered." For years people said, "Where is God and what is he doing and why is he allowing this to go on?" But God says: take the longer view; you can sing even now: "Woe to him who plunders" You can sing it now because God is still on his throne.

We saw pictures of Berlin at the end of the war, and when I went and saw the heaps of rubble, the artificial hills that were made of shattered buildings, and the chancellery where Hitler finally committed suicide and had his body burned with petrol: "Woe to him who plunders." God is still in charge and even when they are plundering, you can sing the "Woe" song.

The next "woe" is this: "Woe to those who become rich by dishonest gain." People think it brings security, but it has a boomerang effect. What you get that way will boomerang on you. Woe to him who does that, and you have done it. The third verse refers to the practice of the Babylonians in taking their captives back to their capital city, and using slave labour to build a magnificent city. Babylon was one of the Seven Wonders of the world. The hanging gardens of Babylon were so famous, that wherever you went in the then known world, and said "Babylon", people would say, "Oh, those hanging gardens, I have heard about them."

Nebuchadnezzar, strutting around that city which he built with slave labour from other captive nations, said: "Is not this great Babylon, which I have built with my power, for my glory". Mine is the kingdom, the power, and the glory forever and ever. Amen (Daniel 4:30). God heard that and within months Nebuchadnezzar was like an animal. His nails and his hair were long, he was eating grass in a field and he lost his reason.

Babylon – famous? "The earth will be filled with the knowledge of the glory of God as the waters cover the sea." Fame? Babylon is now a pile of dust and rubble and only the archaeologist goes there. But the knowledge of the glory of God will cover the earth, the fame of God, the reputation of God. Babylon was built to be famous. Do you remember the year that the Beatles said, "We are more famous than Jesus"? Look at them now.

The next "woe" is about those who take advantage of others' weakness to humiliate them, to degrade them. The Babylonians had a trick—they used to make their captives drunk for entertainment so that they would strip and the Babylonians could watch their naked cavorting. The

Babylonians loved to use their prisoners to make sport and entertainment, as Samson was made entertainment of by the Philistines. We are reminded of Psalm 137:

> We hanged our harps in the willow tree because our captors in Babylon said, "Sing us a song. Sing us the songs of Zion. Entertain us." But we hid our harps in the willow tree. How can we sing the songs of Zion in a strange land? If I forget you, O Jerusalem, may my right hand forget how to play this harp and may my tongue cleave to the roof of my mouth so I can't even sing.

To be exploited for entertainment. God is declaring: "Babylonians, woe to him who does that. For disgrace will cover your glory. You will grovel. You'll be laughed at. You'll be ridiculed. You'll be brought low.

A little aside here: the Babylonians were cursed by God for destroying trees. Isn't that interesting? You know, in the Old Testament, when the Jews went to war, they were forbidden to destroy the trees. They were fighting people, not trees. But the Babylonians, wherever they went, cut down the trees. The same thing the Americans did in Vietnam with acre upon acre of foliage, they just destroyed it chemically. Vietnam marks the beginning of the end for America as a world superpower.

You see, I am trying to help you realise that God is still the God of the nations. You can read your daily newspapers, as well as reading Habakkuk, and you can see all that I am saying. Unless we see that, we shall just have little tunnel vision and go from one conference to another and one meeting to another, and just see our little problems and our little needs and our little spirituality. But get the larger view in space and the longer view in time.

The last thing that God curses in the Babylonians is this:

he curses them for making their own gods, for deciding what shape of a god they want and making god that shape. That is the most common sin in the whole human race. All should acknowledge that there is one God who made us all and who gave us our conscience – we know he is a mighty, moral God, who made everything that is. Paul says in Romans 1 that everybody can see creation and everybody has a conscience; therefore everybody ought to know there is one mighty, moral God. They don't need a Bible to know that. They just need to look at creation and look into their own heart.

But many people don't like a mighty, moral God and so have their own ideas of God. In ancient days and some places today, people make images of wood and stone. More often in the Western world, we make them of ideas. We have the image in our imagination. People say, "Well I don't think God is like that. I think he's like this." Of many of the things I have been affirming in this study, I am sure that many would say: "I can't accept a God like that; that sounds like the Old Testament God; I don't think of God like that." People have all sorts of images of God as a kind of almighty Santa Claus, who sits up on a cloud with a long, grey beard and pats us on the head when we go wrong and says, "All I want you to be is happy; let's forget it." That is not God.

You see, when you have got an image of God there is only one snag: you can talk to it, you can shout at it, you can pray to an image, but the image can do nothing for you. The Babylonians were very religious, but they did not like the moral, mighty God. No, they were going to have their own images and they made them. They made their images then they shouted to the images and said, "Wake up. Wake up. Wake up." It is almost laughable, isn't it? You can afford to laugh at other gods, you know, because they don't exist. They won't be heard; it is alright. They do not even exist.

I think of Elijah on Mount Carmel and all the prophets of

Baal. Elijah said, "Let the God that answers by fire be the real God." The prophets of Baal shout. They cut themselves. They gash, they cry from morning until afternoon, full of religious fervour, but nothing happens. There is no reply. Elijah says, "Go on. Shout louder. Maybe he's on a holiday, maybe he's sitting on the toilet; you never know where he is." That is literally what he says. I am afraid it is cleaned up in our English Bible which just says "Maybe he's turned aside." That is Hebrew for "gone into the bushes", and he says, "Maybe he's gone into the bushes." He is laughing, you see. We can afford to laugh at idols and all the images of God that people have, because those images are not real. They don't reply.

But let me say something now that may hurt a little. We often treat God as an idol by doing all the talking. We are no better than a primitive savage in front of a block of wood, doing all the talking. We have a God who replies. We learn here that the idol doesn't give you any guidance but our God does. If you really believe in the living God, what is the appropriate thing? Is it to be shouting at him and saying: wake up; what do you think you are doing? What is the appropriate attitude to the living God? "The Lord is in his holy temple. Let all the earth shut up. Let all the earth keep silence before him." Listen for the living God. You need to do all the talking if you worship an image, but with the living God, why not shut up and do a bit of listening.

What a rebuke to Habakkuk. There was Habakkuk: how long, Lord, are you going to let this go on? Lord, Lord, I'm sick of the violence. How long? And I don't agree with you. How could you let that happen? They'll come and they'll just take us like fish in a net. You can't let that happen.

Habakkuk let all the earth keep silence. Shut up, Habakkuk. Notice the emphasis on *all* the earth. The larger view keeps coming through. Habakkuk, you are just looking at your nation. The earth will be filled with the knowledge of the glory of God. Let all the earth keep silent before him. It is not something we do very often, is it? We are shouting to our image of God: wake up; do something. God says: shut up; I am doing something and you missed it.

That answers a very big problem that Habakkuk had, "How could God let the Babylonians get away with it?" God is saying he is not going to let them get away with it, not in the long run, and you can start singing the "Hallelujah Chorus" now. Woe to Babylon. We can sing now "Woe to Islam" – that false prophet teaching, which is so subtle; the most subtle threat to the Christian faith because it has got a mixture of truth and falsehood in it, and it is a post-Christian religion. We can sing "woe" now. We can sing, "Hallelujah" now.

The other side of the problem –"Lord, how are you going to stand by and let the wicked triumph?" – well, that has been answered now. But how are you going to stand by and let the righteous perish? Almost in an aside, God slips in just one phrase, which has become perhaps the most important phrase at any rate, to the inheritors of the Protestant Reformation and, more than that, to the inheritors of Paul's gospel: "The righteous will live by faith." That is all that needs to be said.

It begins with one of those lovely little words in the scripture: "But". We were all under wrath. We were all the children of disobedience. We were all under the power of the prince of the air, but God being rich in mercy.... Whenever you get to the word "but" in scripture, underline it. It is very important. The Babylonian is puffed up, filled with greed, "but the righteous will survive by faith" (2:4b).

Let me try to tell you what that phrase means. In the Hebrew first, before we go into the New Testament because we have heard this phrase so often through the New Testament that we, perhaps, have missed the basic meaning of the Old Testament on which the New Testament understanding of the phrase builds. You cannot leave behind what the Old Testament meaning is, otherwise you might be led into an awful misunderstanding which I am going to mention in a moment.

The word, "faith" only occurs twice in the whole of the Old Testament as a noun. It is all over the New Testament, "by faith". The noun "faith" in the Old Testament means, "faithfulness; fidelity". It is used of a husband and wife who stay together for better, for worse, for richer for poorer, in sickness and health, until death do them part. That is faith in the Old Testament sense. It is truth.

The other time it's used is when Moses was praying and Aaron and Hur were holding his hands up. *Keeping it up* was faith. The reason I am emphasising it is this: faith is never one step. It is always keeping it up. It is no use, your taking a step of faith ten years ago and then living on that for the rest of your life. That faith does not save; it is not biblical faith. The faith that saves is the faith that keeps it up. It is the faith that holds on. It is the faith that survives until the end. It is: "He that endures to the end shall be saved" because that is the only kind of faith that does save. Anything less than that is not faith. Faith is hanging on to God. Faith is keeping faith with God.

Now I know what it is to be brought to the brink of atheism, to be brought to the brink of doubt. I am not talking about years and years ago either. I know what it is to be brought to that horrible blackness where you look over into hell and you see the result of losing faith. In God's amazing grace, he gives that faith back again to hold on. When the Babylonians are coming, when everything is going wrong, when it looks as if there is no God in his heaven and all is wrong with the earth, then faith holds on and says, "I believe there is still a righteous God in charge." That is faith and

Habakkuk is told: The righteous will survive by keeping faith with God, by holding on to a righteous God. That is what it means here in Habakkuk 2:4. Not the people who were converted and who have got a testimony of a step of faith they took twenty years previously, or a decision card which they signed then, but those who are hanging on to God. They are the righteous and they will survive. For a righteous person is one who is holding on to a righteous God. Do you begin to understand the meaning of the phrase? In spite of everything to the contrary, in spite of everything appearing to suggest that there is no God in heaven and that the world is totally unjust, in spite of that, the righteous says: "I still believe in a righteous God. I am still trusting him."

Now that phrase, as you know, is taken up three times in the New Testament; it is taken up in Paul's letter to the Galatians where he is talking about those who try to be righteous by keeping the commandments. He is teaching that it is not keeping the commandments because that is in your own strength; that is you trying to do it. The just shall live by faith. That is hanging on to a God who will do it. You see the difference there? See how he is using the phrase, how he is taking Habakkuk's little sentence. You don't do it by keeping the commandments because you are not strong enough to keep them. You will never be righteous that way. But by holding on to a righteous God, you are righteous – that is how it's done.

But the other two references are very significant and underline that misunderstanding I have mentioned: that faith is just something you do once and you are alright; as if as soon as you believe, God gives you a bus ticket to heaven and all you do is stand at the bus stop and wait to go to glory. That is not faith – not saving faith. The only faith that saves is the faith that hangs on.

In the other two quotations of this phrase in the New

Testament, it becomes crystal clear. In Romans 1:17 Paul says, "For the gospel is this: it is righteousness from faith to faith," or, "faith from first to last." That is the faith that saves: from faith to faith, not once and then you're in, it is the faith that holds on. It is from faith to faith; it's faith from first to last. The faith that saves you is the faith you will hold on your dying day, not the faith you hold today. Otherwise, we get this kind of easy believe-ism – as long as you just made a decision at some time you are okay. That is not the teaching of scripture. The whole of Matthew's Gospel has a very strong emphasis on this – that it's not those who began; it is those who finish who have got faith.

The virgins who ran out of oil didn't get into the wedding feast. It was the virgins who were going to hold on and who had enough oil to hold on to the end who got in. This is a very important teaching of scripture. It is so misunderstood and I am afraid we preachers are responsible for the misunderstanding. The faith that saves is the faith that you will hold on to until your dying day. That is the faith that saves. It could begin right now but believing is a process, not an act.

This is so important. The just shall live by keeping faith with God, by holding on to a righteous God. In the pressures that come, and in the judgments of God that are abroad in the earth, and in the disasters that could begin to touch these islands that have not touched them for so long, the righteous will live by holding on to our righteous God. The other mention of this phrase is in Hebrews 10: "For in just a very little while, he who is coming will come and will not delay, but my righteous one will live by faith, and if he shrinks back I will not be pleased with him. But we are not of those who shrink back and are destroyed, but of those who go on believing and are saved." There it is again, Habakkuk. Did you notice the emphasis? The righteous will survive everything that is coming, by holding on to a righteous God.

Consider Psalm 11: The Lord is on his heavenly throne. He observes the sons of men. His eyes examine them. The Lord examines the righteous, but the wicked and those who love violence his soul hates. On the wicked, he will rain fiery coals and burning sulphur; a scorching wind will be their lot. For the Lord is righteous, he loves justice, upright men will see his face.

Read Habakkuk chapter 3

What has happened to Habakkuk? Something has happened between chapters 2 and 3. We are going to explore a little of the meaning of prophetic music. When the prophetic Spirit of the Lord is on people, they become creative in new ways. They use the arts to convey what God is saying. Most of the prophets used poetry even more than prose; some of them used street theatre. They used symbolic actions; one of them streaked through Jerusalem, another carried a yoke on his shoulders. They did all kinds of things. When I read some of them, I am relieved that God never repeats himself.

When Arthur Blessitt was told by God to pick up a heavy cross and walk around the world with it, that was prophetic street theatre. He travelled in danger of his life to speak to the leaders of nations. God is wanting people who will be creative, who will use the arts, including music.

There is a close connection between music and God. You know that God is musical. You know that God likes singing to himself. Isn't it wonderful? We are the only religion in the world that has a God who sings. "I will rejoice over you," he says, "with singing." So it is no wonder that wherever the Spirit of God moves, there is a burst of new music.

Charles Wesley wrote six thousand hymns and we have only got a few left, but they were magnificent. One of the signs that the Spirit was moving during the mid twentieth century was the fact that the earth was encircled with new songs, new choruses, new scripture set to music. But most of the music in the renewal thus far has been either worship or fellowship or evangelistic music. Where is the flow of prophetic music?

Let me give you a little biblical background. After the people of Israel got through the Red sea, Moses the prophet, and Miriam his sister, the prophetess, thanked the Lord. Miriam produced some prophetic music. You can read it in Exodus 15. The words and the music came from the Spirit. Deborah, the prophetess in Judges 5, was a singer. So often the seer of the Old Testament was also a singer. Seers and singers often went together. Here are three of them: Asaph, Heman and Jeduthan are all called "seers" and "singers." They saw things from God's point of view so they could sing prophetically. Samuel: music inspired his prophetic ministry. When he was wanting to speak a prophetic word, he was stimulated by deep music that stirred the heart, so that he might prophesy.

Elisha did the same. When Saul, in his better days, was anointed to be the first king of Israel, what happened was that he met a bunch of prophets who were playing with harps, tambourines, flutes and lyres, and Saul was filled with the Holy Ghost. People said, "Is Saul also among the prophets." Why? Because he was singing and dancing with the musicians. I could mention Ezekiel who was quite handy with the guitar; there are many others.

But the supreme example and one who is often overlooked is King David. Hearing his name, do you think of a shepherd? Do you think of a warrior, a fighter? Do you think of a king or do you think of a prophet? On his deathbed David did not thank God that he had been king. He did not thank God that he had been a shepherd or a fighter. He praised God that he had been a prophet.

HABAKKUK

On the day of Pentecost, when Peter was preaching and mentioned King David, there was only one thing he had to say about King David: "But David was a prophet." It is from David that we have got more songs than from anybody else in the Bible. He is the seer and singer par excellence.

You may have a musical gift if you like to receive songs and work at them, and by the way, if the Spirit gives a song that does not mean no hard work. He gives the essence of it, the kernel of it and you will need to work at it to knock it into shape. But please will you listen to God for prophetic music? We have music about the Spirit and music about Jesus and we have our choruses, but *prophetic* music will be about God primarily. It will be strong, deep music. It will be "shigionoth" – that is the word at the head of this chapter. Do you know what it means? The scholars argue about it, but as near as I can get, it means deep, stirring music – not frothy, not jiggy. There is a place for our little dancing choruses, but *shigionoth* is much deeper than that. Prophetic music is not set to jigs. It is stirring. It gets right down. It is a kind of music that is neither very joyful, nor very sorrowful but just deep, that touches you deep down, that makes you bigger in your feelings, in your vision, in your soul.

I am longing to hear some *shigionoth* to come out of the renewal. But prophetic music will always be music for today; it will never be the music of yesterday, for the prophetic word is what God is saying now.

I haven't even touched the New Testament and the prophetic music there, but Paul says, "Go on being filled with the Spirit. Don't get drunk. If you want a night out, get filled with the Spirit and then get into song." The book of Revelation, you must realise, is not only the most prophetic book in the New Testament, it is the most musical through and through. That is no coincidence and it is filled with new songs and you hear the thunder of thousands of voices:

"Hallelujah, for the Lord God omnipotent reigns."

O God, give us some more shigionoth. Give us some deep, stirring music that is as big and as deep as the vision of God.

This is a very emotional chapter because at last God is getting the last bit of the citadel of Habakkuk's personality. He has got his mind; he's given him the larger and the longer view. He has got his will because Habakkuk is now willing to go and tell. If chapter 1 is getting hold of Habakkuk's mind and chapter 2 is getting hold of his will, chapter 3 gets hold of the heart, the feelings, the will. Never be afraid of emotions; be terribly afraid of emotionalism. My, you can tell when something is being worked up, can't you? You know it immediately. I would rather there was no emotion in a meeting, than somebody trying to work it up.

I have the feeling that Habakkuk is pretty quiet for a bit. After all, if God says to you, "The Lord is in his holy temple; let all the earth keep silence before him," you are not going to go on talking, are you? It is our perpetual problem that we keep talking. Peter saw Jesus transfigured, filled with such glory that the light in his body shone through his clothes and made them transparent, and Peter offered to get three shrines, three tabernacles built there. It thundered and the voice from heaven said, "This is my Son. Listen to him," and I guess Peter was quiet after that. "Habakkuk, let all the earth keep silence."

When he started to talk to God again, it is a different Habakkuk. He prays at first. It is not long before his prayer turns to praise. Now somehow, his soul, his spirit is not so agitated. He has found rest for his spirit. He still prays strongly, but how different from the Habakkuk that said, "Lord, how much longer are you going to make me look at all this? How much longer are you going to leave it alone? Why don't you do something?" Now he's saying, "Lord, I've heard of what you've done in the past. Please, I am not content with hearing it; I want to see it."

He is not asking for replies now, he is asking for results now. He is not asking for an answer, he is asking for action. Habakkuk is now acknowledging the Lord is the mighty, moral God. He knows what he did in the past and what he is going to do in the future. But in his day, right there in the middle, he wanted to see the Lord operating. Do you ever share that prayer? You hear of all God's mighty works in the days gone by in the Bible. You hear of what he is going to do at the end of history when Jesus comes again. Your soul responds to both, but your cry is: "Lord, please, we want to see you now. Do these things in our day, in the middle of the years. Don't just be the God of the beginning and the end."

I remember reading about a little boy who went up to bed to sleep. His mother tucked him in and came downstairs. Then there was a frightful thunderstorm crashing outside the house. The mother who was scared stiff of thunder, was sitting downstairs shaking, wondering how the little boy was and she went up to see him. Of course, you know, most of the fears that we have in life, we pick up from mothers. We are not born with a fear of thunder and lightning, but we pick it up from people around us. But she went up, and wisely she didn't rush in to see how the boy was; she just waited at the open door and listened to see if he was asleep, but he wasn't. He was sitting up in bed. There was a big clap of thunder and the little boy said, "Now another one, Lord, now another one." Then there was a huge clap of thunder and the little boy clapped and said, "Stout fellow. Do it again, Lord – now another one."

The Welsh Revival of 1904 is no use to me. Do it again, Lord. I don't want to be living in books of some golden age of church history. I don't want to get stuck in the Reformation or among the Puritans or among the eighteenth-century revivalists. I say, "Lord, do it in my years, please. Do it now.

If you're the God of Elijah, where is the God of Elijah now? Do it in the midst of our years. You have done it in the past; you're going to do it again. Please Lord, do it now. Let us see in our lifetime your mighty arm laid bare."

Then he comes to a prayer that really touches God's heart: Lord, when you do come in wrath, please remember mercy. Do you know, if you use that little word, "mercy" you touch the softest spot in God's heart? As soon as anybody appeals to that, I say it reverently: "They've got God." They really have. "In your wrath, remember mercy." God so responded to that prayer of Habakkuk's.

The rest of the chapter is a psalm of praise, it is not a prayer any more. He doesn't ask for another thing. The song divides very clearly into three parts. You can divide it by the personal pronouns and you can see the progress of the psalm through those personal pronouns. The first third is all, "He" – God in the third person. Then something happens and Habakkuk moves to saying "You". Then he moves again and finishes by saying "I". You can praise God impersonally and say "he is great"; "he is marvellous"; "he is mighty." That is only the first step in praise. Then comes the second step where you say "You are mighty." But the third part of praise comes when you yourself are so caught up in it that you say "I".

Let us see how this happened to Habakkuk. We look then at the opening of the song. There's something a little wrong in most English Bibles: all the verbs in chapter 3 are in the present tense, not the past. Unfortunately, in my Bible they have put them in the past, as in "His glory covered the heavens". Well just mentally turn it into the present tense and you have got the Hebrew, "God comes, his glory is covering the heavens, filling the earth." It is present tense; it is a vision. Habakkuk's eyes are seeing God answering his prayer.

It is not happening in fact yet, but the prophet is a seer

and the prophet can see the past and the future as if it is the present. That is why most Hebrew prophecy is in this most unusual tense: the prophetic present. Even when a prophet describes something that may not happen for another thousand years or more, he describes it in the present tense because in God, in the Spirit, he is transported through time. He sees it happening and he describes it as it happens: "I see God coming. I see his glory filling the heavens. I see his praise filling the earth." I can see it; it is happening.

That is how the prophets saw the creation of the world. That is how Moses got Genesis 1. He saw it happening. He went back beyond recorded history and he saw the beginning. That is how John, in prison on Patmos, saw the end of the world. He saw it happening; he saw it all before his very eyes. The prophetic spirit has no boundaries in time. The God who was, and who is, and who is to come, and the God who is from eternity to eternity can place the prophetic spirit anywhere in the timeline and it is present to the prophet. Something very exciting is happening here. If you have a vision for the future, you will see it as if it is happening now and you will describe it that way. People will get the reality of it because they have had an eyewitness account of something that has not yet happened.

It is all about God and the time of the exodus, which happened centuries before. God is coming and the mountains are trembling. I have never been in an earthquake but I remember a man vividly describing to me what it was like. He said the most frightening thing was that there was nothing to hang on to. He ran out into the street from the house that was falling down and the ground beneath his feet was shaking like a feather in the wind. He saw it open and a car disappear down the crack. He said, "I really was frightened." There were earthquakes when the children of Israel came through Sinai. The mountains trembled and the children of

THE MINOR PROPHETS

Israel became "quakers" on the spot.

Did you know that is the origin of the word "Quaker"? They are not called that today because they don't look like that today. They look like the Society of Friends, but in the early days, when God was so real to them, they sat on their pews and they shook, they trembled; they quaked before almighty God. Just now and again I have seen that – just little glimpses God gives us. I have only once been in a meeting where a tongue of fire sat on everyone's head – it was in a Bible college. I have once or twice seen people actually shaking because God was there. Habakkuk sees the mountains trembling and the oceans trembling, "God is coming." It takes shigionoth music to describe that.

It is a vision and he says, "I saw", but in the Hebrew it is "I see"; he sees nature trembling. He sees the Midianites trembling; he sees everybody trembling because God is coming. That is the real presence of God. His whole senses are heightened: his spiritual senses, his physical senses. To go back to an earlier study, this is theism, pure and simple. This is a God in total control of nature and history. This is he who we forget can bring mountains crumbling, who can send a tidal wave up, who can shake the whole earth. That is the God whom Habakkuk sees.

When you are asking God to come and do something, are you sure you know what you are asking? Are you sure that "light at the end of the tunnel" isn't an oncoming train? When you say "God visit us", do you realise what might happen? Do you realise that the building in which you pray might be shaken? Oh we say, "God, what are you doing?" God could say: "Are you sure you want me to come and do something? I am God, you know, and everything is shaken when I come." We are told in the New Testament, as well as the old, that God will shake everything that can be shaken because only the things that belong to him cannot. The only thing that will stay when everything is shaken is his kingdom. All the other kingdoms will be shaken when God comes. He just shakes everything.

But Habakkuk is seeing all this and now, after a little pause, a little Selah, he moves on into talking to God personally as "You". From the third person he changes to the second person. He's getting into the vision. He is still asking questions. Habakkuk is a curious fellow; he is full of questions. Thank God for people who go on asking questions, but what different questions: Habakkuk 1 – why are you doing nothing? Why do you tolerate wrong?" Habakkuk 3 – were you angry with the rivers? Did you rage against the sea? What did you feel like, Lord, when you parted the Red Sea? Were you angry with the water? You know, God is waiting for people to ask him how he feels.

If there is one thing he revealed to the prophets, it is how he felt. The prophets are full of the feelings of God – not their feeling about God, but God's feelings about them. Listen to Hosea crying out: "How can I give you up, O Ephraim? How can I let you go? How can I treat you like Admar? I couldn't come and be angry with you because I'm God, not man." Can you not feel the feelings of God in that? Can a woman forget the little baby that she brought forth from her own womb? Could she forget that baby? Yes, even that can happen, but God cannot forget his people. He can forget their sins, but he can't forget them. Don't you feel God?

"Were you angry with the rivers, Lord? How did you feel when you were doing this when you came with your bows and arrows, with your thunder and lightning, when the sun and the moon stood still at your command? How did you feel telling the sun to stand still? How did you feel?" He is getting into God. The prophetic ministry is someone who is into God; that's all. Who is feeling God's feelings? Who is understanding how God is feeling? We are so preoccupied with our own feelings even in our spiritual meetings. Whereas God is saying: where is the man or the woman or the young person with whom I can share my feelings? Who will then sing my feelings, not theirs? Who will not sing, "I'm h-a-p-p-y", but who will sing about God's feelings? That is what he is looking for. Habakkuk is getting right in.

Habakkuk is saying: "Lord, when you came in such wrath, in such anger, in such rage, you came to deliver your anointed one. You came to rescue us. You came to get us out of Egypt. When you were angry with the Red Sea blocking our way; it was to get us out. In wrath, you remembered mercy, Lord,"

Then he moves to the very personal section: "I". He makes two statements about himself. Both of them begin with the same three words: "Yet I will". He is describing the effect of this vision on himself. It has put him in a new place. If you have had a vision of God, you can never be quite the same again.

I only met Arthur Blessitt for one evening, but as soon as I met him, I knew that he had had a vision of the Lord Jesus. You could see it on his face: there is a man who has seen Jesus. Only months later, when I read his book, did I read how it happened, how he and a friend went walking by a lake one evening. As they walked and talked, Arthur looked out across the lake and saw Jesus walking across the water. He couldn't believe it, so he turned away. He looked back and the figure was still there, coming nearer. Arthur was frightened. He turned to his friend to see if he could see anything and realised that they could both see Jesus. The Lord just walked very close to them across the water, smiled at them, and disappeared. Arthur went home and the friend went home. Arthur went to his flat, went in, and his wife took one look at him, screamed, ran into the bedroom, slammed and bolted the door. He had to spend the night on the couch in the living room. Only in the morning would she come out, and he asked: "Why? What was the matter?"

She said, "Your face, it was just shining." When he met his friend later that day, the friend's wife had done the same thing. If you meet the Lord you can never be the same again. If God has shown you something of himself, of his power, his majesty, you will never be the same again.

The two pressures that could have come on Habakkuk at this point and spoiled the vision for him were these: first, the internal pressure of his own emotions; and second, the external pressure of his circumstances. He knew that either of these pressures could rob him of the objectivity of the vision he had had. Habakkuk resolves before God that he will allow neither of these things to rob him of what he has seen.

Take the first—there's a description now of a man who is going to pieces emotionally, whose lips are quivering, whose legs are turning to jelly – who is going to pieces through sheer emotion, which has taken over his body. Commentators seem to suggest that it was the emotion of fear. I don't think so because that doesn't make any sense of what he says: "Yet I will wait patiently." That is not something you say if you are scared stiff. It doesn't relate at all. I believe the emotion he is feeling is the sheer excitement of having seen what God is going to do, and wanting him to get on with it. You would get emotionally excited and that would throw you.

I have met people who in the Spirit have seen something of what God is going to do; or if they have had a clearer vision of the second coming of our Lord – there is a need to guard against that vision being lost in emotional panic or excitement that wants it to happen immediately. When you have had a vision of some purpose of God, you can get so excited, so worked up, and just drop everything, drop your job – because it is going to happen.

This happened to the Thessalonians. They really got a clear vision of Jesus coming again and they were resigning from their jobs, and Paul had to correct it and put them right. The real reaction to getting all excited about the visions of what God is going to do is to say: yet I will wait patiently for it to happen. Don't let the internal pressure of emotion drive you into unbalanced attitudes.

Habakkuk is growing visibly; maturing before our very eyes. He is getting excited about God and yet he has realised that that emotion must not throw him off balance: Yet I will wait patiently for this calamity to come on the nation that is going to invade us. Gone is the impatient Habakkuk, "Lord, how long?" and in its place is the patient Habakkuk who would say: Lord, I don't care how long it takes. I know you are going to do it. I have seen you and I am one of the righteous who is going to hang on to a righteous God however long it takes. Isn't that a lovely balance? God is shaping this man to be a prophet.

The other thing that can rob you of the vision of God is when everything around you seems to be going wrong. When the fig tree stops blossoming, when the vines have no grapes, when there are no sheep in the fields and no cattle in the stall, when there is economic disaster and you don't know where the next meal is coming from; when there is nothing outside you to encourage you, when things seem bleak, blank; when there is no encouragement whatever through your physical eyes – what do you do about that? If you have really seen God, you say, "Yet I will rejoice in God, my Saviour." Everything I see may be depressing. Everything around me may have gone dead, but I have seen God and I rejoice in God, my Saviour.

As Habakkuk gets right into this, and gets the balance right, and gets the response right, and realised that it is this vision of God and his faith in this righteous God that can hold him, he doesn't care what his emotions are going to be like. He doesn't care what his circumstances are going to be like. He has got into the place of security now because he has got right into God. He is a man in God; he is in the Lord. So he finishes by saying in this lovely way, "I am sure footed and I am lighthearted. I feel I've got the feet of a deer." If you watch a little gazelle in the Middle East, that is probably what he was seeing at this moment, you see them just jump with their little matchstick legs and their tiny hooves. They jump from bare rock to bare rock and they go leaping up, and up to the heights. Habakkuk is saying that is how he is now.

He began as a man way down in the valley, "Lord, how long?" He was depressed, frustrated, angry. Now he is a deer; jumping up on the heights, he's got deer's feet. I recommend a book by Mrs Hurnard, a missionary from Israel: *Hinds Feet in High Places* – a lovely book, a little allegory about the spiritual life, how to get hinds' feet in high places. How to get where Habakkuk got, so that instead of being in the valley of depression, doubt and despair he is now leaping from rock to rock. It is not that he has an emotional high, he is clear-headed, sure footed and lighthearted. He is like a gazelle on the mountains. Do you wonder that he instructed the choirmaster to set that to music and sing it? This is prophetic praise.

Now I return to the question: what happened to Habakkuk? Let us run through it. He is praying and he is asking God to come in power. He receives a vision. He extols the mighty works of God. He has a tremendous emotional release and he starts singing. What has happened? He has been baptized in the Holy Spirit. That is what has happened. Did you guess? Did you spot it? He has been plunged into the Spirit of the Lord, the prophetic spirit that leads people to see visions and dream dreams, the prophetic spirit that releases music, the prophetic spirit that touches the emotions and gears them to God, guarding them at the same time against being swept away by those emotions but releasing them and turning prayer into praise. He is at last a prophet of God. He has been moulded, melted and filled; he is God's man.

I believe God has spoken to you through this simple study of Habakkuk. You may wish to obtain my teaching on Jeremiah as well. They were contemporaries and they spoke to the same situation. If God has laid on you a burden for the nation at this time, then I would urge you to follow through on that because God is the same God who spoke to that same situation through Jeremiah as well as Habakkuk. But if God has spoken to you, there is only one thing for you to do now. Say, "Lord, what would you have me do about it?"

You have to do something about a burden. You can't keep it in there. If you try, you'll be like Jeremiah. You will say: your word is like a hidden fire shut up in my bones; I am weary from forbearing; I can't contain it. I have to let it out – and you have got to if the Lord gives you a burden. It must be passed on and shared. So may the Lord show you how.

ZEPHANIAH

ZEPHANIAH

Read Zephaniah
We know very little about Zephaniah. He is not mentioned elsewhere and the focus is on the message rather than the messenger when we get to the prophets. The only biographical details are in 1:1 where we are told his name and his genealogy. The name Zephaniah really in Hebrew is Sephen Jah, which means hidden God. We don't know whether that means that God had hidden himself – he certainly had not spoken for about 70 years – or it could mean that Zephaniah had been hidden by God. I think that is the more likely explanation of his name, and I will explain why. But his genealogy is interesting. He is the only prophet who traces his ancestry back four generations: the son of; the grandson; the great-grandson of – and then the great-great-grandson of. Once you get back to that fourth generation he is related to Hezekiah. He is therefore of royal blood. He is a descendant of King Hezekiah who was the last good king of the two tribes in the south. (By now the ten tribes in the north have gone; taken away to Assyria, and the two tribes in the south are in danger of following them if they don't learn the lesson from what happened to the other ten tribes.) Hezekiah was a man after God's own heart, he did what was right in the sight of the Lord and he feared God and was humbled before God. Now all that makes a good king.

So what has been happening since Hezekiah? The answer is some very bad kings, and the man who followed Hezekiah could not have been a greater contrast. He was a very bad king. His name was Manasseh and it is really too horrible to read. He rebuilt all the pagan altars on the high ground. He re-erected those dreadful phallic symbols and the Asherah poles and he encouraged the people to go back to the fertility cults, with of course their sexual overtones. He introduced the worship of Moloch and introduced child sacrifice and killed his own sons to this god, and he offered these boys to the god Moloch in a valley called Hinnom, or Gehennah, a valley just south of Jerusalem. Jeremiah cursed that valley and Jesus later used it as a picture of hell. It became the rubbish dump and the sewage dump after that. All through the early years of Manasseh's reign there was a prophet called Isaiah who tried to stop it, and do you know what Manasseh did first? He forbade Isaiah to preach so Isaiah wrote his prophecies down and they were circulated in written form, and that is how we got the book of the prophet Isaiah. When Manasseh heard this, he was so furious he ordered Isaiah to be bound and pushed inside the trunk of a hollow tree, and then he ordered people to saw the trunk of the tree in half. That is how Isaiah met his death – he was literally sawn in half. He is mentioned in Hebrews 11 where there is a phrase, some were sawn asunder, and that is a direct reference to how Isaiah met his end under this very bad king.

Manasseh got involved in astrology, he got involved with spiritist mediums, and this spiritual confusion of course led to moral chaos. Idolatry always leads to immorality. God actually says of Manasseh in Chronicles that he was more evil than the original Canaanites. Can you imagine how God feels, because he got rid of those evil Canaanites to make room for his holy people, and now they are worse than the people they replaced. That was a very dangerous situation. Manasseh died after reigning for 55 years and was succeeded by a man called Amon, a very weak character who did nothing to put the situation right and Judah simply became more evil. There was great intrigue and treachery and finally

ZEPHANIAH

Amon was assassinated after only two years on the throne. The whole nation is in moral chaos now and when Amon was assassinated it meant that a young boy only eight years old became king, and his name was Josiah. The question was: how would Josiah shape up? Now because he was so young the real ruler in the early years was Hilkiah the High Priest, but as Josiah the boy developed, the big question was: would he go the way of Hezekiah, his great-grandfather, or would he go the way of Manasseh, his grandfather? That is when God sent Zephaniah the prophet, and really Zephaniah's task was to try under this boy king's reign to pull the nation back before it became too late and they were taken off as the ten tribes had been taken off already.

So that is the setting. I believe that Zephaniah as a boy had been hidden, just as Moses had been hidden, as others had been hidden, and that is why his mother gave him the name "hidden by God", Sephen Jah. That is my theory anyway, because the little boys were all being sacrificed to Moloch and his mother saved him. He was a royal prince and the other royal princes were being sacrificed so I think his mother hid him and brought him up.

Now Zephaniah comes with a very strong message all of which revolves around the day of the Lord. That is not a 24-hour period. It means the day of God's judgment, the day of putting things right, the day of vindication of righteousness. It is the day when wrongs are righted, when wickedness is punished. The day is coming and you might say that the whole of Zephaniah revolves around this day of the Lord when God is going to settle accounts with people, and as the day gets nearer, as it must be doing, then God's people must be getting ready for it, or should be.

I am sure you know that there were four Quarter days in the English calendar which used to be for settling accounts. There is Lady Day, March 25th; Midsummer Day, June 24th;

Michaelmas Day, September 29th and Christmas Day, December 25th. All debts had to be paid on those days and all finance brought up to date, and that was when fraud was revealed and punished. It was the audit day, and that gives us a kind of picture of the day of the Lord when all accounts are examined, audited and settled, and fraud is punished. So the day of the Lord is coming.

I told you there is a direct connection between prophecy and music, and there is a lot about singing in the prophets and I am sure this is the chorus that Zephaniah would want us to learn:

That is the day, that is the day when the Lord will judge, when the Lord will judge.
We will regret, we will regret and be sad in it, and be sad in it.
That is the day when the Lord will judge, we will regret and be sad in it.
That is the day, that is the day when the Lord will judge.

Now that is I think what Zephaniah would have wanted to sing – not a cheerful one.

I divide the book into three sections which are very clear. In the first section he is concerned with the foreign religions which have got into Judah and he announces judgment and makes four basic statements about the judgment of the day of the Lord that is coming. That judgment is deserved. It is now declared. He then describes what it will involve and what will happen to them when God judges, and then he offers them the possibility that even at this stage judgment can be deflected from Israel and turned away by repentance. It is the same message all the prophets have. To us, when we read one prophet after another, we say: well, that is the same message as the one we have looked at. Of course it was because God repeats himself when it is necessary. But bear in mind that whereas these prophecies in the Bible come next to each other there was often a gap of 70 years between them, and therefore they had to be said all over again. So Zephaniah was saying that is the day when the Lord will judge, and it is getting very, very near and still you are going down the wrong path, and look what is happening in the nation – and you could see it, they didn't need to be told what was happening.

After this first section on foreign religion we turn to a second section in which he also spreads the net of judgment to other nations – the nations all around – and he includes them and says the God of Israel will not only judge us but he will judge you too and he boxes the compass. On the west side of Judah was the land of Philistia (or Philistines) and the word "Palestinian" is directly descended from the word "Philistine". Then on the east side Moab and Amman, on the south side Egypt and even as far south as Ethiopia, and on the north side Assyria is still the world power, the biggest power on the Tigris and Euphrates rivers. Babylon has not come on to the scene yet. Assyria is the nation that has taken away the ten tribes in the north so most of the people of God have gone now, and just little Judah is left surrounded by these nations. But Zephaniah has the courage to say these nations also will be judged by God. He is the judge of the whole world and especially, you remember, they will be judged for their attitude to Israel, those that have had contact with her.

The Philistines became a real thorn in the side of Israel, right through to King David. David was really the one who dealt them a death blow, though they still kept raiding even after that. It was always the Philistines. Samson had to deal with the Philistines, and indeed the word has actually become proverbial in the English language for someone destructive.

I have already mentioned that God brought the Philistines into the land at the same time as he brought the Hebrews. In Deuteronomy God explains. He said: I have brought them to test you. If you keep my word, you will keep them at bay and they will be no problem to you. But if you disobey me I have brought them to be an instrument of discipline for you, and when you are doing wrong they will overcome you. God has his way of disciplining his people. God is a Father to his people and a good father disciplines his children when they go wrong. In fact Hebrews 12 says if the Lord doesn't discipline you, then you are not a true son of God, you are a bastard. One of the proofs that you are a child of God is that he does punish you, and as we shall see the choice really is: do you want the punishment of God now or later? If you become a child of God now, then he will punish you now, life won't be easy and when you go wrong he will deal with you. Whom the Lord loves he chastises, but he does that so that you don't need to be punished afterwards. Becoming God's people does not mean escape from his punishment, it just brings it forward a bit, but it is much better to have it now and be a son of God and be chastised when we have been naughty so that we remain in the family, than not have any punishment from God now and have it all later. Now many people don't realise that is the choice – have it now or then – and I would much rather have it now, would you not? That is why Christians can expect life to be a bit tough here. Believe me, I can never believe those testimonies when people get up and say "I came to Jesus and all my troubles were over." I used to believe them and it depressed me. Now I know it is not true. My testimony is a little bit different. I came to Jesus and my troubles began. Then I got baptised in the Spirit and my troubles got much worse. That is my testimony. But I am glad because it fits the promises of Jesus. He said in the world you will have big trouble, but he said cheer up, I am on top of it. I said to a friend of mine some time ago: how are you? He said: I am very well over the circumstances. I thought: that is a Christian talking. Yes, Jesus promised us trouble in this life. There will be trouble in the world which hates God. But there will also be trouble from God. God loves you too much to let you off, and if you steer away from his path then expect trouble from him. That is his loving way of getting you back into his way and his line, and because he loves you now he will do it now. Much better than to store it all up for later, which is what the world is doing. So, by and large, that means that God's people are going to have a rougher time than other people in this world. But in the next world – totally different.

We move on to the third section of Zephaniah. In the first section he really hit hard this indulgence in fertility cults, superstition, astrology and spiritist mediums, and sacrificing babies to Moloch. He really goes hard after that and declares with great force, God is irritated by this. It is an interesting word. God is intensely irritated, and from that word actually came a song that was sung in many churches in the Middle Ages called Dies Irae – and "Irae" is the Latin from which we get "irritate", "ire" or anger. The day of God's irritation. The day when God has had enough. The day when God boils over.

The Bible says God's anger is simmering now. I believe it is simmering over our country and if you really keep your eyes open you can see it because the signs of God's anger simmering are an increase in unnatural sexual relations, an increase in antisocial behaviour, an increase in breakdown of family life, and increase in people becoming slaves of their appetites and addiction. Now all that is there, and that is God's anger simmering, and Zephaniah is saying: look, can't you see that God's anger is simmering now and the day is coming when it boils over, and that is what is meant by the day of wrath in the New Testament as well as the Old. God is holding his anger in, but it is simmering and the symptoms of it simmering are there for all to see in a society going downhill and, it is there for all to see in our country right now, and throughout the western civilisation I believe. One day it is going to boil over and it is that day that we must deflect if we possibly can, and put off by repenting and getting things put right. God's anger is simmering. But suddenly, quite quickly, the day of his wrath comes and his irritation boils over and he explodes. You see when you are irritated by something or someone it builds up, doesn't it? It builds up entirely; finally you let it out, and it comes out very quickly, and even unexpectedly if you have not been aware that it is building up.

In the last section, 3:1–20, there is a strange tension or ambiguity between cursing and blessing, between God's justice and his mercy. It is almost as if Zephaniah is saying: choose, which are you really going to have? Which do you really want? God's justice to boil over in anger? You are intensely irritating God right now and it is building up and it has got to explode at some point and when it explodes there will be nothing but justice and judgment, and yet God is full of mercy and what he wants to do is have mercy on you and show you his mercy. That is what he really wants but he can't do that without your co-operation because God only gives mercy to those who ask for it. He loves to give mercy. What thrills me is when people use the word mercy – God be merciful. You only use that prayer if you think you are pretty bad. It is only bad people who ask for mercy, and we are all bad, and it is because of his mercy that we are not consumed and his mercies are fresh every morning. But you only think of God's mercy if you feel bad enough not to deserve anything good; and nice, good churchgoing people don't often ask for mercy. They are not bad enough.

But there was a great revival in the prisons because bad people were asking for mercy, and they were getting it because God is merciful to those who want his mercy. So we have a mixture here of justice and mercy and Zephaniah is saying now: which is it to be? In the first half of chapter 3 he really faces them with the possibility of a day of divine justice coming and he tells them how obstinate they are. They have rebelled against God quite deliberately and they are resisting God's appeal. He accuses them of rebellion and resistance. They are an obstinate people. I feel another song coming on! I read a little verse in Zephaniah which said that morning by morning he dispenses justice and I found myself singing this to myself.

> Great is thy righteousness,
> O God all holy;
> There is no error of judgement with thee.
> Thou changest not; thy commandments
> They fade not
> As thou hadst been thou forever wilt be.

> Great is thy righteousness,
> Great is thy righteousness;
> Morning by morning by justice I see:
> All that is merited,
> Thou has requited;
> Great is thy righteousness;
> Lord hear our plea.

Now I will tell you why I have done this: because so often we love to sing the nice songs – the songs about God's faithfulness, the songs about this is the day we will rejoice and be glad. We like all that, but there is another side to God, and balancing God is very important. Paul says behold then the goodness and the severity of God. Both goodness to those who believe, severity to those who do not; and goodness to those who go on believing is the right translation, and severity to those who do not go on believing. You see it is going on believing, it is not the faith you start with that saves, it is the faith you finish with. It is going on believing. John 3:16 properly translated reads like this:

For God so loved the world that he gave his only-begotten Son that whoever goes on believing in him will never perish but go on having eternal life.

Has that changed that verse for you a little? It is the faith that goes on which saves. Well, he says if you go on rebelling and resisting there will be a national disaster. God's anger will boil over; the day will come. He also says that same anger will boil over towards the nations and obliterate them, but then how often even the most hard prophets, the most tough prophecies, end with a note of hope – as if God always wants to make a last appeal with good news. Amos was a very tough prophet. He was the second last prophet to the ten tribes in the north before they disappeared, and his message is a tough message of God's justice, but the last word to the north was Hosea, a message of God's mercy and love, and it is almost as if God's last word to us is: won't you have my mercy? Interesting isn't it. God doesn't want to punish. He has no pleasure in the death of the wicked, he wants to show mercy, and so many of these Old Testament prophets finished on a good note – of hope for the future; a note of mercy, and his note of justice here was both for the nation and the nations. His note of mercy is for the nations and then the nation. His note of mercy for the nations was that out of every nation he is going to have people who love him. Out of every kindred, tribe, tongue and people – God doesn't want a single ethnic group on earth to be missed out. That is why he told us to preach the gospel to all ethnic groups, and

ZEPHANIAH

make disciples of all ethnic groups, and that is important.

There has been a great move of God among the gypsies in this country, and my videos have been used to teach those gypsy preachers who could not read or write and could not read the Bible. Just a few months before I gave this talk I was with 160 gypsy preachers and they told me that there was not a gypsy family in England without a Christian in it, and it may well be the first ethnic group in Britain to be entirely Christian. God wants every ethnic group in this family and his mercy will ensure that there will be some out of every nation who are godly. That is a promise of God's mercy. Isn't that exciting? Heaven is going to be multiracial, but we are all going to be "colour blind".

But then he finishes up with the national gladness, with the possibilities of blessing for Israel itself. Nine times in this last little section God says "I will". They may break his covenant, but he will never break it, and he talks about a wonderful future when he will quiet them with his love. Isn't that a lovely phrase? He will quiet us with his love, calm us after all the stresses and strains of this world. Then he says God will sing about his people – he will rejoice over them with singing.

What Zephaniah is saying is take your punishment now, while God's anger is simmering. Don't have it later when it boils over. God's people have the opportunity to be judged now and to get right with God now. The nations will have to be judged later and that is a principle that goes right through into the New Testament, and Peter writes in his epistle: For it is time for judgment to begin with the family of God. If it begins with us, what will be the outcome for those who do not obey the gospel of God? You see? That leaves us with one question about Zephaniah. Did Josiah take any notice? Was his prophecy effective? Josiah came to the throne at the age of 8, in 640 BC, and he reigned for 31 years. At first he was heavily influenced by the High Priest Hilkiah, and priests tend to keep the status quo, but then he began to be influenced by Zephaniah. At the age of 16 he destroyed the altars in Jerusalem. At the age of 20 he ordered all the pagan altars to be destroyed throughout the whole country. At the age of 28 he noticed that the temple of God was in bad repair and needed spring cleaning and repairing, so he ordered the temple of God to be put right, and while they did that somebody found in a dusty old cupboard a copy of the law of Moses and they realised they had not been studying it or reading it for years. It is like finding a dusty old Bible on a shelf. They came to the king and said: look what we found in a cupboard. He read it through and was horrified. He said: no wonder God is warning us, we have got to put this right, and at the age of 28 he ordered the law to be read again and done. But it was too late. As I have said, you can't make people good by Act of Parliament. You can't impose righteousness from above. I know many people would like our government to pass laws making people behave in a Christian way. It doesn't work, it has got to come from the heart, and although Josiah did his best to clean up the country, he failed, and then he made a big mistake. He decided to go to war against the Egyptians and God didn't tell him to, and he met the Egyptian army, who weren't going to attack him, they were simply passing through the Promised Land to go and attack Assyria and he should have just let them go through, but I am afraid he said you are not passing over my land. He met the Egyptian army at Meggido, at the crossroads of the world, and he died, killed in battle. It is a sad tale.

There was a young man actually the same age as Josiah, now 28 when Josiah died, and that young man was told: you have got to pick up this prophetic burden and you have to tell it to the people because the reform of Josiah isn't working. That young man's name was Jeremiah and that is how the

ZEPHANIAH

prophecy of Jeremiah came to be.

So Zephaniah failed. He tried hard, and Josiah tried, but the people didn't listen. Twenty years later, Habakkuk saw the situation getting worse and worse.

Before we leave Zephaniah there is one more thing I would note, namely a similarity between the structure of Zephaniah's prophecy and that of the book of Revelation. Both Zephaniah and Revelation start with judgment on God's people – in this case Israel, and the church in Revelation chapters 1–3. They move on to judgments on the nations, then to the day of judgment, the day when the anger or irritation of God boils over – 3:1-8 in Zephaniah; chapter 20 in Revelation. But the last word is the final bliss of God's giving a place to his people where they can live forever: 3:9–20; 21–22. In Zephaniah it is of course the old Jerusalem, but in Revelation it is the new Jerusalem. In Zephaniah God comes as King but in Revelation Jesus comes again as King. But isn't that remarkable? There are over 400 allusions to the Old Testament in the book of Revelation, but the closest connection is with this minor prophet Zephaniah.

HAGGAI

HAGGAI

Read Haggai 1

About 2,500 years ago there lived in China a man called Confucius. We know a great deal about his life. He spent many of his years both speaking and writing words of wisdom and there is no doubt that he had a great brain and he used it to think. From his lips came many practical words of wisdom including something that we still say very frequently, namely: "What you don't like done to you don't do to others" – the negative form of the golden rule. It took another five hundred years for Jesus to come along and turn that word of wisdom into a positive one, "Whatever men you would have do to you, do also to them." But Confucius was a wise man. Mind you, his books which you can still read are full of inaccuracies – especially historical inaccuracies which cause the scholars of Confucius to have some real headaches as they try to work out what he said.

At the same time as Confucius was pouring out words of man's wisdom, there was another man many hundreds of miles to the west at the eastern end of the Mediterranean not pouring out a flood of words but just giving a few words which were historically accurate and which are words that are the words of God. His name is Haggai and the contrast between these two men who lived at the same time is very marked. For years, Confucius poured out his words. Like all human oratory and wisdom it is not infallible. But Haggai spoke only five times over a space of three or four months from September to December in the year 520 BC, and on each occasion he only spoke for a few minutes and on one occasion he only said four words.

Yet still these words come across as being infallible words of truth. The circumstances in which he was speaking have long since disappeared. Nevertheless, I am going to go back into those circumstances to enable you to get the feel of the Word of God that came through this man about whom we know nothing. We do not know where or when he was born. We don't know how long he lived; we don't know what kind of a person he was. We don't know if he was married or unmarried. He was just a mouthpiece at a critical juncture in the history of God's people. So take your seat for a little history lesson.

Come with me for a little trip back into history. In the year 586 BC Jerusalem fell. The city for over four hundred years had been the centre of God's people, the capital of Israel, the city of David—not only where the king lived but where the king's King lived in a house next door. It was where the house of God had been built by David's son and it was a magnificent building, the finest they had ever seen. If you can imagine God's house with the people's houses clustered around it, and in the year 586 the armies of Babylon came to that city and razed it to the ground. They pulled down the houses, they broke the walls, they took the people up in chains. They killed the babies by taking them by the feet and dashing their brains out against the stones.

The house of God was destroyed utterly – that magnificent temple which had taken so many years to build, so much labour and so much money. Jerusalem was left empty. The people of God were taken away in chains into slavery.

But thank God that he does not finish with people like that. It was their own silly fault, there is no question about that. Prophet after prophet had come to that city and said that the way they were treating God was disastrous. If they went on like that they would lose this city and the land and go far away into an unknown land as slaves. They did not listen. They laughed. They thought: this is ridiculous – prophets of doom. They had their own preachers who said it would be all right – don't get worried about judgment, God's not like that. But God is like that and there always comes a point where God's patience is exhausted with people's folly. God was saying to them: You cannot treat me like that. You are my people and I have set you in this land to be a light shining to the nations; I have put you here as an example of my blessing; you are to demonstrate me and you can't get away with this.

So they went away and they had lost their city and the stones they built up one upon another were pulled down to the foundations, and the place was left empty and ruined but God had not finished with them. He still hasn't. When God chooses a man or a woman or a nation, he may discipline them, he may punish them, and that is a proof that they still belong to him. It is the sons of God who are chastised by him, not the others.

God would bring them back when they had learned their lesson, when they realised why this had happened, why things had gone wrong, why they had lost their city, and why the house of God was in ruins.

Bring them back he did. In the year 538 BC, fifty thousand of them came back across the desert. Can you see them, coming back, looking for the green hills of Judea, seeing in the distance the hills surrounding Jerusalem, climbing those hills? Then can you imagine them looking down from the Mount of Olives and seeing before them the wreck of a once lovely city? So they began to rebuild. That fifty thousand got back in the first wave of immigration, but they began to build a house of the Lord again, slowly, stone by stone, but what a gigantic task it was, fourteen acres of it.

Some of the stones weighed a hundred and ten tons and you can still see some of them. It was a gigantic task and after a bit they lost heart. It was too big for them and so they began to concentrate on building their own homes. That was a task that they could cope with. The house of the Lord didn't even get the foundations finished – mind you they were pretty big. So they got their own homes' foundations laid and they got the walls up and they got roofs on and still they didn't go back to the house of the Lord. They even began to decorate their own homes in fancy style. In those days they didn't have double-glazing and all sorts of other things that we have today but they did have wooden panelling, and that was considered the status symbol of those days. They began to have wooden panelling lining the walls and ceilings, and still the house of the Lord had an unfinished foundation. Then things began to go more wrong. Inflation hit them and the cost of food spiralled. They found it more and more difficult to make ends meet and the harvest began to fail. The wheat didn't produce what they had hoped, and the oil wasn't there. When they got their wages it seemed as if the money lost value overnight. They were putting it into a bag with holes. Does this make you feel sympathetic with them? You understand their situation, and though they lived in better homes than they had lived in for many a long year, yet somehow they were becoming obsessed with just making ends meet and trying to get enough money to keep going, just to keep body and soul together. Into this situation came this unknown man with a word from God.

The word was simply this: do you not see any connection between your neglect of God's work and your problems with inflation? What a message. This bold little man came into that nation and spoke to the religious leaders, Joshua the high priest, and to the political leaders, Zerubbabel the governor, and he said: Listen, God has something to say about your situation. Haggai had just two things to say, but how powerfully he said them. The first is: God's work must have priority.

If we are going to be free from the anxiety of what we eat and what we wear, then God's work must have priority. Jesus said it too: Seek first the kingdom of God and his righteousness and all these things will be added to you. Why are you so worried about making enough? Why are you becoming obsessed, caught up with just staying alive; seek first his kingdom and his righteousness. The second thing Haggai said, we will see in chapter 2: God's workers must have purity. Here are the two great needs if God's people's needs are to be met: that God's work must have priority and God's workers must have purity. When those two things are present then God's people will find that they have enough to live on.

Let us look at the first. The basic sin of this people even after they had been through this dreadful experience of exile in another land, even after they had got back into God's land, was to say "some other time". That was what they were doing when they were confronted with the needs of God's work. "Yes I'm interested. Yes I'd like to help and maybe sometime I'll be able to, but the time is not right now. The circumstances are not right now. It's too difficult to do it now. Someday when things have eased up I'll do it."

I have discovered in my life that life never eases up. If you say "God's work can't be done now because I'm under too much pressure", then you will go on saying it for the rest of your life. You will never get back to your priorities. I remember when I was under pressure, taking my degree exams at college. At the same time I was also called to be a lay preacher and had certain exams to pass there. I remember it was the easiest thing in the world to say something like this: "I've got to get my degree now, that is all important."

Someday when I had my degree and passed those exams I would get back to the preacher's exams.

But first things first and I remember that the Lord rebuked me and challenged me on this. What is first in your life? Your career or God's kingdom? So I had to get things balanced up again and made quite sure that those preacher's exams got done and that I didn't say: when my degree is over then I can get back to God's work. Because when my degree was over I did not find life eased up. Each hurdle you come to, you think this is the busiest stage of your life and most demanding. "Once I get this over, I'll get back to God's work." But it never works out like that and this is what the people of God were saying here: some day we will rebuild the house of the Lord but it just doesn't seem the right time; we are having such a struggle to keep ourselves going; we have got to get our own houses built. The house of the Lord lay waiting for builders.

So Haggai came with the word "consider". I have discovered that the most frequent comment I have after preaching is: "Well, you've certainly given us something to think about." It is usually said in terms of mild reproach as if, you know: "I didn't come to church to use my brain. I came to relax. I came to rest." You maybe thought (and you shouldn't have really done) that it was an intrusion to the service.

"I came just to worship..." but the Word of God says: consider. Sit down, use your brain, use your nose (that is Greek for common sense). Exercise the gift that God has given you to see why things are happening. God's word is not just to tell us what is happening, but *why* certain events are taking place. On Sundays we come to hear the word of God, to ask "why", to think it over, to consider the ways of God. In God's Word is the answer. Haggai says consider. Look what your life is. You are chasing after just keeping alive. You are finding it increasingly difficult to keep body and soul together. Your money is going nowhere. Have you ever considered why this is happening? The economist might give you his reason. The politicians have theirs. None of them seem able to put their finger on it. Could it be that we are neglecting God? Could it be that the reason why we find it so difficult to make ends meet is that God is not first and not even second or third but very much last in our order of priorities? "Consider," says Haggai. Think it over. Do you see no connection between the contrast of God's house and your homes?

Today we think of the comfort of our homes, the labour-saving devices, the time we spend decorating, and God's work gets what's left and there isn't much left and there isn't much to spare. Do you see no connection between your struggles and God's work neglected?

It is a serious word. Haggai is saying that God is behind all this. Prosperity depends on God. He is waiting and willing to provide for your needs, to look after your physical needs, to look after these things you are so desperate to have. He wants people who will put first things first and get on with his work and he has promised that the rest will be supplied. God keeps his word. The message is very simple: get your priorities right. Get first things first. God's house is more important than yours. God's work is to be done by his people. In this way we are tackling the cause of our problem not the effect – tackling the disease and not the symptom.

How do we apply that to our day? Well first I am very tempted to apply it to our nation. I have lived through a world war. Have you noticed the pattern that follows when we pass from war to peace? During wartime we have room for God. We have national days of prayer. We see churches crowded with people pleading with God; ministers and preachers of the gospel were exempt from military service because the nation regarded their work as so important.

I don't think that will ever happen in another war, but people prayed then. We needed God and then we came back from war to peace and within a decade we were living for the things that we had to do without during the war. We were becoming more and more interested in better homes and the things that money could buy, and we became an affluent society – and therefore and afterwards a permissive society. No one has ever from the top suggested: "Let's get back to God and ask him to sort out some of these problems of ours." I think there is a message here for our nation. Only the nation that puts God first can ask and expect him to do something about the other problems. But I believe that this word is to be applied rather to the church than to the nation. It is to God's people that Haggai came, not other nations. It is to God's people that his message comes about priority. Have you got your priorities right? Some people take Haggai's word and apply them to the church building. Well it is certainly nice when you have a church building that is as comfortable and well cared for and looked after as our own homes, and that is as it should be. It always worries me when I see an old, dirty down at heel church building when I know that the people who worship there have lovely homes and look after their homes. They are almost saying: for God anything will do but my home has got to be right. But I am going deeper than this. I don't think this prophecy applies to the building of the church, nor do I believe it primarily applies to the church programme, as if the priority must be meetings of the church, though I think there is an element of truth in there. But I believe God's house today, which needs building up in this land, is made up not of the building and not of meetings but of people, and that the desperate need for God's people today is to build God's house in this land. That house is going to be made of people. In a word "evangelism". The people of

Israel were told to go up into the mountains and get timber, and come back and build the house of God. We are to go out into the highways and byways and bring people back to build a house of God. I believe that that's our priority call.

Which are we really concerned about: our business or God's business? I had a fascinating chat with an Australian Anglican minister from Sydney. He said a revolution happened in his church. He said, "One day I just looked at the congregation and I saw gifted businessmen who in their particular sphere have used their gifts to build up commerce and have been successful. All they were doing in church was taking the collection. I began to see that we have got it all wrong. They saw me as the minister, as the one to do the work of the church, and themselves to keep me going. So I decided to do something." He made a lunch appointment with every businessman in his church. He travelled miles to the cities where they worked. He found he had lunches in the best clubs in town. Sometimes they even had a working lunch, when he took sandwiches and sat and talked to the man over his desk in his office, but he just had one message for each of these men: "Who has the priority in your life? Is God just getting what's left over? Are you thinking you are just supporting me to do the work of God? Or do you see it as *your* work, to which your business ability, all your gifts and energy, could be directed."

He said that a revolution took place. "They didn't wait for me. They just got together and said: as businessmen we are going to be in the Lord's business. We are going to use the gifts that God has given us, the experience that God has given us – of selling, of getting in contact with people, of organising – and we are going to get men together and tell them about Jesus Christ." And off they went.

Five of those men are in full-time evangelistic service. God has met their needs. That Anglican minister had been a

Haggai. He had taken the message of chapter 1 and said to those men: Does God's business get what's left over or could you say, "I'm a businessman. I'm going to give my business ability to building God's house to get a hold of people for the Lord"? Oh, the potential of those who get first things first. What God can do with those who give him priority!

So that is the message of chapter 1. How did Haggai get on? It was not a very popular message. After all they were very comfortable looking after themselves, but he said, "consider". For about three and a half weeks nothing happened. Nothing happened that you could see, but when you plant God's Word in human hearts it is alive and it germinates, and something begins to happen and God's Word goes on acting. I am so glad that Haggai had no immediate response because that can be so often due to the emotion of the moment. Deep in the hearts of God's people the word of Haggai was burning.

The message of Haggai went on working in these people's hearts and three and a half weeks later the political leader Zerubbabel came, the religious leader Joshua came – and thank God when it hits the leaders as well. All the people came. What a revival, and that is how it began. The Lord stirred up the spirit of all the remnant of the people, all of them came, and they said: we are going to get on with God's business. Get on with it they did, and they began to build.

Haggai had a second message for them. On the first day he said: get your priorities right and get God's work done. On the twenty-fourth day of the same month he came and he said this: "I am with you," says the Lord. That was the shortest sermon he ever preached. The presence of the Lord among his people is conditioned by their willingness to put *his* work first, and the business of building his house at the top of their list of priorities.

Lest you think that I am using the Old Testament to say

something to Christians that doesn't have New Testament sanction, may I take you to the last chapter of Matthew's Gospel where Jesus told the church what the first priority was and what our top task is: "Go into all the world and make disciples of all nations and lo, I am with you even to the end of the age." Same message: seek first my kingdom and you'll have my presence. Go out and win others for Christ and build up the house of the Lord and I am with you.

That is the secret of the presence of the Lord. Are you feeling you have lost a sense of the presence of the Lord, that he is not as real to you as once he was? Then could it be that you've got your priorities wrong? Get on with building God's house, winning people, and building them into a structure in which the Lord can dwell, and you will find the presence of the Lord will be with you. He is never so near as when you are talking to someone else about him.

Read Haggai 2

Now the people and their leaders have been busy building God's house. They have been at it for four whole weeks and have made hardly any impression on it. Now it is the day of the "harvest festival" and they are holding it in the ruins of the temple, surrounded by what little they have built.

The older people among them remember the great occasions in the past when the temple was complete, and they are discouraged and depressed. It is not unknown for God's people to get depressed. What depresses them? I have seen four things in this chapter that got them down. First of all they were depressed by the huge task. They had worked for a whole month and had only just scratched the surface. They had not even completed the foundation platform. They were discouraged by the size of the task. It is easy for us too to be discouraged by the size of a task. When we consider the millions there are to reach, and the race against time that there is, we could be discouraged by the size of our task. The second thing that discouraged them was the slow progress compared with what was yet to be done – they seemed to have done so little in the whole month. We too can get discouraged: even though we see people coming to know God. We look out at the millions who don't. A third thing that was discouraging them was their limited resources.

When Solomon had built the first house of God he was the richest king there had ever been. Now they have come back from exile with nothing in their pockets. They could get stone and wood, gathering the stone from the hills and chipping it and chopping the trees down for wood, but where was the gold and where were the cedars of Lebanon, and where were all the riches that they needed to restore the splendour of this building? They did not have it. Their limited resources were causing discouragement and depression. If only we had the money that Solomon had! God's people today can get discouraged in the same way because the resources are limited. Missionary societies cry out for more resources. You can get discouraged about such things.

The fourth thing that was discouraging them was odious comparisons. This was coming from the older people present who should have known better. May I say a word in love to older church members: do you realise what a power you have to encourage or discourage those who work today? How easy it is to say, "Oh you should have been in the good old days. I'm not impressed with what's happening today. I go back to the great days of So and So." "Which of you remembers the former glory and what does it seem to you today; does it not seem to you as nothing?" says Haggai.

Some draw comparisons and talk about the past as the good old days and are not impressed with what is being done in the present. I beg of older folk: don't live in the past; don't discourage people by reminding them of what once was, and regretting that the present is not the past.

A crisis arose, for discouragement stops work and despondency leads to loss of service, so Haggai came into that situation again with another message from the Lord: take courage. Take the courage that comes from God. Take courage Zerubbabel, the political leader. Take courage Joshua, the religious leader. Take courage you people. It is all right. Don't get downhearted. Don't get despondent. Don't be discouraged.

If you are going to cheer people up you have to give them reasons to cheer them up. It is no use telling them to whistle in the dark. You have to tell them that the situation is not as bad as they fear.

The two things Haggai tells them from God are: I am; I will. Those two phrases are among the most encouraging phrases of the Bible when God speaks them. Look at what he says first under "I am". I could summarise the meaning as: I am with you; when I brought you out of Egypt I promised to be with you and I don't go back on my word. I'm still around. My Spirit is abiding with you. Do you think I have let you go? All right, what you're doing doesn't seem very great at the moment but I'm with you and I'm great.

It means take your eyes off the visible and look at the invisible; take your eyes off the material and look at the spiritual; take your eyes off the earthly and look at the heavenly. When God's people get down it is because they are looking at the visible, earthly, material things. God is letting his people know that he is in this thing.

Then he says, "I will." What is he going to do? He says: "I am going to shake the earth. I am going to shake everything. I am going to shake the nations.

He is going to take the nations by the feet, hold them upside down, and shake them until the money drops out of their pockets. "I will shake the nations and the treasures of the nations will flow into this house for the silver and gold is mine."

Just let this sink in: every bit of money in the world is God's. Every last penny everywhere is God's and he can redistribute wealth as he pleases. That is the most amazing thing, and he is always doing it.

You see, you are looking at your resources. What about his? "All the money in the world is mine, the cattle on a thousand hills, the gold, and the silver." Are you worried about your resources? Yes, your resources are limited but not mine. I will shake the nations until they have to let that money go. "The latter splendour of this house will be greater than the former." When God says something like that you know it is difficult to believe but it is going to be true – and it did come true. Not immediately. The trouble is we are in a hurry and God isn't, but it came true. By the time Jesus came, the temple which Zerubbabel had rebuilt was greater and grander than it had ever been in its history. The remarkable thing is that it had been brought to that splendour by a heathen man called Herod – a descendant of Esau, not even one of God's people. But God had shaken that man and his money had poured into that temple. When Jesus was walking the courts of that temple it was still being rebuilt on a grander scale than ever before.

When God makes a promise to those who are struggling in a day of small things and says that the future is going to be better than the past, you can rely on that promise.

So we look forward to the latter splendour of the house. As we build God's house we may see a conversion here, a conversion there, and that is another brick in God's house, but you know you are building a house that is going to be glorious, larger, greater than anything that has ever yet been seen. Does that pick you up? Does that give you courage?

I am quite sure that Haggai saved the situation. There is

no room for despondency among God's people. If we are going to do God's work then let us expect prosperity. Let us just tie together two things we have said so far: God's work must have priority; God's work will have prosperity. These two things follow as night and day, and they are cause and effect. If God's work has priority it will have prosperity. Here we have a simple statement of Scripture.

Now let us move on to the second great principle which Haggai enunciates. At 2:10, with confidence they pressed on with the work and another two months passed. By now they were beginning to see the building rise again. God's house was beginning to take shape. Actually it was going to take them about three or four years altogether.

They must have worked their own land when they could, but the priority was given to God's house. Haggai had said: the cost of living is going up, the harvest is failing, your larders are half empty, if you only build God's house you would find that this situation would be put right – and it didn't happen. For three months they worked hard on God's house and at the end of three months the financial situation was no better than it had been at the beginning, and Haggai had to face this very honestly. Did he have doubts? Haggai faced them honestly. He had said that if you give God's work priority you won't lack food. You will have enough to live on and it just wasn't happening after three whole months. Can you see the crisis looming? Haggai went back to the Lord and waited on him – you said if we got on with your house we would have enough to live on in our own houses; Lord, why?

Then he realised. God showed him that there were two things that were needed, not just one. This is so like God, he doesn't give it to us all at once. He gives us one thing to put right and when we have put that right he will tell us the next thing to put right. If he gave it all at once we would be overwhelmed or discouraged. But God says something is needed and when we give him that he then says another thing is needed. There were just two things needed. Number one, God's work must have priority. Number two, God's workers must have purity. Suddenly Haggai realised clearly what was wrong. They were doing God's work but in the wrong way and it still was not acceptable to God.

It came to this message in the form of a question, a conundrum, which was to be directed to the priest and when we first read it we think, "Well, it is purely a ceremonial technicality. It is simply a bit of casuistry. It is simply the priest arguing about the details of their ritual, because a vital part of Jewish ritual was the distinction between clean and unclean. The priest had to say which things were clean and which things were unclean and how people got clean and how people got unclean, and they laid it all down. So Haggai went to the priests and asked them two questions and they gave him the answers expected. We might dismiss this and say it is a bit of Old Testament priesthood or ceremonial, but it is not. It concerns a vital principle of life, both in our world and in the church. The principle of life is this: holiness is not contagious but evil is.

Now I want you to let that simple principle sink in because even if we are busy doing God's work we can be spoiling God's work because we have forgotten that simple principle. Let me illustrate it very simply. I want you to imagine that there is a large room with a nice rug in it and somebody comes in who has got a frightful cold – sneezing, blowing their nose, coughing. Only one person has that cold and five hundred others in it are perfectly healthy. Do the healthy people cure that person of his cold or does the person with the cold give it to the healthy people? That is the question. One person with cholera can fill a city with fear because all the healthy people in that city cannot take away the cholera.

One rotten apple in your loft can make all the rest rotten. The good ones don't make the rotten one good. This applies morally and spiritually. Christians, may I give you a warning? It is so easy to think that if we go and mix with evil people freely, that our goodness will rub off on them but according to the Bible your goodness is not infectious but their evil is. That is why Paul says quite simply: bad company ruins good morals. Yes we have got to go into all the world and preach, but don't kid yourself that you can enjoy social life with evil people and be an influence for good upon them. It is evil that is contagious, not good.

Now what has this got to do with building God's house in Haggai's day? Simply this. If unholy people try to do holy work the holy work does not make the workers holy. The unholy workers make the work unholy. Do you follow this? It is a delusion to think that if we are busy doing God's work that makes us better people. We may be having the opposite effect and spoiling God's work. Have you ever taken your car to the garage to be serviced and it has come back with oil on the steering wheel, the seat all covered with dirt, and you just feel, "Oh, they've done the job but look how they left it." Or take another simple illustration. When as children we offered to help our mother to make pastry, somehow it always came out a delicate shade of grey. God is saying: I am glad you are building my house. I am glad you got on with the job but why do you make such a dirty job of it? In other words: you are doing my work and you think that because you are doing my work, which is always a holy work, this is a holy house you are building, that you are holy people – far from it. You are unholy people and you are making a dirty job of my house.

I remember being in a church building once when it was under construction and there were some subcontractors doing a job on it. They were only there for a short time but they came in and their language was blasphemous and filthy, and I thought: don't they realise they are building something for God – and it seems so incongruous? Then the Lord turned that back on me and said, "Well, what about you?" Because we are doing a holy job it doesn't make us holy. We could be spoiling God's work – the building of God's house – by what we are. You see, it is possible to do something for God, a holy work for God and be proud of doing it and you have spoiled it in God's sight. It has become a dirty thing in God's sight, an unholy building. You could be doing it for God and you could be jealous of someone else because they are doing it better. Somehow your bit of building is spoiled, it is dirty, and it has become an unholy building for God.

The two things that God's work requires are priority and purity. God is not just wanting his work done, he is wanting it done by people who are fit to do it. It is a holy work to build God's house, to do his work, to get on with his business.

Haggai could now see what was wrong. People were giving God priority but not purity; doing his work but not fit to do it. So they were leaving it dirty and in a mess and staining it with their own selfishness in it all. What a message! At this point in the sermon comes the most unexpected thing – so unexpected that it hits you. I would have thought that God would now say through Haggai, "As soon as you've got clean hands to do my work, I'll bless you and I'll give you what you want." But God said no such thing. He said: "I'm going to bless you today." Let me just state it quite bluntly so that you get the message: though God requires holiness in his workers he does not wait until they are holy before he blesses them. Now just think that through. Haggai says "consider"; "think it over." Well, I sat down and I thought it over. What a remarkable thing for God to do. If he wants clean work and clean workers, then surely he will have to wait until they are clean before he allows them to work – but no, listen to what God says: "I'll bless you today. From the very first day I've told you this I'll bless you."

Now what do I think about that? I considered it and three thoughts struck me. Thought number one was: you are taking an awful risk, God. If you withheld your blessing until we were fit to do your work then that would make sure we were fit, but Lord, if you bless us from this day, from the day of telling us that you require this, you are going to run the risk that we won't follow after this – that we will go on as we are.

Then I realised that God takes that kind of risk. My second thought was this: thank God. Lord, if you waited till I was perfect before you blessed anything I did, you would be waiting an awfully long time. Thank you that you are going to bless now, even though you require us to be fit for your work.

My third thought was this: how like God. He is not a God who bargains; he is a God who blesses. God is not going to say, "I'll wait until you get up here and then I'll respond." He says he is going to begin right now. Yes, he wants us to be holy. Yes, he wants you to be fit. But he is prepared to bless us now. That is grace. Do you know, that is how you begin the Christian life with what's called "justification", and that means quite simply that God is prepared to accept you as you are and bless you. He's not going to wait till you are perfect. Isn't that a lovely message? Yes, God's work requires priority. Yes, God's work requires purity. But God says, "I will bless you now" and that makes us thoroughly ashamed of ourselves. It makes us very small. It makes us realise that we can never say: "You know, I was good enough for this blessing." Let us never make the mistake of thinking that blessing means we are better than any other. It doesn't.

Finally on that same day on the twenty-fourth day of the month of what we now call December, another message came – a little one. No longer for all the people but for one man,

Zerubbabel. Now what do we get from this last little message from Zerubbabel? We know a little about him. We know he was the governor of this little struggling group of people, fifty thousand trying to rebuild a nation. But we know that when Zerubbabel heard the Word of the Lord, Zerubbabel took the lead and gave an example and said, "Let's get on with it." We know that it was Zerubbabel who really was the prime mover. We know that he risked losing his job and that a report went back to the ruler of the empire that he was doing this – a critical report. But Zerubbabel was a man who was prepared to risk his job to do what the Lord said, and Zerubbabel was a man who responded to Haggai's call.

Consider Zechariah chapter 4:6–9:

"This is the word of the Lord to Zerubbabel: 'Not by might nor by power but by my Spirit,' says the Lord of hosts. What are you O great mountain? Before Zerubbabel you will become a plain. He shall bring forward the top stone amidst shouts of grace, grace to it. Moreover the word of the Lord came to me saying the hands of Zerubbabel have laid the foundation of this house. His hand shall also complete it. Then you will know that the Lord of hosts has sent me to you, for whoever has despised the day of small things shall rejoice and shall see the plumbline in the hand of Zerubbabel."

What does that tell you? It tells you that one man led the rest. It tells you that one man heard the Word of the Lord and one man got on with laying the foundation and enthused the people. One man saw it through even though it was a day of small things. God was saying: Zerubbabel you started it, you will finish it. Zerubbabel you will put the top stone on with the plumbline in your hand and those who despise a day of small efforts, those who laughed at the beginning of your work and said, "That's nothing," they will see you finish it.

What a message! I have found that again and again in God's work, when the word of the Lord comes to a group of God's people, very often it is one person in that group of people who says "Let's get on with it" and leads the others forward. You study Christian work. Study church history. You find that even though the people hear the word of God, it waits for one person to say, "I'm going to get on with it. Who will come with me?" Zerubbabel was that man. So God had a word for Zerubbabel through Haggai – the man who got on with it and encouraged others to do it by doing it himself. What was that word? It is a simple word: that God would never forget him. What is a signet ring (see v. 23)? It is a reminder of someone. It is worn even when that person has disappeared from the scene. The kingdoms of the earth – you feel you are just a tiny little group in history – but God is going to shake these kingdoms, and kings off their thrones. He is going to shake the nations, but in the day when they all disappear Zerubbabel will be like a signet ring. Zerubbabel will not be forgotten by God.

This life will soon be past and only what is done for Jesus will last. It gave me a thrill in my heart to turn to the New Testament and to read again the genealogies of Jesus. The genealogies of scripture are precious. I hope you have learned the spiritual secret of studying the "begats". In Matthew 1 and Luke 3, there is the family tree of Jesus – that line of people which includes all kinds of people. It includes a prostitute, it includes a foreigner, but there in the middle of both family trees, in Matthew and Luke, there is Zerubbabel, son of Shealtiel. This man was part of God's plan to prepare for the coming of Jesus. I give you the same promise in the name of God: that if you hear the word of the Lord, to give his work priority and you will step forward as Zerubbabel did, and you will say: let us lay the foundation;

let us get on with it. Come on, let's do the work of God. Who will come with me?

Then I assure you that your work will not be forgotten, nor will you. "Therefore my beloved brethren be steadfast, immovable, always abounding in the work of the Lord, knowing that in the Lord your labour is not in vain."

MALACHI

MALACHI

Read Malachi

The background to Malachi is much the same as for Haggai and Zechariah, only worse. We have now gone 100 years after the return from exile in Babylon, and I am afraid things are not good. Jerusalem is still deserted; the people living in the country around them still don't want them back; the land is still largely barren and uncultivated; there are poor harvests and they are getting locust swarms. Life is hard and precarious. The building of the temple is finished but it is such a small thing compared with Solomon's (it was finished in 520 BC). The walls which were broken have been built up by Nehemiah, but people still prefer living out in the country and it is a job getting them back in to town. They have not built a palace because they don't have a king. They have the royal line but the family of Zerubbabel is living in a poor house. They are not allowed to reign. The Persian governor is still their ruler. There is still just a little hill town and surrounding villages there, nothing like the kingdom of David, so the people are disappointed, disillusioned and even despairing, and they are beginning to ask whether it was worth it. They have been back 100 years, and where was this kingdom they were going to build? So they were asking a question which I am afraid people ask today. I can put it very simply: they were saying why bother; and therefore they were becoming complacent, contented. They were settling down, and this depression was having a devastating effect on their religious life for a start.

They had learned the lesson about idolatry in the exile. They never again went after other gods or changed their religion, but their religion had become a formality. They still went to the temple but it was largely out of tradition. It was ritual without reality; it was no longer a priority and they were now asking what was the minimum amount of time they need spend on religious activity and what was the minimum amount of money they could get away with. How small a coin could they put in the temple collection? A tip, instead of a gift, and I am afraid the fact is the more you put in to your faith the more you get out of it, and the less you put in to your devotions the less you get out of them. The priests were like the people, I am afraid, by the time Malachi came along. The priests were just doing it for a living. They were honestly not bothered about how many people came to attend the services as long as they just got through it and got their living – I am afraid that is also true today – and they were neglecting teaching the scripture, they were just keeping the services going in a casual and careless manner as if anything would do for God. No longer did they offer the best, they just kept it going. Not only had this an effect on their religious life, but when you get that attitude to your religious life it begins to affect your moral life too, and sure enough this was happening. When you say why bother about God it is not long before you say: why bother trying to be godly? Or, to put it more simply: when one generation gets this way about God (why bother about God?), the next generation will be saying "Why be good?" And we have lived to see that in our lifetime because we are now in the third and fourth generation away from church.

I remember going in to a factory canteen to speak to the men, and a man got up and challenged me at the end. He said: "I am not boasting, but you ask the other workers here who they go to when they are in trouble, and who helps them? They will say me."

He continued: "I am not boasting, I am just telling you a

fact. Come to our street and ask all my neighbours: who is the man who helps the most when they are in trouble, and they will say me." Now he said that he did not go to church, he did not read the Bible. He did not say prayers. How did I explain that? He was taking the old line: I can be as good a Christian without going to church. He asked me how I explained that. He was saying: I do not bother about God but I live a good life.

I had to ask the Holy Spirit to give me a word of knowledge. I said, "Your grandfather went to church, didn't he; and your grandfather prayed with his Bible, didn't he? He said yes.

I will tell you something more: your grandchildren won't be like you, because if you don't pass God on you cannot pass goodness on, and, you see, you can live for a couple or three generations on the faith of your forefathers but then it runs out and goodness disappears when God disappears. This is what Malachi was finding, and so the people were just saying: look after yourself, look after number one; make as much money as you can and give as little to God as you need. They had got into trading, and Jews are good at this. Even though they knew trading was wrong on the Sabbath they built out of town supermarkets just outside the gates so they could open them on the Sabbath. Isn't it interesting? Consumerism took over, it had a devastating effect on family life. "Why be faithful to God?" soon becomes "Why be faithful to your wife?" and so especially when your wife gets older and loses her sex appeal – "Why not trade her in for a later model? which is what they were doing, and it is all happening again. Furthermore, they were rather short of women, because most of those who had come back from Babylon were men, and in the shortage of women they said: well, nothing wrong with marrying outside of the people of God – Solomon did; why shouldn't we? So not only were they divorcing and remarrying but they were remarrying non-Jewish women against the law of God, so I am afraid the city of Jerusalem was being filled with abandoned wives and there was no state welfare then. They had a pretty rough time – widows, orphans and abandoned wives.

When times are bad you have got to find someone to blame, haven't you? Got to find a scapegoat. We have all got one: we have got the government, and they are honestly a very convenient scapegoat. Of course they did not have a government to blame, but they did have a God to blame and that is precisely what they did – and they said God is not bothered about us so we are not bothered about him. It sounded very impressive. They said: God has stopped loving us so we have just stopped loving him. They said: we can't believe in a God of love; look at the situation we are in – we are having to look after ourselves, he has abandoned us so we might as well just look after number one.

Now their criticism of God had two sides to it. On the one hand they said God does not reward good living, and on the other side he doesn't punish bad living – so why bother? This seems so real and relevant. There are so many people who think and talk like this, or if they don't talk like it they live like it. They don't bother about God because they say that he doesn't bother about us, how we live – and God seemed to be doing neither. So why bother to keep his laws? What is wrong with bending his laws? Now Malachi had to deal with this situation. His whole prophecy is in prose, not poetry, and that to me is a very serious indication of something: it indicates that God has lost his feelings for his people, and that is precisely what had happened. God had lost his feelings for his people and he was not going to talk to them again for another 400 years. This was his last word. It was a very cool word, not a warm word. It is not a heart word, it is a head word – argument. Malachi is unusual in that he is the one prophet who had arguments with people, and he obviously spoke this word and was heckled because he reports the heckling. They were offended by his preaching because his basic message was: you started all this; it was not God who stopped being bothered about you, you did it first. That is much the same as Haggai. You stopped bothering about God, that is why he is not bothered about you – and that is how God responds to a human situation. Romans 1 again. Paul says men gave God up, so God gave men up – that is fair, isn't it? And when a nation gives God up, he gives them up.

Some decades ago it was reported that Britain is the second most godless nation in the entire world. People aren't bothered, but when people are not bothered about him I am afraid he doesn't bother about us, and look what is the result. That is when violence, selfishness and pride take over.

Malachi could point out that the people had lost interest in the Lord – their lack of real love for him was the basic problem. They did not believe him; they were terribly offended. There were repeated protests of innocence from the congregation – it is not as bad as you make out. They felt insulted and indignant, and they argued, and they said: how did we stop caring for God?

You know, it is much the same in the parable of the sheep and the goats in Jesus' teaching, when he said: I was in prison and you didn't visit me, I was hungry and you didn't feed me. So how? We never saw you in prison, we never saw you hungry. Oh yes you did, he said, because I live in my brethren – when you are doing it to my brothers you are doing it to me. He had much the same reply – how did we not bother with God? How did we stop loving him? How did we stop caring? Malachi takes them through it step by step and his whole prophecy is an argument with them to show them how they did it, how they stopped caring about God and therefore caused him to stop caring about them.

Malachi has five very unusual features. First, there are more "God words" in Malachi than in any of the other minor prophets: 47 out of 55 verses (85%) are the direct words of God, and that is among the highest proportion in any prophetic book. The second is that this prophecy is anonymous. I know you thought Malachi was his name but it is not a name – it is the word "messenger" and that is all. It could have been his name but it is never known as a name anywhere else in the Old Testament, but it is frequently used. In fact, within this book he uses the word "messenger" of prophets, priests and kings, so he is just an anonymous messenger – a nobody bringing God's last word to his people Israel. The third feature is that this dialogue takes the form of sharp exchanges between prophet and people. He was heckled; 12 times it says "but you say". They argued, interrupting his sermon, and said: that's not true, that is exaggeration, you are making us out to be worse than we are. He had to deal with every objection, which he did very effectively.

The fourth feature I have already mentioned: it is prose, not poetry, because God's feelings have run out, dried up. God feels drained. He feels exhausted with his people and therefore he won't talk to them for another 400 years. You need to see God's heart here. Wouldn't you be fed up if, having taking them to exile and brought them home, they now cannot be bothered about God.

The fifth feature is of course that this is God's last word. Perhaps the Christian order of the books in the Old Testament is right after all, because this was God's last word and the last word is "curse", and to this day, whenever the Jews read Malachi in the synagogue, they do read the last verse lest he "smite the land with a curse", and then they go back and read v. 5 again so they don't end with the word "curse". Isn't that interesting?

You go to the synagogue, and when they read Malachi that is what you will find. So here we are dealing with God's last word to his people Israel for 400 years.

Malachi announced that God had loved Jacob and hated Esau. How many of the deepest divisions today go right back into history? The whole Arab-Israeli conflict goes back to Ishmael and Isaac, and here we have a conflict that goes right back to Jacob and Esau, those twins, but having said that I want you to know that in the Bible "loved" and "hated" do not mean what we mean by these words, and therefore we get a wrong impression. To love someone is to care for them and seek their highest good, it is not to feel good about them and to "hate" someone in Bible language is not to care for someone and not to seek their good. When Jesus said you are not worthy to follow me if you don't hate your father and mother, he did not mean that you are to have bitterness and resentment towards them, he means you are to care for him more than them. Now that is rather important, otherwise we can be misunderstood.

Furthermore, God is not just talking about way back in the past – Jacob and Esau – he is really talking about the two nations Israel and Edom, and he is reminding them that over the previous hundred years he has done nothing but good for Israel and he has punished Edom; that is what he is really talking about, not the distant past but the recent past, and the recent past is this: when the Babylonians came to take the Jews away and to destroy Jerusalem, the Edomites, descendants of Esau living over the Jordan on the hills the other side, were thrilled to bits and they joined in and they said Hallelujah! They are finished! And they really came and they took the babies of the Jews by the heels and they bashed their brains out against the Jerusalem wall. This was the Edomites taking advantage of the Babylonian invasion. It is all there, and in exile they wrote a song. It is a terrible song which goes something like this: "We hung our harps in the willow trees; how could we sing the songs of Zion in a foreign land? May my tongue cleave to the roof of my mouth and my hand forget its cunning if I forget thee, O Jerusalem". It ends: happy shall he be who dashes your babies against the stones, Edom. You get a picture there of what happened. It was not just that the Babylonians took them and Edom joined in; the descendants of Esau came against the descendants of Jacob. Since then, God has punished Edom.

Petra is where Edom lived. It is now an empty ruin that was Mount Seir. That is where the descendants of Esau lived and God threw them out of there by bringing the Arabs to throw them out and they had to go and live in the desert, where there were no crops, and had to scratch a living as virtual Bedouins – travelling Edomites, as wanderers in the desert of Sinai. God says: Esau I have hated. He had done that to them for what they did to his people. Remember that I have loved you and I haven't cared for them. Herod, a descendant of Esau, managed to persuade the Romans to sell him the kingdom of Israel and he was king when Jesus was born. The unfolding history is intriguing, isn't it? Now what Malachi is saying is: just think about your survival. Looks what happened to Edom for what they did to you. Look what I have done for you: I have loved you, I have hated them – you should be grateful to me.

In other words, when you are complaining about God just think about what he has done to other people and think about what he has done to you, and you will be jolly grateful. It is on that basis that he then begins to deal with the accusations that they have stopped bothering about God and we will look at that later.

Behind all Malachi's preaching there is a concept of God. There is a "God framework" and it is important to outline that framework before we look at the individual prophecies.

He sees God in three functions as the whole Old Testament does, but I am afraid those who don't read the Old Testament tend to forget these three things. We read the New Testament and think God is the loving Father, and he is, but these three dimensions of God are vital: he is the Creator in our past, the King in our present and the Judge of our future. We must come to all things with this "God framework" of God in mind. That is the picture of God here, as it is in the whole Old Testament, and in the New Testament the loving Father side supplements this but it does not substitute for it. It is very important to have this godly sense of God as the background.

The first people he has a go at are the priests, and he has two goes at them. It is interesting that here God is seen as Father and as Master, and should be respected, but instead they are treating God with contempt, and familiarity breeds contempt.

Again, may I dare to say it, I miss the fear of God in many services today where God is treated with familiarity but not with reverence and respect.

He said: you priests are bringing God into disrepute and dishonour; you are giving him a bad name – you should be reverent. But you are not reverent and I am not going to call you because you don't reverence God. They said: How are we showing contempt for God?

In two ways. They were offering cheap sacrifices instead of choosing the best lamb. They were choosing the worst, accepting blind and crippled animals to offer to God what nobody else had any use for – and approving this offering, to God less than the best. That was showing contempt for him. You would not go to the Persian governor with a blind, crippled lamb as a present, yet you go to God with that. That is a devastating argument, isn't it? You give God what is left over; you give someone else the best you can give. He said: that is how you do it; and he said God's name is great among the nations, but not among you – the Gentiles have more reverence for God than you do. Quite devastating.

Then he said that the second way in which you show contempt for God is preaching popular sermons. You are supposed to be God's messenger but you give the people what they want to hear; you are supposed to be teaching them the law, you are supposed to be God-fearers, not men pleasers.

Here we have again a fundamental temptation and pressure on those who have served God in the church. It is so easy to give people what they want to hear and not to disturb them, because if they are disturbed you will not be invited back. So here is how he specifically challenged them. He said: you are showing God contempt. And they said: how do we show God contempt? He said in this: you are giving him less than the best as a sacrifice and you are preaching sermons that are not what God wants. You are preaching what the people want.

These things are not out of date, are they? He reminds them of God's covenant with Levi, with the priests, that they would not need to work, that they would be supported by the others provided they taught people to fear the Lord. He said: you get the living still but you are not teaching people to fear the Lord; you are not teaching them all reverence – you are to be an example too. The levitical priests were told that people must be able to look at their lives and see it, not just hear it with their ears. He says: your lips and your lives must be giving the same message, and they are not, and he says: you are already under a curse and there is worse to come because many of you, your children, are going to die and your priesthood will come to an end, and your family will no longer be part of the priesthood if you carry on like this. Quite a severe word. In other words, they had become careless and casual. Again, I am disturbed at how casual some people treat the worship of God. This is Almighty God we are coming to worship. They were doing the right thing but doing it in the wrong way.

Next, Malachi moved on to the people, and there were five things which showed that both their belief and their behaviour were slipping. The first two examples are examples of broken faith; broken covenants. The first basic thing was mixed marriage. Their young people were marrying out of the people of God, which God said must never be. That is as true for the church as it is for Israel – we are not to be unequally yoked with unbelievers. The chief Rabbi of this country some decades ago said the greatest anxiety they have is that so many Jewish young men in this country are marrying Gentile girls that Jews are likely to lose their identity in this country in another ten years or so. It was happening then. It is happening in the church, too. If you marry a child of the devil you are going to have problems with your father-in-law. We should be telling our young people this. It leads to a lifetime of unequal yoke which chafes and rubs and causes great unhappiness.

The second thing was heartless divorce. It had now become rife. People changed their wives. They had got into what we call consecutive polygamy. Simultaneous polygamy is where people have more wives than one at the same time; consecutive polygamy is where they have as many wives as they want provided they have them one at a time. This is now right inside the church. Pastors are changing wives now. But why is it worse for them than church members? We are all brothers in Christ. This was happening in Malachi's day. There were divorces and remarriages going on all over the place within the people of God, and this hurt God because every marriage is in God's sight. Whether it is in a register office or the Garden of Eden or a church, every marriage is holy matrimony in God's sight, and every marriage comes under the law of God, and God's law, according to Jesus, is that whoever divorces and remarries commits adultery. But most preachers today are scared stiff of quoting that, much less preaching it, because it would upset too many people. One pastor of a church in the USA actually pinned me against a brick wall because I read that verse in a service, and he said, You've upset half my congregation." Actually, I found out it was him as well (he was on his third). Malachi had faced this and we have to face it too, but it is probably the most unpopular thing to face in today's church.

God simply says "I hate divorce". When we read the Bible right through in our church, one lady whom I didn't know asked whether she could read for fifteen minutes. I said yes, she put her name down, and she came to the church to read for her fifteen minutes – and then she was going straight afterwards to her solicitor to get a divorce. She read Malachi and she found herself reading "I hate divorce", and the result was that she never got to that solicitor. Coincidence? No. God knows how to deal with people.

Then Malachi deals with the people's doubtful questions. You see, he accused them of breaking covenant and they said: how are we breaking covenant? He said they were breaking the covenant with each other because marriage is a covenant and you are breaking the covenant by marrying outside the people of God. You know, these people he was talking to thought they were innocent and they did not like this preacher accusing them. How do we do this? But he spelled it out in detail and I find actually people don't mind you making general statements, it is when you spell it out in particular ways, that is when it hurts and that is when people say to the preacher: "Shut up." Doubtful questions. We learn from Malachi that this is wearying God.

You might be saying, "How can you believe in a God

of love when this is happening?" How dare you ask such questions. You ask where the justice of God is. How dare you ask that question? Judgment will come and it doesn't come by next Friday, it doesn't come immediately with God – that is his patience with us – but don't ever accuse God of being unfair, and of being indifferent to bad things going on.

But there will be an even bigger surprise when he does come to punish bad people, because the purging will start in his temple. As the New Testament says, judgment begins in the house of God.

Malachi knew that people were crying out for God to deal with bad people, but when he does, it will be you he deals with. He says the priests will go, and then lots of you will go, and he makes a list of what they were doing. He says these are the people who don't fear God and will go if God comes to judge: sorcerers, adulterers, perjurers, those who are defrauding labourers of wages, those who are holding cash back when they owe it, those who oppress widows and the fatherless, and those who deprive immigrants of justice. He says that when God comes to purge, they are the ones who will go. It is pretty direct talking.

Now at this point there is a change of tone, and in all this accusation there is an appeal from God, and God speaks from his heart just for a little while and says: it is because I don't that they are not restored; it is because I am amazingly patient that I don't judge quickly. You have a long history of unfaithfulness but I am still faithful. You may break my covenant but I never will. I am still committed to you. You may have turned away from me, but you can still turn back. Return to me and I will return to you. There it is again. You see, when we get away from God he gets away from us, but when we return to him he returns to us. God is in a dynamic two-way relationship with his people and he responds to them all the time. When they give him up, he gives them up, but when they return to him he returns to them; when the prodigal returns home, the father runs out to meet him. God is constantly meeting us where we are, responding to us, reflecting our attitude to him. That is this dynamic relationship which we have with God. Some people think of God as sitting way up in heaven far away, and just making decrees and pushing us around like puppets. That is not the Bible picture. The Bible picture is of God who is responding to us all the time, who changes his mind when we change, who repents when we repent, who returns to us when we return to him – that is the dynamic picture. It is a very live relationship.

Now Malachi says: you are stealing from God. How? We have never stolen from God. Oh yes you have: unpaid tithes and offerings. See how Malachi pins them to the ground, they object and say they are not like that; he says yes you are, and he spells it out and they cannot say a thing. They have not kept up the tithe to God or the voluntary offerings and he says therefore you are under a curse because the law of tithing and the law of Moses says if you pay, God blesses you, and if you don't, he curses you to the third and fourth generation.

Praise God, Christians are not under that law. I have never preached tithing in my life. I have preached giving because in the New Testament we are to give out of gratitude and the Lord doesn't want your gift if you don't want to give it. But in the Old Testament they had to tithe. It is not a Christian practice, but it was a Jewish practice. My wife and I sat and listened to a young man in a church preaching on tithing – which he should not have done – but at least he was honest. He gave them the whole story and he said to the congregation: if you don't tithe, your grandchildren and great-grandchildren will suffer, because the law says to the third and fourth generation, he said, you will be under the curse, and he will put your grandchildren under a curse – do you want to do that? Then let us take up the offering for this morning. They got the biggest offering I think they had for years. But I said afterwards to the leaders of that church: that was wicked teaching. If you are going to teach tithing you have got to teach the curse of not tithing as well as the blessing of tithing, and the Jews you could say that to, but to say that to a Christian congregation is wicked and it makes people give out of fear, but the Lord loves a cheerful giver under the new covenant.

I throw that in because too many churches teach tithing and it is not the law for Christians. We are to give out of sheer gratitude to God, and frankly churches that are taught giving give far more than tithing. For some people tithing would be far too little, and for others it would be far too much, and we need to be more flexible.

But they were under this law and he says: you are already under the curse because you haven't brought the tithes. And he said: if you want blessing again then you know how to do it – bring all the tithes into the Lord's storehouse and see if I don't open the windows of heaven and pour out such a blessing as cannot be contained. Unfortunately it is that verse that Christian preachers get hold of, and they ignore the verse in front about the curse, but that is being "pick 'n' mix" related to the Old Testament. We should not do it. But what does he mean by the "windows of heaven"? He means, literally, clouds and rain because the curse had brought drought to them. He says: I'll open the windows of heaven and pour out – and he means: I'll give you rain again if you just do what I've told you to do and bring them all in.

Then he accuses them of slanderous talk, and they say: how have we slandered God? Malachi, with that sharp razor of his tongue, says because you say it is useless to serve God, it's futile, it doesn't pay to be religious. That is a libel on God. They were saying that even evildoers prosper so it doesn't pay; those who challenge God seem to get away with it, so why bother? He said that is a slander on God.

Now did all this have any effect? Was Malachi as effective a preacher as Haggai and Zechariah had been? Did the people respond? The answer is some did, and some went away from hearing Malachi's prophecy and they got together in a house group here and a house group there, and they didn't have roast preacher for supper as so many do; they didn't discuss the messenger, they discussed the message, and they repented and said that preacher meant us – we have got to put things right. Only a few did that, and they did it in little groups in homes, and it says God wrote their names down in a book. They talked about God so God said: I am writing them down; I am noting who responded to the message. Quite a thought, isn't it? God writes down the names of those who hear and talk about it and do something about it.

So they discussed it among themselves and the Lord listened to their conversation. He wrote their names in a book of remembrance. You see, God writes names in books and if your name is not written in the Book of Life when the book is opened at the end of time it would be better for you if you had never been born. God notes names down – of those who hear the message and receive it, talk about it with each other and say: we are going to be different.

So we come to the final section of this prophecy. There is going to be a separation within the people of God. Within Israel there is coming a day when they will be divided into two, right down the middle. It is called the day of the Lord. Here is the day coming up again, as we remember it from Zechariah and other prophets like Amos and Joel. They too talked about the day of the Lord. It is a day of reckoning, a day of settling accounts; it is the day of Judgment, and on that day there will only be two groups: the righteous and the wicked; those who serve God and those who don't; those who revere God and those who despise him; those who are humble before God and those who are arrogant about themselves.

On the one hand, there are the righteous. I love this next description. I used to get up at 4 a.m. to milk 90 cows. There were two of us who did that, and during the winter we kept those cows indoors. It was in Northumberland and the weather was not fit to leave them out, so we brought them in each autumn, and then we fed them cake and hay for months, and then came the day when we let them out for the first time in the spring. If you know anything about country life you know what happened next. Even the oldest cow gambolled like a lamb, and the old, big fat cows would jump around the field for joy. They would just go wild. Calves do it naturally at any time of the year. Have you ever seen calves suddenly getting excited? Horses sometimes do it in a field, and suddenly gallop around the field, but calves do it and even cows will do it. It says on that day the righteous will be my treasured possession, and they will leap like calves let out of the stall. I just see that picture. I have seen it so often that I can just see some people leaping for joy on that day – perhaps you can even see me doing it, but you know people will be so thrilled, so excited, like calves let out of the stall. We always did it when the sun was strong enough on a sunny day, and it says the sun of righteousness will rise with healing in its wings. It is a spring picture, it is poetic language, but the sun is shining and people are leaping for joy and it is the spring – life.

But those who are rejected on that day are like stubble burned after harvest. It is not legal to do it now in this country because smoke pollutes the atmosphere and drifts over roads, but until recently after the harvest did you ever see a whole field of straw being burned and crackling fire running through? All that is left is ash. Just as the calves leaping in a green field under the sun is a picture of the righteous on that day, the ashes of stubble is a picture of the wicked – those who have not responded to God.

There are three notes that are sounded here which I would just sound at the end. Israel as a people will survive. There will always be an Israel. As Malachi said on behalf of God: I don't change; I don't go back on my word. But that does not mean that every Jew who has ever lived will be saved. It does not mean that the Jews don't need the gospel. We do need to preach to them because there are hundreds of them dying and going to hell now. The second thing that is clear is that some in Israel will be lost. The third thing that Malachi makes clear is that some outside Israel will be saved. The Goyim – that is what we are – is the word for Gentiles. It says some in Israel will be lost and some outside Israel will be saved – that is us.

Now we get to the last three verses, a postscript, and it is built around the greatest two men in the Old Testament – Moses and Elijah. It is God's last appeal to his people of Israel in the Old Testament days; last word for 400 years. He says: remember Moses; get back to the maker's instructions he gave you. God is your great king, get back to Moses, and then he says God will give you another chance. He will send one more prophet to you, Elijah, and he will come as a forerunner, and he will come to challenge you. Now Elijah was the first major prophet to challenge the idolatry and the immorality of Israel. That was his greatness. He was the first of a long line: Elijah, Elisha, Amos, Hosea, Isaiah, Jeremiah. Moses was the prophet who led them out of Egypt and who gave them the covenant and the law, but Elijah was the first prophet to say: you have broken it and you need to get back to it.

So the Old Testament closes with that, and says if you

don't listen to Elijah then the land will be smitten with curse. That is the last word in your Old Testament: "lest he come and smite the land" – it should be "... the land with a curse." They would get one last chance before the day of the Lord, one more prophet to prepare the way of the Lord; an Elijah calling for repentance who would reconcile the generations and bring family life together again, and reconcile fathers to sons and sons to fathers – one more chance, and for over 400 years they waited for that to happen. They were occupied by Persians first, then Egyptians, then Syrians, then Greeks, then Romans. Then the chance came, and suddenly there was a man dressed like Elijah, eating the same diet as Elijah – locusts and wild honey – and the country said he has come. They flocked out to hear this man, and he preached the message that Malachi said he would preach; he called people back to wisdom and back to family life – and Elijah had come, but he had only come as a forerunner to prepare the way of the Lord to come.

When you turn to the New Testament you find that there was a great debate about whether John the Baptist was Elijah or not, and in fact Jesus came in to the debate twice and he said Elijah has come; he was my cousin John. So Malachi and Matthew go side by side in our Bible because that was the very next thing God said, and Matthew tells us how Elijah did come in the person of John the Baptist and he deliberately wore the clothes of Elijah and ate the food of Elijah. This was the revelation of God's next move, and I think it is lovely that when Jesus reached that watershed after two and a half years, took the disciples to the foot of Mount Hermon and said "Who do people think I am?" They said: some think you are a reincarnation of Jeremiah or somebody else. And he said, "But who do you say I am?"

Peter saw the truth that Jesus had lived before, but not down here: "You are the Christ, the Son of the living God."

Then Jesus said to Peter, James and John: come with me up the mountain. They went to the top of the mountain and Moses and Elijah appeared and talked to Jesus. Malachi promised it, and it all came together.

All these Old Testament examples are written for our use and we must let the New Testament interpret the Old Testament. We are not under laws like Sabbath and tithe, but we are under the law of Christ; we are under his law which is stricter than the law of Moses on divorce and remarriage, and on many other issues, and we are not to lose the fear of God. That is the danger if you forget the Old Testament, you lose the fear of God.

Above all we must remember that judgment begins at the house of God. The New Testament writers say, like Malachi, that when God comes to judge he first judges his people, and then he judges everybody else. We need to remember that. There will be a separation even of people in church, so let us not drift away; let us not neglect the faith; let us not commit apostasy – let us stay with it and go on believing, and he who believes to the end will be saved.

EPILOGUE

I want to refer to an important question that arises from all the Old Testament prophets, and especially those we have been looking at. Most of the Old Testament prophets make predictions about the future of the nation Israel, the Jewish people, and yet you can go to many churches in this country and other countries and never hear about any future for God's people Israel, and there is a reason for that. It is that there are different ways of treating these predictions about the future of Israel, three different ways in fact, and possibly the majority of Protestant churches in the West treat these predictions differently from the way I have taken them. Things that are promised about the future of Jerusalem and the future of Israel, and their place among the nations and so on – will these actually come true?

Now the three positions are these. First of all, one group of Bible interpreters say that all these promises were conditional; they were always conditional on Israel being faithful and obedient to God, and that therefore, because they were not, all these predictions have been cancelled – they have fallen to the ground; they will never happen because the conditions attached to them were not fulfilled. In other words, these things can happen if you co-operate, and that having not co-operated, and in particular having refused Jesus as their Messiah, the Jews have now forfeited their entire future, and all these predictions have fallen to the ground; they will never happen. They might have happened in the past but in fact they never were fulfilled and never will be. That is one reason why some preachers never talk about Israel or its future.

The second approach is that they were unconditional. It is not a case of they will happen if..., but they will happen whether or not; that they are unconditional – that God has said "This is what I intend to do and I will do it". But even within this group of those who take these predictions as absolutely certain to happen, there are two totally different ways of saying how they will happen, and probably the major way in which churches say they will happen is to say that they are already happening to the church and that these predictions are already being fulfilled in a symbolic or spiritual way in the church. This is the view we call "replacement theology" – that the church has replaced Israel, and therefore all the predictions made to Israel are now to be fulfilled in the church and are being fulfilled in the present but in a spiritual way, not in a literal way. So that we are being brought to the heavenly Jerusalem, not an earthly one, and the promises of fertility and blessing are seen in church growth and so on. It is intriguing. I cannot help being a bit sarcastic here, because all the predictions of blessing are applied to the church but all the predictions of cursing are quietly put in the waste paper basket, and this seems to me an awful way of treating the Bible.

The old Authorised Version, if you go through the prophet Isaiah, of every blessing promised it says "Blessing on the church"; and every curse promised says "Curse on Israel". This seems to me a bad case of prejudice, but it would probably be the majority view in many churches. It would probably be the majority view in many churches that the church has replaced Israel; that God has finished with Israel altogether. We have to evangelise them like we evangelise any other nation, and that is all there is to it – they don't have any future as a people, but individual Jews who get converted have a future along with us Gentiles in the church. The habit of calling the church "the new Israel" is very common, and yet the name "Israel" occurs 74 times in the New Testament and not once is it clearly applied to the church. In 73 of those it is clearly applied to the Jewish people. There is only one verse that could be a little ambiguous. Now that is not enough to apply the name "Israel" to the church, and I believe we should not call the church "the new Israel". The New Testament does not do it. That is that second view. So it says these predictions made to Israel are now being fulfilled in the present in the church but in a spiritual way and therefore, are fulfilled by Christ's first coming.

The third and last view and the view, which I have taken when I have been teaching the prophets here, is that those predictions were unconditional; they will happen, but that they will happen literally to Israel, as God said they would, and that therefore most of them are still future. The phrase "all Israel will be saved" is taken by those other people to mean the church will be complete; but here it is that Israel will be saved – therefore the fulfilment of these predictions tends to focus on the second coming rather than the first coming of Christ.

There are three positions, and you must work your way through and come to your own conviction about these, but some of the decisive factors to me include, particularly, Paul's section in the letter to the Romans, and particularly Romans chapter 11, where he says: "Has God finished with the Jews? – never!" They may have rejected him but he has not rejected them. Then there is the fact that people like Malachi write "I hate divorce" – God doesn't give up that easily on a people. He said to them again and again: you may break my covenant with you but I will never break it; and the fact that Israel is still around I believe to be proof that God keeps his word – they are still his chosen people even in unbelief because he chose them, and he doesn't go back on his promises.

I have given away my position. Therefore, the second coming seems to be a focus for much of the fulfilment of all this, and I do find that many who hold the other positions have a very hazy view as to why Jesus is coming back. If you ask them whether they believe Jesus is coming back, they say "Oh yes!" Then you ask them: why? What do you think he is coming back to do?

"To take us to heaven," they reply. But you will already be there if you have died. Why does he have to come back, and why does he have to bring all of us back? Why do we have to live on earth a second time? You do realise that, don't you? That when he comes he will bring with him all those who have fallen asleep, so that all Christians are going to live on earth – this earth – a second time. That is where we are going to get our new bodies. You don't need a new body in heaven but you do need one to live here, so why are we all coming back and getting a new body down here?

There is some great purpose to be fulfilled here long before there is a new heaven and a new earth. I believe the answer to the question "Why has Jesus to come back?" is: to reign over all the nations. Then we will shout: Hallelujah! The kingdoms of this world have become the kingdom of our God and of his Christ and he shall reign for ever and ever!

ABOUT DAVID PAWSON

A speaker and author with uncompromising faithfulness to the Holy Scriptures, David brings clarity and a message of urgency to Christians to uncover hidden treasures in God's Word.

Born in England in 1930, David began his career with a degree in Agriculture from Durham University. When God intervened and called him to become a Minister, he completed an MA in Theology at Cambridge University and served as a Chaplain in the Royal Air Force for three years. He moved on to pastor several churches, including the Millmead Centre in Guildford, which became a model for many UK church leaders. In 1979, the Lord led him into an international ministry. His current itinerant ministry is predominantly to church leaders. David and his wife Enid currently reside in the county of Hampshire in the UK.

Over the years, he has written a large number of books, booklets, and daily reading notes. His extensive and very accessible overviews of the books of the Bible have been published and recorded in *Unlocking the Bible*. Millions of copies of his teachings have been distributed in more than 120 countries, providing a solid biblical foundation.

He is reputed to be the "most influential Western preacher in China" through the broadcast of his best-selling *Unlocking the Bible* series into every Chinese province by Good TV. In the UK, David's teachings are often broadcast on Revelation TV.

Countless believers worldwide have also benefited from his generous decision in 2011 to make available his extensive audio video teaching library free of charge at **www.davidpawson.org** and we have recently uploaded all of David's video to a dedicated channel on **www.youtube.com**

UNLOCKING THE BIBLE

A unique overview of both the Old and New Testaments, from internationally acclaimed evangelical speaker and author David Pawson. *Unlocking the Bible* opens up the Word of God in a fresh and powerful way. Avoiding the small detail of verse by verse studies, it sets out the epic story of God and his people in Israel. The culture, historical background and people are introduced and the teaching applied to the modern world. Eight volumes have been brought into one compact and easy to use guide to cover both the Old and New Testaments in one massive omnibus edition. *The Old Testament: The Maker's Instructions* (The five books of law); *A Land and A Kingdom* (Joshua, Judges, Ruth, 1&2 Samuel, 1&2 Kings); *Poems of Worship and Wisdom* (Psalms, Song of Solomon, Proverbs, Ecclesiastes, Job); *Decline and Fall of an Empire* (Isaiah, Jeremiah and other prophets); *The Struggle to Survive* (Chronicles and prophets of exile); *The New Testament: The Hinge of History* (Mathew, Mark, Luke, John and Acts); *The Thirteenth Apostle* (Paul and his letters); *Through Suffering to Glory* (Hebrews, the letters of James, Peter and Jude, the Book of Revelation). Already an international bestseller.

OTHER LANGUAGES

Unlocking the Bible is available in book, video and audio formats and has been translated into other languages.

 WATCH DAVID'S INTRO
www.davidpawson.com/utbintro

 WATCH
www.davidpawson.com/utbwatch

 LISTEN
www.davidpawson.com/utblisten

 PURCHASE THE BOOK
www.davidpawson.com/utbbuybook

PURCHASE THE EBOOK
www.davidpawson.com/utbbuykindle

PURCHASE THE DVD
www.davidpawson.com/utbbuydvd

PURCHASE USB
FLASH DRIVE INCLUDING:
- ALL VIDEO (MP4)
- ALL AUDIO TRACKS (MP3)
- CHARTS (PDF)

www.davidpawson.com/buyusb

THE EXPLAINING SERIES
BIBLICAL TRUTH SIMPLY EXPLAINED

If you have been blessed reading this book, we have more books available in David's Explaining Series. Please register to download for free by visiting
www.explainingbiblicaltruth.global

Other booklets in the *Explaining* series include:
The Amazing Story of Jesus
The Resurrection: *The Heart of Christianity*
Studying the Bible
Being Anointed and Filled with the Holy Spirit
New Testament Baptism
How to study a book of the Bible: Jude
The Key Steps to Becoming a Christian
What the Bible says about Money
What the Bible says about Work
Grace – *Undeserved Favour, Irresistible Force or Unconditional Forgiveness?*
Eternally secure? – *What the Bible says about being saved*
De-Greecing the Church – *The impact of Greek thinking on Christian beliefs*
Three texts often taken out of context: *Expounding the truth and exposing error*
The Trinity
The Truth about Christmas

They will also be available to purchase as print copies from:
Amazon or **www.thebookdepository.com**

JESUS: THE SEVEN WONDERS OF HISTORY

This book is the result of a lifetime of telling 'the greatest story ever told' around the world. David re-told it to many hundreds of young people in Kansas City, USA, who heard it with uninhibited enthusiasm, 'tweeting' on the internet about 'this cute old English gentleman' even while he was speaking.

Taking the middle section of the Apostles' Creed as a framework, David explains the fundamental facts about Jesus on which the Christian faith is based in a fresh and stimulating way. Both old and new Christians will benefit from this 'back to basics' call and find themselves falling in love with their Lord all over again.

OTHER TEACHINGS
BY DAVID PAWSON

For the most up to date list of David's Books
go to: **www.davidpawsonbooks.com**

To purchase David's Teachings
go to: **www.davidpawson.com**

www.ingramcontent.com/pod-product-compliance
Lightning Source LLC
Chambersburg PA
CBHW071214080526
44587CB00013BA/1369